Democratic Destiny
and the District
of Columbia

Democratic Destiny and the District of Columbia

Federal Politics and Public Policy

Edited by Ronald Walters and
Toni-Michelle C. Travis

LEXINGTON BOOKS
A division of
ROWMAN & LITTLEFIELD PUBLISHERS, INC.
Lanham • Boulder • New York • Toronto • Plymouth, UK

Published by Lexington Books
A division of Rowman & Littlefield Publishers, Inc.
A wholly owned subsidary of The Rowman & Littlefield Publishing Group, Inc.
4501 Forbes Boulevard, Suite 200, Lanham, Maryland 20706
http://www.lexingtonbooks.com

Estover Road, Plymouth PL6 7PY, United Kingdom

British Library Cataloguing in Publication Information Available

Library of Congress Cataloging-in-Publication Data

Democratic destiny and the District of Columbia : federal politics and public policy /
edited by Ronald Walters and Toni-Michelle Travis.
    p. cm.
ISBN 978-0-7391-2716-2 (cloth : alk. paper) — ISBN 978-0-7391-2717-9 (pbk. : alk.
paper) — ISBN 978-0-7391-4435-0 (electronic)
  1. Washington (D.C.)—Politics and government—1995- 2. Washington (D.C.)—
Politics and government—1967-1995. 3. Home rule—Washington (D.C.) I. Walters,
Ronald W. II. Travis, Toni-Michelle, 1947-
  JK2716.D46 2010
  320.9753—dc22

                                                                    2009042332

∞ ™ The paper used in this publication meets the minimum requirements of
American National Standard for Information Sciences—Permanence of Paper for Printed
Library Materials, ANSI/NISO Z39.48-1992.

Printed in the United States of America

Contents

Acknowledgments   vii

Foreword   ix
 Eleanor Holmes Norton

1   Introduction: An Administered System of Government   1
 Ronald Walters

POLITICS

2   Home Rule for the District of Columbia   21
 Michael K. Fauntroy

3   Walter Washington: Mayor of the Last Colony   45
 Toni-Michelle C. Travis

4   Marion Barry, Jr.: A Politician for the Times   61
 Wilmer J. Leon III

5   Sharon Pratt Kelly: The Reform Mayor   87
 Toni-Michelle C. Travis

6   The High Tide of Pragmatic Black Politics: Mayor Anthony
 Williams and the Suppression of Black Interests   103
 Daryl B. Harris

PUBLIC POLICY

7   The Mayor as the Head School Master   121
       ReShone L. Moore

8   Can Washington, D.C., Youth Speak? Youth, Education,
       and Race in the Political Socialization Process   137
       Darwin Fishman

9   Banished: Housing Policy in the District of Columbia and
       the Struggle of Working Families   157
       William G. Jones

10 Democracy and Its Impact on Rehabilitative Resources in
       the District of Columbia   181
       Kevin L. Glasper

11 The Dynamics of Poverty in the District of Columbia   205
       Angelyn Flowers

12 Communicating Liberation in Washington, D.C.   225
       Jared A. Ball

13 Conclusion   255
       Ronald Walters and Toni-Michelle C. Travis

Index   263

About the Authors   277

Acknowledgments

The editors would like to express their appreciation for the unique manner in which this project was conceptualized by a number of new doctoral graduates from various area universities. While interns together in 2007 at the Black Leadership Forum in Washington, D.C., the premier coalition of African American organizations, contributors Kevin Glasper and Darwin Fishman and their colleagues conceptualized this project. As editors we refined the philosophy of the project and added contributors to complete the structure of the work. It has been a singularly positive experience in producing with them what we believe is a substantive contribution to the intellectual analysis and understanding of the politics and public policy of the District of Columbia. Coeditor Dr. Toni-Michelle C. Travis was not only born in the District but has done substantial work accumulating original papers and interviews on the life and legacy of Mayor Walter Washington. Coeditor Dr. Ronald Walters was chair of the political science department at Howard University, has been a faculty member there for twenty-four years, and has been a persistent analyst of politics and policy of the District.

In the production of this work, we note with appreciation the resources made available online by the D.C. government, as well as the records in the Washingtoniana section of the D.C. library system. Moreover, we would like to thank Danielle Olsen, Dr. Travis's research assistant. Most important, however, was Joseph Barry, acquisitions editor for Rowman and Littlefield Publishing Group, and his belief in the possibility of the project. We were assisted in the production effort at Rowman and Littlefield by associate editor Patricia Stevenson, assistant editor Bethany Blanchard, and editorial assistant Tawnya Zengierski. Finally, we all thank Delegate Eleanor Holmes Norton for taking time from her impossibly crowded schedule, especially during this session of the House of Representatives, to write a foreword that is a substantial contribution to the work.

Ronald Walters, Ph.D.
Coeditor

Toni-Michelle Travis, Ph.D.
Coeditor

Foreword

Eleanor Holmes Norton

Coeditors Ronald Walters and Toni-Michelle C. Travis have gathered a talented group of scholars to offer a rare "critique of the issue of democracy in Washington, D.C." during the modern era of self-government. However, considering the birth of the nation in 1787 and of the city in 1801, readers may find it astonishing that except for a brief period after the Civil War, the era of self-government for the District of Columbia, permitting residents to elect their own mayor and city council, began only in 1973. Equally surprising is how little basic information has been available to Americans about the generations of citizens denied democracy in their own nation's capital. This volume is especially valuable in light of the paucity of published work devoted to the enigma of a capital bereft of democracy where the leaders of "the free world" conduct their business.

The citizens of the District of Columbia have been in a struggle with the Congress of the United States for democratic self-government and for voting congressional representation ever since the city became the official capital in 1801. In only the twenty years I have represented the city in the House of Representatives, we have tried to achieve representation in every existing way—through statehood, through votes in the Senate and the House, and currently through the D.C. House Voting Rights Act, which would grant the District a voting representative in the House.[1] Today's effort for a mere House vote so late into the history of the nation speaks to the incrementalism that characterizes the city's long struggle for basic democracy. Similarly plodding was the coming of the era of self-government, or "home rule," in 1973 that began only with a presidentially appointed school board, then a mayor and city council, also appointed by the president, before local residents were permitted to elect their own leaders.[2] Today, the city has home rule on all matters. The Congress, nevertheless, retains paternalistic and unnecessary control over the District's right to govern itself on purely local matters.[3]

Almost as frustrating as the slow walk toward democracy has been the lack of knowledge, even among educated Americans, concerning the long absence of democracy in the nation's capital before the Home Rule Act of 1973 and the continuing interference by Congress into many important matters essential to self-governance.[4] It is difficult to blame Americans considering that published works, like the chapters in this volume on the District government since home rule, are still rare. The city's most recent national campaign for voting rights encountered near universal surprise that District residents have no congressional voting representation. The voting representation issue is more visible today, thanks to the work of District residents themselves, especially the citizen-created organization DC Vote—with comic assistance from Stephen Colbert, who took to having me on "The Colbert Report" to make fun of my voteless status as the District's delegate to Congress and in the process unwittingly helped popularize the voteless condition of nearly 600,000 American citizens.

The most recent phase of the city's struggle for democracy mirrors similar efforts by District residents for two centuries. The invisibility of the denial of self-government and of voting congressional representation are linked to this failure to become a subject of national conversation. The near absence of democracy in the nation's capital mostly escaped national notice, despite hometown protests for more than 150 years. Washington has long been a high-profile capital, but the District of Columbia has been all but obscured under the brilliant spotlight on federal Washington. Beneath the shadows, Southern congressional Democrats adopted and used the city for their own purposes for two centuries. First, Southerners, led by George Washington, waged a successful fight to locate the new capital below the Mason-Dixon line that divided the newly independent nation between the regions that enforced segregation and those that were reluctant to do so. Then, congressional Southerners used their authority to ensure that the city would reflect Southern culture on race, including segregated schools and public accommodations.

However, the District has always had a strong freedom-seeking population, particularly in its African American residents. Many identified with the civil rights movement long before it assumed national dimensions. Rev. Walter Fauntroy, who was to become the first modern-era elected District of Columbia delegate to Congress in 1971, was an important lieutenant to Dr. Martin Luther King, Jr. The city provided a major platform to secure rights for many other Americans during the 1960s, while D.C. residents were denied their rights, only adding to local aspirations for citizenship rights. District citizens participated in the Poor People's Campaign on the National Mall and in the historic March on Washington in the years leading to the Home Rule Act. They quickly saw the national civil rights movement and the changes it was bringing to the country as leverage in their own fight for self-government and representation in the nation's capital. The national liberating effect of the 1965 Voting Rights Act became the catalyst for a natural political coalition that developed between District residents and African Americans in the sixth congressional district of South Carolina. The Black South, empowered by the new voting rights law, defeated John L. McMillan—an avowed segregation- ist—who for years had been chair of the Congressional District Committee, the overseer of hometown D.C.

Fatefully, however, the modern self-governing years for the District of Columbia began during perhaps urban America's most turbulent years. These were the years when urban riots occurred in almost all of the big cities of the nation, including the District. The majority of the city's residents had been white for most of the District's two centuries of existence, but the white exo- dus from the great cities everywhere, as in the District of Columbia, began in earnest in the 1960s. White flight accelerated after the District, one of the five Brown vs. Board of Education cases, desegregated its schools in 1956. Soon the District had a black majority.

However, the decline of the old cities and the growth of the new suburbs meant fewer taxpayers of every race in big cities. As a result, governing as- sumed nearly unprecedented challenges. Many cities that had become pros- perous because of industries built and sustained by their residents saw their hometown companies head south or overseas. With corporate flight went the low-skill, high-paying jobs that had built the American middle class. A new urban economy emerged, spawning a lucrative drug sector that replaced the income-producing industries and jobs that were fleeing. Finishing school became less attractive than the more immediate rewards offered in job-poor cities by the underground drug economy.

Into the new self-governing District of Columbia, fraught with novel prob- lems, emerged new rulers, elected mayors and city councils. They found in the District an urban crisis both similar to and different from what other great cities were experiencing. The District had no industry, but it was the home of the federal government. Unlike the companies that abandoned the great cities, the District's home company could not leave the capital. Cabinet agencies, by law, must be in the nation's capital. However, as home rule came, the federal government was undergoing such a large expansion and need for skilled em- ployees that the city could not contain all parts of all federal agencies. Many federal agencies had to be placed in the nearby suburbs of Northern Virginia and Maryland counties. The region, in turn, also attracted a new government contracting sector, as well as other industries drawn by federal agencies, especially the high-tech industry that settled in the Virginia suburbs. The national capital region became one of the most prosperous in the country and a magnet for highly educated workers.

The home rule mayors also benefitted from the expansion of the federal government. Job loss was not the problem for the District that it was for many cities. However, the white collar jobs that grew during this period demanded solid secondary education and, increasingly, college training. Many in the District's black middle class followed their white counterparts out of the District as urban problems became more visible. Ironically, these migrating blacks became the core of the most prosperous black community in the United States, Prince George's County, Maryland, just across the District line. Hometown Washington was left with a diminished highly educated white and black population, a growing proportion of low-income, poorly educated African Americans, and good middle-income jobs that increasingly went to suburban residents. Elected local officials arrived just as the drugs moved in, along with the crime and blight that accompany economic and social dislocation.

Greater political and civic democracy had brought citizen rule and participation after nearly two centuries, but self-government alone could not remedy urban problems and a declining tax base. The District of Columbia proved to be in many ways like, but in others very different from, other cities. The city's evolution from a Southern, segregated, nearly invisible urban hometown, without voice or vote, was a fascinating departure from the stories of other American cities. Even so, hometown D.C. has attracted little popular or scholarly attention.

In some ways, the ironic plight of the capital city fits a nation that began by declaring that "all men are created equal," and then wrote a Constitution enshrining slavery and patriarchy. The evidence, however, is that the Framers envisioned a capital like Paris or London, not one that would be denied the chance to govern itself. However, the generations who inherited the vision of the Framers proved less revolutionary than those who created the nation. Although the citizens who lived on the land given for the nation's capital rallied under the war slogan, "No taxation without representation," they could not have imagined that they would lose what democracy they already had in the states from which they came, as well as the vote in Congress they had fought to attain. They lost the self-governing power they had had as citizens of Maryland and Virginia, the two states that ceded land to form the capital, and in the cruelest of all ironies, these Americans who became citizens of the District of Columbia also lost the chance to vote—for which they had gone to war. They lost representation in Congress.

The struggle for full democratic self-government and for equal congressional voting rights in the House continues unabated. Nevertheless, self-government has brought the first record by which to take a measure of the District as a self-governing city. The authors of these essays look at some of the major issues that comprise that record. Opponents of full self-government for the District of Columbia have sometimes been fond of using urban issues against the idea of self-government in the District itself. It does not matter that the problems cited are typical of those experienced by great cities besieged by the nation's urban crisis. However, these authors take a fresh look at how the elected officials who governed the District of Columbia defined self-government for the city amidst the problems and dilemmas they found. The nation should be grateful to these authors for what their insights tell us about government in the modern nation's capital and, inadvertently, about the nature of governing in the nation itself.

NOTES

1. The residents of the District of Columbia pay the second highest per capita amount of federal income taxes, but have no voting representative in either of the two legislative chambers. *See* U.S. Census Bureau, Census 2000 Summary File 3, fact finder.census.gov/servlet/GCTTable?_bm=y&-geo_id=D&-ds_name=D&-_lang=en &-redoLog=false&-mt_name=DEC_2000_SF3_U_GCTP14_US9&-format=CO-1. Consequently, the city has adopted for its license plates the slogan, "Taxation without Representation." D.C. residents also have fought and died in every war, including the Revolutionary War, which was fought based on a derivation of that slogan.

2. *U.S. House of Representatives: Governance of the Nation's Capital: A Summary History of the Forms and Powers of Local Government for the District of Columbia, 1790 to 1973,* November 1991, p. 53. In the early nineteenth century, the District had a popularly-elected local government, which was revoked by Congress in 1871. That year, Congress granted the District a nonvoting delegate in Congress, but the federal government abolished the delegate position in 1874. Nelson F. Rimensnyder, *Local Government in the District of Columbia: Congressionally Chartered Government for the Nation's Capital, 1801-1871* (Committee on the District of Columbia, U.S. House of Representatives, 1977), pp. 3-6.

3. Congress still has oversight over the District's locally raised budget and laws. However, Congresswoman Norton has introduced legislation to allow the District of Columbia to enact its own budget and laws. *See* District of Columbia Budget Autonomy Act of 2009, H.R. 1045 *and* District of Columbia Legislative Autonomy Act of 2009, H.R. 960.

4. As the city's representative in Congress, Norton's formal titles are "delegate" and "Congress member." As such, Congresswoman Norton has every privilege of the House except the final vote on the House floor. In 1993, she wrote a memo that argued that

she should be able to vote on the floor in the Committee of the Whole just as delegates have long voted in other committees. This right was granted by the House and later affirmed by the courts. Today, in addition to voting on some matters on the House floor and on all matters in all the committees on which the delegate serves, she chairs one of the subcommittees of the House.

1

Introduction: An Administered System of Government

Ronald Walters

There is considerable understanding that the citizenship of residents of the District of Columbia is devalued by the extent to which they are not able to be represented properly in Congress. They therefore have less access to the republican form of government envisioned by the framers than others in this country. Less well understood is the fact that the constitutional relationship between the Congress and the District of Columbia also complicates the citizenship of residents by limiting their participation in the policymaking process in ways that affect their needs and desires.

The modern history of local government in Washington, D.C., has, since the mid-1960s, been concerned with instituting the missing accoutrements of democracy and the establishment of effective governmental practices in an effort to enhance the empowerment of local residents. In this sense, they have been part to the general perception that democratic practices, such as the right to elect local officials and to participate in national government, were linked to the ability to provide the kind of effective local government that was not only representative but that delivered the services necessary to assist individuals and families to achieve social and economic viability.

The struggle for voting rights and representation by the District of Columbia is one of the important political legends in America. In fact, as this volume is being written, another chapter in that saga finds that the Congress is considering whether to grant full voting rights in the House of Representatives to the delegate from the District and whether to give the District government autonomy over the consideration of its legislative program. But while this struggle (complete with Mayor Adrian Fenty, like others, having led demonstrations to highlight the importance of this issue) has received considerable public attention, comparatively little is known regarding how the federal relationship has affected the nature of democracy for local residents. This volume explores the question of "democracy" as it is structured by the unique relationship with the Congress and the District, examining what the normalization of that relationship to the Congress and the greater control of politics and public policy by the District could mean to its citizens.

Before 1974, the character of city government in the District reflected a strongly administered paradigm. Theoretically, Braybrooke and Lindbloom say that one of the chief characteristics of such administered systems is that the locus of decision-making power is located in the system and that it tends to be impervious to outside influences but highly responsive to hierarchical control.[1]

The question of whether there would be an expansion of local civil rights that would empower not only the home rule majority but all citizens in the District through a regime of home rule was partially settled by the passage of Public Law 93-198 by Congress, which was signed into law on December 24, 1974, by President Richard Nixon. It provided for an elected set of officials who were supposed to establish a city government that could tend to an agenda of public needs in the exercise of its normal function. However, of the nearly eighty thousand governments in the United States, the District of Columbia is unique, having state-like authority, in the guise of a thoroughgoing urban government, but under the paternalistic control of the Congress.

With regard to policies that promoted equality and human needs on a universal level, the federal government has exercised more authority because of the reluctance or inability of states to do so. Over time, however, the normal distribution of responsibility and power between the federal system and states in general, Baumgartner and Jones say, has shifted, such that the states and localities are more receptive to policies directed toward the enhancement of the local human and physical infrastructure.[2] Now, many states accept such responsibility except where they are reluctant to accept federal mandates in these areas without the attendant revenue to carry such policies out.

Thus, if the District were considered a state, it would likely be able to exercise more responsibility for human needs issues because of the heavy socioeconomic needs of its predominant African American demography. Race affects the construction of public policy for the District in two ways. First, since African Americans are traditionally viewed as both a dependent and a deviant group, as Ingram and Smith suggest, policy for dependent groups is constructed with them as a secondary target, but with the agencies that care for them as the primary targets of both funds and responsibility.[3] Resources very often are provided in amounts less than needed, and the content of policy is burdensome because of the assumption that the intended population can do less for itself than others, which evokes the autocratic management of lives and interference with the quality of their citizenship. Policy is constructed for deviants groups very often with punishment motives in mind, often "making easy scapegoats for the problems of our society."[4] The authors say that sanctions and force are looked upon as the preferred tools of policy in areas such as criminal justice with the intended effect of devaluing the citizenship of such groups to the point that they cannot threaten society. As a result, Ingram and Smith suggest that "policies should be designed as much with their effect on citizenship in mind as with their technical and political feasibility."[5]

The public policy environment and its output that flows from the lack of not only voting rights but political autonomy is the foundation of unstable and unaccountable public decisions about the vital issues. The fact that such issues are presented to government and solutions proposed are then rejected by the federal establishment has made the fight for expanding democracy in the District involve the ultimate objective of achieving statehood. Although it is clear that politicians in the federal government have justified their intervention into District affairs by virtue of the constitutional control, the symbol of a largely white establishment exercising control over a largely black District is an unavoidable political issue. This relationship has often borne agenda conflict which Cobb and Ross define as such:

> First, agenda conflicts are about whether government will or will not seriously consider a particular grievance issue that initiators bring to it. Second, agenda conflicts are about competing interpretations of political problems, but behind them lie competing worldviews involving how people ought to lead their lives, how society ought to act, what should or should not be done by government, how we should treat the environment and who threatens people's security.[6]

As a consequence of political conflict between two parties, agenda denial is a manifestation of raw political control and the various strategies utilized to affect this may be manifest in both the various policy intervention strategies as well as the lack of decision on policies desired by the petitioning party. In any case, the relative weakness of the District in this game has determined its loosing position in the fundamental issue of who will control its political agenda and as such, we would argue, affects the quality of life of the citizens of the District of Columbia.

The way in which federalism has structured issue conflict in the political system has long been of interest to political scientists, since the work of E. E. Schattschneider's 1960 volume, *The Semisovereign People.* But Lisa Miller has said that

> While the scholarly literature takes account of the federal nature of the U.S. political system as it relates to specific policy areas or subfields, much less work

views federalism as a force that structures group representation, the scope of conflict, and the breadth and depth of pluralistic policy process.[7]

But while issues of political incorporation are satisfied by the extent to which African Americans have been represented in local government, still the federal aspect of that relationship is unique in its constitutional origin and, consequently, in the degree to which the structure of local government has been as effective as possible.

Nevertheless, the racial motive in agenda control is not always obvious; thus Ingram and Smith, and Cobb and Ross, believe that the intended messages of public policy are not always articulated and that the subtle meanings are often more important. In the case of the refusal of Congress to consider formal inclusion of the District representation in the manner of a state or in the limitations or inclusions of policies that are unwanted by the citizens and their representative structure of local government, what results is the phenomenon of agenda denial. In any case, it is widely believed by residents that this denial is somehow related to the racial composition of the District.

DEMOCRATIC OR PATERNALISTIC FEDERALISM

Between 1960 and 1970 black families grew in the District of Columbia by 35 percent, boosting the home rule population to 75 percent by 1970. As a result of federal programs, the black middle- and upper-income group ($12,500 and over) tripled while the group earning $4,000 and under remained constant. This fact presumed that a democratically elected government would be most responsive to issues contained in the history of the subordination of blacks who constituted over 70 percent of the District population at this time. It was a community also marked by a strong pattern of racial segregation as late as the 2000 census.[8] Between 1970 and 1990, the District experienced a substantial loss of population, as middle-class, both white and African American, families with children, as one study said, "changed the character of the city and eroded the resource base that often supports neighborhood life."[9] The study also shows that the loss of population was greater in the African American wards of the city.

One source was led to say that "Washington was in transit from a predominantly white, middle income city to a predominantly black, middle income city—not, as is widely believed, to a black, poor city."[10] Therefore, one could expect that the desire for democratic participation in a system that would deliver resources to a population in proportion to the need would be great.

In fact, Banfield and Wilson suggest as much when they state, "It is not always the size of the city per se which has made the difference (in the thirst for citizen participation); rather it is the empirical correlation between large size and the relative number and political power of the lower class."[11] Politics, indeed racial politics, have been paramount at the hierarchy of the control of District policy. In the House District Committee, governed by Southern Democrats at the time, the District's location in the South was regarded as the purview of Southern members of Congress, some of whom were racially insensitive. For example, at one hearing of the committee on February 8, 1972, Rep. John R. Rarick (D-La.) said that home rule could lead to the takeover of the city by home rule Muslims and that was why he opposed it; committee member Rep. Charles C. Diggs Jr., an African American from Michigan, then retorted, "The gentleman is pursuing a racist line."[12] Furthermore, since home rule supporters voted then as now, overwhelmingly Democratic, Republicans were loath to see Democrats advanced in the District at their expense.

African Americans in the District, like others in the United States, had always suffered from the lack of inclusion into society and the legitimate political system and as such, responded strongly to the emergence of the civil rights movement that accompanied their quest for democratic participation since at least the formation of the Union. To the extent that African American leaders in the District, such as Rev. Walter Fauntroy (an associate of Rev. Martin Luther King Jr.) and others, played important roles in the civil rights movement, it was natural that it should have a catalytic local manifestation.

Moreover, the District was at that time the veritable ground zero for many other struggles for justice that encompassed the emerging Third World countries, opposition to the Vietnam War, justice for the inclusion of women and many others. It provided the dramatic stage for the March on Washington of 1963, the Poor Peoples' Campaign of 1968, the evolution of the Congressional Black Caucus, and other important events related to the home rule community nationally.

In addition, the citizen participation as a part of President Lyndon Johnson's Model Cities Administration placed a strong democratic value on the involvement of citizens in their government, many of whom worked for the Office of Economic Opportunity that funded the local United Planning Organization and other organizations. So, when one looks at other funded programs such as Youth PRIDE, Peoples Involvement Corporation, Community Action Program, Shaw PAC, Adams-Morgan Community Control Educational Project, MICCO, the Black United Front, Concerned Citizens of Central Cardozo, and many others, it is possible to understand the depth of the emerging grassroots thrust for the participation of citizens in their own government.

Thus the mobilization of the local residents through their own civil rights movement to achieve both fair representation and effective government has been a long and persistent affair. It resulted in the right to vote for president of the United States in 1961, which fueled the right of local residents to elect members of their school board on April 22, 1968. Then, on December 24, 1973, Congress passed the Home Rule Act giving local residents the right to elect their own mayor and thirteen-member city council. Democracy advanced in the District of Columbia through the Home Rule Charter which further structured the relation between the federal government and aspects of the city government operations, but the paternalistic element remained unchanged.

The movement toward greater involvement of citizens in this period of history was not exclusive to the District of Columbia, since the citizen participation movement assumed that political incorporation was a good thing that not only increased democracy, but improved service delivery. When Greenstone and Peterson wrote about this issue in 1973, there was a far more robust relationship between the federal government and cities, based on the expectation that incorporation would produce positive results.[13] Since that time, there have been considerable changes leading some scholars to doubt the efficacy of incorporation as the key instrument of black viability.[14] These factors will be reflected in the analyses that are developed, with historical analyses that introduce a primary concern with modern features of government, politics, and public policy and their implications for the future.

Nevertheless, with limited home rule, a great deal of attention has been focused on wielding normal powers of local governance by the administration of various mayors and the city council and the issues that they have confronted. The fight for home rule grew out of the larger civil rights movement, where there was a presumption that black involvement in government would result in the alleviation of a myriad of social problems and that, in fact, blacks had proved, as early in American history as Reconstruction, that they were able to govern.[15]

The modern opportunity arose with the election of a generation of home rule officials at local levels, initiating the scholarship of what Patterson called "black city politics" and which Preston, Henderson, and Puryear referred to as "The New Black Politics."[16] In any case, the issue of governance in the District of Columbia would not be solely grounded in the activities of African Americans, because the constitutional responsibilities of Congress, the role of the president of the United States and the domination of local economic, media and cultural institutions by whites made them the "effective" majority. As in many other states, however, although blacks began to be elected to office as the numerically dominant population, the institutional control over the local political structure by those who controlled the police, fire, courts, media, businesses, etc., limited the use of that power to fully satisfy the needs of the most disadvantaged. In fact, they found that even with relative autonomy it would be even more difficult to truly reflect local policy interests because of encroaching state government intervention which provided something of a parallel to the District-Congress relationship, also as a by-product of conservative politics in the 1990s and beyond.

Although the expectation was strong in the District of Columbia (a pivotal city in the civil rights movement) that incorporation would yield positive policy benefits, the federal relationship between the city and Congress has historically affected the quest. Indeed, changes in national ideology and the political control of government at the national level, Professor Michael Fauntroy has asserted, have led to the erosion of home rule and as such, "the District of Columbia is not well positioned to control its destiny."[17] This linkage or "tension" as it is often portrayed, invites the examination of questions such as: What styles of national and local political leadership have promoted democratic practices in being most responsive to the needs of residents? What has been the relationship of these styles of governance to the leadership of public institutions that have faced critical social problems? What features of citizen participation contributed to promoting excellence in service delivery? What issues remain that might enhance both democracy and government performance in the area of policy effectiveness? This issue will be addressed in the chapters on public policy.

THE PATTERN OF POLICY INTERVENTION

The pattern of policy intervention into the decision-making by the District of Columbia government has taken several forms by various actors in the federal system. It has come from the president as chief executive and from the courts, but most frequently from Congress exercising its direct oversight of the budget and legislative acts of the District.

Over time, *congressional intervention* into the policy affairs of the District after the passage of the Home Rule Act in 1973 was done infrequently because of the desire to let the recently established power of home rule work, but also because the civil rights aura of the District had established allies in the Democratic Party, which was in control of the White House and the Congress in the aftermath. Rep. Charles Diggs, a founder of the Congressional Black Caucus (CBC) was chair of the House District Committee, 1973–1979, and as he ushered in home rule, he also established the pattern of exercising as little interference as possible. The Committee was taken over by Rep. Ronald

Dellums, CBC member from Oakland, California, who served from 1979 to 1993. At the same time, during this period, the District House Appropriations Committee was chaired by CBC member Julian Dixon whose role as a member of the CBC meant that he was also an ally of the District.

In what might be called the "grace period" of home rule, after the Act was passed the concerns brought to the District Committees might be considered frivolous. For example, in a District Committee hearing one member asked why the gas pump at a certain filling station was so heavy that his wife could not manage it.[18]

Presidential Intervention

Presidential participation in intervention into District affairs began a serious phase with the advent of the presidency of Ronald Reagan in 1980. His approach to such issues reflected what would become the Republican agenda in the 1980s and 1990s. A leading issue in this regard was his party's opposition to abortion, and in 1987 he requested that Democratic House Speaker Jim Wright (Tex.) not appropriate funds in the District budget to be utilized for abortion. Taking his cue from anti-abortion activists, Reagan said:

> I am taking this opportunity to reiterate my request that the Congress ensure that none of the funds appropriated for the District of Columbia be used for abortion unless the life of the mother would be endangered if the fetus were carried to term. Thus, I will support an amendment to the . . . bill that restricts the use of both the District's federal and locally generated funds for abortion.[19]

At issue was $52 million in the 1988 budget approved by the mayor and City Council and Reagan's veto of the original appropriation sent it back to the Congress, where it was revised.

Congressional Intervention

By the end of 1981, the use of the veto power by Congress to repeal serious District legislation had only been exercised twice, once to block the enactment of limits on where foreign chanceries should be located and another time with respect to a Council ordinance reforming the District sexual assault laws that would have decriminalized heterosexual and homosexual relations.[20] Then another House committee demanded that no funds be appropriated for a lottery or the printing of tickets for it. Such actions would continue and grow.[21]

Other actions by members of Congress prevented legislation from being considered by the District Committee. For example, conservative politician

Rep. Stan Parris, Republican of suburban Virginia, blocked Mayor Barry's attempt to increase the number of African Americans on the police force, and Democrat William Natcher of Kentucky blocked the attempt by Barry to reduce the size of the police force, one of the largest per capita in the country.

By the mid-1980s, intervention picked up, with Congress using its oversight to attach measures to the city budget that would repeal both a residency requirement for city workers and a law barring insurance companies from testing applicants for AIDS. When a similar proposal by the District was blocked in 1986, Councilman David A. Clarke said not only was there no demonstrated federal interests in this case, but that the move was a ploy by Sen. Jesse Helms, Republican of North Carolina, to find a platform for "conservative interests."[22]

The frequency of intervention by Congress increased toward the end of the 1980s and into the 1990s, pushed on by the rise of conservative government through the Republican party. The 1990 District budget was passed without many of the fetters of the past because the Democrat-controlled Congress defeated restrictions on the use of city funds for abortions, blocked Rep. Parris's legislation prohibiting the city from giving hiring preferences to residents, and allowed the city to prohibit insurance companies from refusing assistance to AIDS patients by testing.[23] Thereafter, the tide of intervention quickened, as Republicans assumed control of the Congress.

- The 1995 budget came under the tax cut strategy as outlined by the D.C. House Appropriations Subcommittee Chair, Rep. Charles Taylor (S.C.), who said: "The intent of this bill is clear—to provide tax and debt relief to the often-ignored District of Columbia residents and taxpayers. What we are about today is not funding the District government bureaucracy."[24] The deep cuts were ultimately not passed, but attached to the bill were cuts in the D.C. city government and a voucher plan that would pay for students from low-income families to attend private K–12 city educational institutions. In any case, the voucher plan would return in 2003, under Republican control of the Congress with funding for 1,700 students.[25]
- At a hearing to reconstruct the city financial structure, Republican Sen. Sam Brownback (Kans.), who chaired the Senate District panel, said that the District financial system was out of control and that the District needed "radical surgery."[26] After assuming control of the Congress, Republicans instituted a Financial Control Board in 1995 to govern the District's affairs.
- The House budget amendment of Republican Rep. Brian Bilbray (Calif.) stated that children under eighteen who were caught with a cigarette

could be arrested, fined, forced to perform community service, and forced to attend tobacco cessation classes.[27]

- Republican Rep. Ernest Istook, Jr. (Okl.) submitted an amendment that would prevent clinics in the District that received federal funds from distributing free needles to fight the spread of HIV/AIDs.[28] A Republican measure appeared in the 2003 budget to promote a zoning measure that would fast-track a proposal by the Girls and Boys Town Assn. to build a facility in the city.[29]
- Republican Representatives Frank Wolf (Va.) and Thomas Davis (Va.), chair of the House District Committee, strongly rejected a proposal to put gambling on a city referendum, saying that it would be rejected whatever the local outcome.[30]

Intervention by the Courts

In some instances, the courts rebuffed decisions taken against the District government. For instance, at the close of the legislative session the following year, the House passed the Armstrong Amendment to the appropriations bill that required the City Council to revise its Human Rights Act so that religious schools could deny funds to gay rights groups.[31] But rather than simply abide by the wishes of the amendment, the Council sued the Congress and a U.S. Court of Appeals panel ruled the congressional amendment unconstitutional, affirming that the Council had the same rights as other legislative bodies in the country.[32]

However, when Congress or the White House were not active in intervening in the home rule rights of the District, they had the support of the courts, which by this time had grown more conservative through appointments made by Republican presidents since the 1980s. Several examples are shown below.

- In 2003, the Congress banned the attempt of the District to institute a commuter tax aimed at residents in the surrounding suburbs who frequently used city services. The ban was eventually upheld by the U.S. Court of Appeals, which refused to question the congressional authority over the District.[33]
- In 1975, one of the early pieces of legislation passed by the City Council was the Firearms Control Regulations Act, known as one of the toughest laws in the country. In 2005, however, Republican leadership stated a goal to repeal the District's gun control law. This measure eventually found its way to the Supreme Court that ruled in the summer of 2008 (*D.C. v. Heller*) that the city's ban on handguns violated the Second Amendment to the Constitution.[34]

- A District law passed in the fall of 2004 to protect citizens from inflated prices for prescription drugs was ruled unconstitutional by a U.S. district judge who held that this was against the wishes of the Congress, which had passed a balanced law governing interstate commerce with respect to drug prices.[35]

Perhaps the most egregious intervention was, as referred to above, the imposition of the Financial Control Board in 1995 to govern the city's finances and, by extension, things that those finances controlled such as the schools, making it the most expansive mechanism of such intervention in urban history.

Although this subject will be covered more comprehensively elsewhere in this work, it should be noted that this measure, supported by District Delegate Eleanor Norton and signed by President Bill Clinton, gave near total authority to the board over decisions by the mayor and City Council. This act of the federal government suspending the home rule experiment was received racially in the District in a manner that split residents, with whites (70 percent) largely approving of the board and home rules (60 percent) largely rejecting it.[36] This proof of the racial attachment of blacks to home rule helps to support the notion that its origin, as argued here, was founded in the wider movement for civil rights.

MOTIVATION FOR INTERVENTION

One source of such intervention had to do with the feeling that the District was badly managed, a view taken by Republican Rep. Frank Wolf, a member of the House District Committee.[37] Other feelings followed the negative image of the city that developed as a result of the legal troubles of Mayor Marion Barry and his close associates. Indeed, since the project of elected government was so new, it was difficult to determine whether such views were objective or race-based. Wolf was concerned about a trip that Mayor Marion Barry had taken where his security team was on-site in New York City, but he had disappeared. Then, on the night of January 19, 1990, Barry was arrested, having been trapped by an FBI sting operation smoking cocaine in a downtown Washington, D.C., hotel. Incidents such as these gave politicians opposed to home rule a sublime opening to both criticize the District and propose their own view of curative measures.

However, what often raised the specter that race may also have been intertwined with politics as a motivational force was the strength of the invective against a black majority city that controlled the District government and the disproportionate role of Southerners in the process of intervention who were partisans of the conservative movement and a key constituency in the Republican party. Republican control of the Congress and the conservative perspective would be reflected by Rep. Tom DeLay (Tex.), majority leader, who was known as a "district-basher" for his persistent complaints about crime in the city, the condition of the schools, the presence of prostitutes, and his view that the city was a "festering liberal hellhole."[38]

However, objections to statehood were revealed that were founded on race and politics. The expectation of democratic participation in a government that would have the capacity to satisfy their needs evolved—as it did in other states—from the contribution of citizens to national crises such as foreign wars and domestic damage. But it also flowed from the contribution of citizens to the tax base, such that the District has not be been an economic ward of the federal government, as it widely believed, but the taxes of its citizens have provided the lion's share of the financial resources for the operation of local government. This is supported by the striking statement by President George H. W. Bush, on March 23, 1990, that he opposed statehood because the city's funding came "almost exclusively from the Federal government."[39] At that time, the federal payment constituted only 14 percent of the District's budget, making the basis of his objection either ignorant of the facts or related to other motives.

THE SHAPE OF THE CITY

As noted above, that the modern origin of the quest for home rule in the District of Columbia took root in the civil rights movement of the 1960s, and that the growth of the black population achieved a majority of city residents, gave added impetus to the demand for democratic participation that would highlight the black population as a key sector of city resident for an improvement in their condition of life by the new form of city government.

Since 1950, the year of the greatest concentration of population in the District, metropolitan Washington, D.C., experienced rapid growth. However, the District lost forty-seven thousand residents in the twenty years between 1950 and 1970 as the black population grew to a majority status. Indeed, race is important here because 61 percent of the region's black population lived in Washington, D.C.[40] Census data indicates that as of 1969, 17 percent (123,000) of the 725,000 city residents were living under the official poverty line, but by 1986, of the total city household population 82 percent were black, and in 1990, although the city poverty rate was 16.7 percent, the black poverty rate was 20 percent, 2.6 times larger than the white

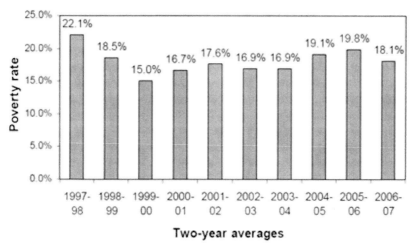

Figure 1.1. Poverty in the District of Columbia

rate.[41] That this group also needed government services disproportionately is indicated by the fact that in 1970, the poverty rate was 17 percent, growing to 20.2 percent by 2000.[42] Indeed, throughout this period, the District was perennially among the top cities in the nation in their poverty rate, and District data show that African Americans suffered disproportionately. In 2007, the white poverty rate was 7.4 percent and the black poverty rate was 22.7 percent.[43]

One could duplicate this comment in terms of the unemployment rate, since the Department of Housing and Urban Affairs reported that 17 percent of central cities, including the District of Columbia, were 50 percent or more above the national rate in 1998 with rates at 6.75 percent or higher.[44]

The following data indicates that except for the substantial decline in the poverty rate in the late 1990s (22.1 percent to 15 percent), the changes since have been statistically insignificant as poverty climbed to 17.6 percent in the 2001–2002 period.

The question one asks is whether or not the form of governance inherited in the Home Rule Act and implemented by various administrations has made an impact on the poverty rate. Because the poverty rate has an effect on so many other conditions of life, such as employment, education, health care, and so on, one can also ask whether the residents have been well served. One asks this question, however, with special relevance to the African American community, which has experienced a condition of low socio-economic status relative to whites as the community that apparently has needed democracy most.

THE APPROACH OF THIS VOLUME

Therefore, we propose to present several critiques of the issue of democracy in Washington, D.C., that focus on the impact of these factors on the effectiveness of local government. This would support the view of the Georgetown University Task Force on District of Columbia Governance that

> [c]urrently, concerns about political representation and democracy have been overridden by the fiscal crisis in the District and the appointment of the Financial Control Board in 1995. Perhaps the solution to political representation and the fiscal crisis may be intertwined. Perhaps with greater political autonomy and representation, the interests of the District would be better served and thus its financial problems would be dealt with more comprehensively.[45]

The theme of this work as stated immediately above will attempt to assess the political character of "democracy" by reviewing the performance of every administration since Mayor Walter Washington, with regard to whether the governing content and style of leaders enhanced democracy. As such, the political focus *will not engage the long-term, explosive quest for congressional representation* that has been the subject of much concern, but on how the various mayors administered the city in ways that were able to enhance democracy. The second major emphasis here is on policy evaluations addressing several important social and economic problems. It will be utilized to provide a concrete basis of evaluation of successful engagement with critical problems faced by the residents, especially those who need government most. Linking political leadership to service delivery is complicated in that the system of governance is the independent variable and much relies, especially in the District of Columbia, upon not only the performance of the official political leadership, but the interventions of the various centers of power as well.

The interventionist relationship of Congress and the White House has often meant that the District has been utilized as a laboratory for federal experimentation. It is not accidental that, for example, one-third of its public school system is comprised of charter schools, more than any other system in America, that its fiscal situation once invited the establishment of a "control board" with unprecedented powers over the entire city administration, that poverty and crime are still substantial among residents in the nation's capital seat, and that the child mortality rate has resembled those in Third World countries. This raises questions of what kind of democracy this unique political system has wrought.

As such, we will approach the analysis of this problem first through a series of chapters on the administrations that have held forth since 1974:

Michael K. Fauntroy provides a chapter on the Home Rule Charter; Toni-Michelle C. Travis presents chapters on mayors Walter Washington and Sharon Pratt Kelly; Wilmer J. Leon III writes a chapter on Mayor Marion Barry Jr.; and Daryl B. Harris writes the chapter on Mayor Tony Williams. Then there will be several chapters on various public policies that have been prominent in serving the District residents who are disproportionately dependent upon government services. ReShone L. Moore and Darwin Fishman analyze aspects of the educational system and its impact on students in separate chapters; Jared A. Ball writes on the impact of communications on District culture; Kevin L. Glasper presents a chapter on crime and rehabilitation; Angelyn Flowers delineates the various dynamics of poverty in the District; and William G. Jones analyzes housing policy.

CONCLUSION

The District of Columbia has attempted to fulfill the mandate of democratic governance since the legislation of its charter in the early 1970s establishing a framework of limited home rule. In a context that confronts multiple centers of paternalistic power with the authority to intervene and socioeconomic challenges that stem from the history and modern dynamics of race, the question remains as to how well citizens of the District have been served. The mobilization of the citizens of the District for the democratic right to have a more autonomous and representative political system has itself been a form of democratic participation. The issue this volume raises is the necessity for it to be achieved if the output of public policy is to truly be the source of a politics that more completely addresses citizens needs.

NOTES

1. David Braybrooke and Charles Linbloom, *A Strategy of Decisions*, New York: The Free Press, 1970, 37–57.

2. Frank R. Baumgartner and Bryan D. Jones, *Agendas and Instability in American Politics*, Chicago: The University of Chicago Press, 1993, 216–17.

3. Helen Ingram and Steven Rathgeb Smith, eds., *Public Policy for Democracy*, Washington, D.C.: The Brookings Institution, 1993, 78–79.

4. Ibid., 80–81.

5. Ibid., 93.

6. Roger W. Cobb and Marc Howard Ross, eds., *Cultural Strategies of Agenda Denial*, Lawrence: University of Kansas Press, 1997, 219.

7. Lisa L. Miller, "The Representational Biases of Federalism: Scope and Bias in the Political Process, Revisited," *Perspectives on Politics*, American Political Science Association, Vol. 5, No. 1, June 2007, 306.

8. William Frey and Dowell Myers, "Neighborhood Segregation in Single-Race and Multirace America: A Census 2000 Study of Cities and Metropolitan Areas," Working Paper, Fannie Mae Foundation, Washington, D.C., 2002.

9. Carol J. De Vita, Carlos A. Manjarrez, and Eric C. Twombly, "Poverty in the District of Columbia—Then and Now," Center on Nonprofits and Philanthropy, The Urban Institute, Washington, D.C., February 2000, 4.

10. *Metropolitan Bulletin*, Washington Center for Metropolitan Studies, George Washington University, No. 9, August 1972.

11. Edward Banfield and James Q. Wilson, *City Politics*, Cambridge, Mass.: Harvard University Press, 1963, 183.

12. Stephen Green, "Rep. Rarick Accused of Racism At Hearing on D.C. Home Rule," *The Washington Post*, February 9, 1972, A1.

13. Cited in Douglas M. Fox, *The New Urban Politics: Cities and the Federal Government*, Pacific Palisades, Calif.: Goodyear Publishing Co, 1972.

14. Robert C. Smith, *We Have No Leaders: African Americans in the Post-Civil Rights Era*, Albany: State University of New York Press, 1996, 127–37.

15. Albert K. Karnig and Susan Welch, *Black Representation and Urban Policy*, Chicago: University of Chicago Press, 1980.

16. Michael B. Preston, Lenneal J. Henderson Jr., and Paul Puryear, eds., *The New Black Politics: The Search for Political Power*, New York: Longman, 1982.

17. Michael Fauntroy, *Home Rule or House Rule? Congress and the Erosion of Local Governance in the District of Columbia*, Lanham, Md.: Rowman and Littlefield Publishers, 2003, 9.

18. Sandra Evans Teeley, "Congress Gets Answers About D.C. Policies," *The Washington Post*, June 8, 1983, Section DC, 6.

19. Ed Bruske, "Reagan: Bar Funding of D.C. Abortions; Budget Change Would Include City Money," *The Washington Post*, August 2, 1987, B1.

20. Ben A. Franklin, "Washington Seeks True Home Rule," *The New York Times*, October 9, 1981, 17A.

21. Ibid.

22. Arthur S. Brisbane, "D.C. AIDS Bill Draws Challenge in Congress; City 'Snookered' on Insurance, Says Helms," *The Washington Post*, June 20, 1986, B1.

23. Michael Abramowitz, "House Democrats Rescue D. C. Budget, Heading Off GOP at the Pass," *The Washington Post*, August 6, 1989, D1.

24. Michael Powell, "House Panel Approves D.C. Budget with Job and Tax Cuts, Vouchers," *The Washington Post*, September 18, 1997, D3.

25. Sylvia Moreno, "House Panel Approves Plan for Vouchers at District Schools; Norton, Who Opposed Bill, Says Member's Absence Affected Result in Narrow Vote," *The Washington Post*, July 11, 2003, B5.

26. Hamil R. Harris, "Key Senator Says D. C. Needs Radical Surgery; At Hearings, Brownback Pans Clinton Aid Plan," *The Washington Post*, May 14, 1997, B8.

27. "Congress, Tobacco and D.C.," *The Washington Post*, August 11, 1998, A20.

28. Stephen C. Fehr, "Clinton Seeks to End Impasse on D.C. Budget," *The Washington Post*, November 2, 1999, B2.

29. "House Panel Asked to Pass Zoning; Williams, Cropp Make Group Homes Plea," *The Washington Post*, June 6, 2002, B4.

30. Spencer S. Hsu, "Lawmakers Say Congress Won't Allow Slots in D.C.," *The Washington Post*, July 13, 2004, A1.

31. Michael York, "City Council to Sue Congress Over Amending Rights Law," *The Washington Post*, November 1, 1988, D5.

32. Pam McClintock, "Appeals Panel Rejects Hill Coercion of D.C.," *The Washington Times*, September 27, 1989, B1.

33. Carol D. Leonnig, "D.C.'s Commuter Tax Burden Discriminatory, Judges Told," *The Washington Post*, April 5, 2005, B2.

34. U.S. 554, No. 07-290, June 26, 2008.

35. Eric W. Weiss, "Prescription Drug Plan in D.C. Barred," *The Washington Post*, December 23, 2005, B1.

36. Yolanda Woodley, "D.C. Residents see a Future at Risk; Blacks, Whites Split Over Plan to Appoint Control Board, Poll Shows," *The Washington Post*, May 5, 1995, A1.

37. Sandra Evens, "D.C. Image Tattered on Hill, Wolf Says: Lawmaker Cites Barry Trip, Housing Shortage, Prison Release Plan," *The Washington Post*, October 12, 1988, B6.

38. Ibid.

39. Ann Devroy, R. H. Melton, and Nathan McCall, "President Opposes Statehood," *The Washington Post*, March 24, 1990, A2.

40. Samantha Friedman, George Washington University, "Behind The Monuments: Taking a Sociological Look at Life in the Nation's Capital," paper delivered at the 2000 Annual Meeting of the American Sociological Association.

41. See "Opportunity Ladders: Can Area Employment Possibilities Improve the Prospects for Washingtonians in Long-term Poverty?" Greater Washington Research Center, 1988, 16. Also, Census Historical Poverty Tables, cph-l-162, "Persons by Poverty Status in 1969, 1979, and 1989, by State," www.census.gov/hhes/www/poverty/census/chl162.html.

42. William Frey and Alan Berube, "A Decade of Mixed Blessings: Urban and Suburban Poverty in Census 2000," The Brookings Institution, Washington, D.C., August 2002.

43. "District of Columbia Detailed Profile, houses, real estate, cost of living, etc.," www.city-data.com/District_of_Columbia-DCV.html.

44. www.huduser.org/publications/polleg/tsoc99/summ-02.html.

45. "Political Representation," Task Force on District of Columbia Governance, Georgetown University, Graduate Public Policy Institute, 1995.

POLITICS

2

Home Rule for the District of Columbia

Michael K. Fauntroy

INTRODUCTION

After a war fought to replace a monarchy with a government that operated with the consent of the governed, the framers of the American constitution and founders of the nation touted representative democracy as the best possible form of government. Great care and attention were given to striking the right balance between giving the people a say in their government while creating a system that could function effectively. A federal system of government emerged that divided responsibility for certain functions between the states and the national government. States have further devolved responsibilities for certain areas to local and county governments. Over time, a form of government has taken root that is, in many ways, the governmental beacon all other nations try to reach.

The District of Columbia sits in a truly unique place in this democracy. On the one hand, it serves as the seat of the national government of the world's longest running democracy. It is a city in which diplomats the world over come to negotiate, legislators and jurists in rising democracies come to learn how representative democracy is implemented, and politicians around the nation aspire to work. On the other hand, it is the least democratic place in the nation as it is denied one of the most basic rights American democracy purports to show the world: full voting representation in its national legislature. This conflict with the American ideal of representative democracy has long been a point of contention among local citizens. This disparity takes on a particular resonance when one considers the lengths to which the United States is fighting to create a functioning Western-style democracy in Iraq and, more broadly, the entire Middle East.

District advocates for greater representation in the national legislature, more governmental autonomy, and even statehood have long worked to end the representational disparity that exists between the nation's capital and the rest of the country. The most significant struggle for greater democracy for the residents of the District of Columbia culminated in passage of the Home Rule Act of 1973, which created the city charter under which the District government now operates. This chapter explores the concept of home rule as a governing construct. It also examines the various eras of District of Columbia governance in which significant changes to the relationship between the national government and the District were effectuated and the fight for home rule.

DEMOCRATIC GOVERNANCE, THE DISTRICT OF COLUMBIA, AND THE CONSTITUTION

Basic democratic theory argues that the citizenry should have a say in their government and nations are deemed more or less democratic based on their citizen participation. Those with little or no citizen participation are seen as undemocratic and, in some cases, authoritarian. Indeed, nations are viewed as more or less democratic based on the extent of citizen participation. As such, self-rule sits at the core of democratic governance and serves as a major characteristic of open government. The United States has served as an example in this regard concerning its Middle East policy. Former president George W. Bush has often spoken about the importance of spreading democracy to new places in the world.

Article I of the U.S. Constitution details the responsibilities, rules, and roles for the national legislature. For example, voters in the respective states select their representatives in the House and Senate.[1] The District is not a state and no specific constitutional provision was made for the representation of its citizens. Indeed, with one exception, the Constitution is silent on the District. Article I, Section 8, Clause 17 states Congress is empowered to "exercise exclusive Legislation in all Cases whatsoever, over such District (not exceeding ten Miles square) as may, by Cession of Particular States, and the Acceptance of Congress, become the Seat of the Government of the United States."

The most likely explanation for the exclusion of the District of Columbia from the representation in the national legislature may lie in the reason why a federal district was deemed necessary. After the Revolutionary War, a group of veterans descended upon the Continental Congress meeting in Philadelphia demanding payment for their combat work. Unable to get protection from state officials, the Continental Congress fled to Princeton, New Jersey. After working there and in two other locations the Continental Congress adopted a resolution that called for buildings and land to be donated for the creation of a national capital which would be under the exclusive jurisdiction of the United States, thereby eliminating the possibility of such an incident occurring again. However, in seeking security for itself, the Continental Congress never settled the representation question for the three thousand people who lived in the territory at the time.

The constitutional silence on District representation has created a contradiction and infirmity in American democracy that exists in stark contrast to that of the rest of the nation. American citizens who live in Washington, D.C., do not fully participate in American democracy. Currently, Washingtonians live within the context of a limited, congressionally allowed home rule government that takes on many, but not all, of the characteristics of representative democracy.

What is Home Rule?

Home rule refers to a governmental status in which authority and responsibility for management of a unit of government (e.g., state, city, county, territorial) falls to that unit of government, subject to the parameters set by a superior unit of government. Domestically, home rule is seen in the context of relationships between cities and states or between counties and states.[2]

As Kneier notes, "home rule for cities means, in a broad sense, the right of self-government."[3] His differentiation between the two types of home rule provides important context for understanding how the District is governed. Kneier identifies the derivation of home rule powers as either legislative or constitutional in origin. Legislative home rule is that which is granted when a legislature abdicates

> its power to interfere in municipal affairs and grants to the cities the power to govern themselves. One difficulty, however, is that legislatures have been unwilling to follow this procedure. They have preferred to reserve to themselves the power to make detailed regulations relative to the government of cities. Even though home rule is granted by legislative act, there is no assurance that a subsequent act of the legislature may not take this power away.[4]

The first grant of legislative home rule was in 1858. By the end of the nineteenth century, a movement toward legislative home rule had begun in the American South.[5] While widely used, legislative home rule can be repealed by the state legislature and city ordinances can be overridden by the legislature. This makes legislative home rule weak, deficient, and always open to acts—predatory or otherwise—by the superior legislature. Consequently, cities with legislative home rule operate under the possibility of state interference, as their derivative powers can be revoked at any time.

Constitutional home rule "refers to the power of self-government conferred upon cities by constitutional provision."[6] This type of home rule can
be protected through court action and clearly establishes lines of demarcation
between the city and state because they are drawn in the state constitution.
Constitutional home rule cannot be abrogated by the legislature without
amending its constitution. Because it ensures and protects the freedom and
autonomy of the city, constitutional home rule is more advantageous for a city
than legislative home rule, which cannot offer the same level of security.

The District was afforded legislative home rule, the weaker of the two
forms; the Home Rule Act of 1973 did not change the U.S. Constitution.
The Act allowed Congress to grant autonomy to the local government, while
reserving the ability to intervene and overrule the District at any time. Functionally, the U.S. Congress, for the purposes of this discussion, serves as the
state to the District.

FIGHT FOR HOME RULE

The current form of home rule for the District of Columbia, which dates to
the passage of the Home Rule Act of 1973, was the culmination of decades
of work and strategy. For generations, Washingtonians—especially home
rule activists—had grown to resent the House District Committee in its role
as the gatekeeper for D.C.'s political and economic existence. Most home
rule advocates saw recalcitrant Southern conservative members of the House
as the main barriers to increased local autonomy. These conservatives were
personified by committee chair John L. McMillan (D-S.C.). McMillan, who
represented a rural district in South Carolina, benefited from laws—both
written and unwritten—that kept his African American constituents away
from the ballot box. Consequently, McMillan could act with impunity on
racial issues without fear of voter retribution. McMillan's maneuvering made
him "a symbol of congressional resistance to home rule for the city, and for
the domination by White Southern congressman of the affairs of a city with
a majority of Black residents."[7]

As former district delegate to Congress Walter E. Fauntroy noted, the Voting Rights Act of 1965, which opened the ballot box to African Americans
throughout the South, helped set the stage for passage of the Home Rule
Act:

> The passage of the Voting Rights Act of 1965 was the defining moment that
> changed the stranglehold the Federal City Council [and other opponents of
> home rule] had on District policy. It was critical because it opened the door
> to change the composition of the District Committee by registering Blacks in

the South who would vote for candidates who would be more favorable to the District of Columbia. This was particularly helpful with respect to McMillan, who saw registration efforts in his district result in an increase in the percentage of Blacks registered to vote from three percent in 1964 to twenty-eight percent in 1972.[8]

The Voting Rights Act helped open the door to the implementation of a strategy that would propel the home rule movement to new heights by adding more African Americans to voter rolls in the South. Many of these citizens had relatives who migrated to the District and, consequently, could be counted on to support the home rule movement. The role of African American voters in this regard is profound, and the capacity of racial conservatives to control the South was damaged by the Voting Rights Act. These new voters changed the composition of the Congress in such a way that home rule stood a much better chance of gaining legislative support. This led to a bold strategy by Fauntroy, who sought the defeat of McMillan, a fellow member of Congress from his own party. Fauntroy believed that defeating McMillan would eliminate the single most important barrier to home rule.

Fauntroy developed a network of activists throughout the South during the 1960s, through his organizing efforts in support of the civil rights movement. Fauntroy called upon those activists to help register Southern African Americans to vote, but focused particular attention on congressional districts in which African Americans could provide the margin of victory. These were not districts in which African Americans were in the majority—and could elect home rule candidates if they wished—but areas where they could decide who would win by their action (voting in large numbers) or inaction (staying home on election day). McMillan represented one such district.

Fauntroy reasoned that McMillan could not win reelection if home rule supporters turned out in large numbers in his district. He then led an effort—coordinated largely through home rule churches—to register and turn out to vote thousands of African Americans in support of Claude Stephens, an African American physician who challenged McMillan in the 1970 Democratic Party primary. McMillan won the primary with 49 percent of the vote, but was forced into a run-off primary because he did not cross the 50 percent threshold. In the second primary, however, supporters of McMillan and Bill Craig, the third place finisher, joined together to give the election to the incumbent. He later won the general election, and returned to Congress for another term.

Even in defeat, the framework for defeating McMillan had been set. As Stephens noted in defeat, "the 6th Congressional District will never be the same; the people here have shown that hopelessness does not exist . . . and big odds do not deter further efforts."[9] Furthermore, home rule in Washington, D.C., had been placed on the agenda in the sixth district of South Carolina as Fauntroy and other leaders and residents from the District of Columbia went to South Carolina to campaign against McMillan.

Realizing that it would be virtually impossible for an African American to win the seat held by McMillan, Fauntroy and others searched for a white candidate capable of unseating the incumbent. Settling on John Jenrette, Fauntroy continued his registration efforts in McMillan's district with an eye toward the 1972 Democratic House primary.

The effect of McMillan's defeat on the home rule movement was profound, as it opened the door to self-determination for District residents. It also showed that African Americans could compete in the world of brass-knuckle American politics. As Fauntroy noted in a press conference after McMillan's defeat, "this victory serves as a warning to those who oppose self-determination for the District."[10] Members who represented districts with similar profiles as McMillan's and who shared his worldview were put on notice that they could be targeted as well if they did not support home rule for the District.

The ideological makeup of the House District Committee in the wake of McMillan's defeat was profoundly changed. As indicated above, McMillan had surrounded himself with like-minded conservative Southern Democrats on the District Committee; in 1972, seven of the fifteen members were from Southern or border states, including McMillan and the next two ranking Democrats. By the start of the next Congress, six of those seven Southern or border state members left the committee, either voluntarily or, as in the case of McMillan, by electoral defeat. The path to home rule had been established.

HOME RULE ACT OF 1973

The Home Rule Act of 1973 proved to be an exercise in political compromise—neither side got everything it wanted, although the end result was a bill that needed future legislative attention. One editorial called the bill a "product of the 'process of accommodation' that takes place within the House, where bargaining is the name of the game, and where the hopes of Washingtonians can become merely incidental in the maneuvering for votes."[11] Home rule came with strings attached—so many that the system designed in the early 1970s began to be exposed just over a decade later as insufficient for allowing local officials to manage city affairs. Given the political context of that period, it is reasonable to assert that the Home Rule Act of 1973 was the best bill that could be passed at the time. As Senate District Committee chairman and home rule supporter Thomas F. Eagleton noted, "It does not give the citizens of the District of Columbia what I would call true home rule, because it does not give them the power of the purse, [but] it is a significant step forward."[12] It is unlikely that many viewed the Home Rule Act as the final step in the march to complete local autonomy on par with that of the cities around the country. More likely is the contention that the Act was a means to an end:

> To those who have insisted for so long—as we have—that Washingtonians should be accorded the democratic rights of full citizenship, this grant of a modified franchise is not fulfillment, not the true rule that other American communities enjoy. But it is a genuine opportunity for the people of the nation's last colony to seize new local initiative toward that end.[13]

The bill was a good start toward correcting the governmental wrongs that had been perpetrated against the District for generations.

The chief negotiator for the bill was Representative Charles Diggs (D-Mich.) who succeeded John McMillan as chairman of the House District Committee. The Home Rule Act allowed the residents of the District to elect a mayor to serve a four-year term with no term limits; a thirteen-member City Council with one member representing each of the city's eight wards, and five members (including the Council chair) elected at-large, also serving four-year terms. As a concession to minority parties in the overwhelmingly Democratic District, a provision in the Act mandated that no political party could nominate more than one candidate for the two at-large seats each election year. All acts of the Council would take effect after a thirty-legislative-day layover in the Congress. In reality, this period could take over two months, as weekends, holidays, and other days in which Congress did not convene did not count toward the legislative layover period.

The Home Rule Act had many provisions, with the most notable dealing with the power of the mayor and City Council, budgeting, and the makeup of the judiciary. The mayor would have broad power to appoint officials and administer the government, while Congress would retain control of how the District spent its money by requiring the city budget to pass through the congressional appropriations process each year. The mayor could also veto legislation passed by the City Council, though the legislative body could override such action with a vote of two-thirds of those present and voting.

The president would continue to appoint local judges instead of transferring that authority to an elected mayor. This was a major concession on the part of Representative Charles Diggs, chair of the House District Committee, because many local home rule supporters asked for local control over the courts. This was proposed in early 1973, but was removed after withering criticism by Republicans, as well as, in an unprecedented move, some local jurists. When originally proposed

> [t]he chief judges of the Superior Court and the D.C. Court of Appeals charged that a home rule bill shifting judicial appointments from the President and Senate to an elected city government would destroy the independence and integrity of the local courts. The proposed change, the judges said, would also subject them to political pressures from which, they said, they are now insulated.[14]

This concession was indicative of the Diggs-led negotiations that formulated the Home Rule Act, yet led to cries of "sell out" by some advocates of a stronger self-government bill. Diggs made six major concessions to home rule opponents:

1. Retention of line-item congressional control over the city's budget;
2. Election of the [City] Council and mayor on a nonpartisan basis rather than by partisan elections;
3. Specific authority to the president to take over control of the local police force in an emergency;
4. Confirmation of judges appointed by the mayor to the D.C. Court of Appeals and the D.C. Superior Court by the Senate rather than the City Council;
5. A prohibition on the City Council from making any changes in the criminal code; and
6. Provision that no Council action would take effect until thirty days after enactment to give Congress an opportunity to veto it.[15]

Some critics argued that the overwhelming vote in favor of passage—343 to 74—demonstrated that Diggs could have made fewer concessions and still got the bill through the House.

The Senate, which passed numerous home rule bills over the years, passed the 1973 version by a sixty-nine to seventeen vote. Twelve of the seventeen votes against the measure were cast by senators from Southern and border states: James Allen of Alabama, John McClellan of Arkansas, Samuel Nunn and Herman Talmadge of Georgia, James Eastland of Mississippi, Samuel Ervin and Jesse Helms of North Carolina, Henry Bellmon of Oklahoma, Strom Thurmond of South Carolina, John Tower of Texas, and Harry Byrd Jr. and William Scott of Virginia.[16]

The House-Senate conference version of the bill was adopted by the House on a 272–74 vote, and the Senate on a 77–13 tally. Opponents of home rule, while ultimately unsuccessful in preventing any local autonomy for the District, were very effective in weakening the city's ability to fully control its government in the conference version of the bill:

> The Senate-passed bill and the House version originally reported by the House District of Columbia Committee would have given the city much more control over its own affairs than the final bill. However, House District Committee Chairman Charles C. Diggs, Jr. (D-Mich.) had agreed to take the compromise version to the floor when it became apparent that the original House bill would be defeated or amended out of recognition by the House.[17]

The compromises that led to passage of the home rule bill in the House helped create a system that eventually collapsed in the 1990s, causing the District considerable governmental crises.

The Home Rule Act had a number of strengths and weaknesses. On one hand, the Act expanded democracy by allowing District residents to elect representatives of their choice to run their local government. In addition, the elected officials changed the face of District government by expanding the contracting base to include African American businesses which had been traditionally locked out of such opportunities. There was cultural significance as well given the place Washington, D.C., has held in the history of black America. In that regard, home rule provided an opportunity to instill pride in African Americans, not just in the District, but around the nation.

Conversely, the compromises that led to passage of the Act helped create the fiscal crisis that engulfed the District a decade and half later under Mayor Marion Barry. Because Congress retained final control of city budgets, it prevented the city from a number of revenue options, including the ability to impose a commuter tax on nonresidents who work in the District. Prohibitions in acting in certain ways on given problems represent the largest weakness in the Act. Congressman Charles Diggs (D-Mich.), chairman of the House District Committee and lead House negotiator, noted during the debate on the Home Rule Act conference report:

> *Mr. Speaker, when we examine the conference report it should be noted that we have reserved the right of the Congress to legislate for the District at any time on any subject* [emphasis added]; we have retained in the Congress the authority to review and appropriate the entire District budget, set up authorized audits and so on; we have preserved the court system. We have insured that planning by the local government may be vetoed by the Federal Planning Agency if it affects the Federal interests. We have prohibited the local Council from among other things, enacting tax reductions and increasing height limitations on buildings and affecting the functions of property of the United States. We have prohibited them from regulating the courts and the U.S. Attorney's office and the marshal's office . . . . This legislation is a reasonable and rational accommodation between

the interests of all Americans in their Nation's Capital and the basic principle that government should be responsible to the governed.[18]

The powers retained by the Congress, particularly those related to revenue generation, while constitutional, created a financial structure for the District that proved to be untenable. The result was a devastating fiscal crisis.

Those deficiencies severely undercut the ability of the city to protect itself against poor fiscal times. Further, those deficiencies were exposed and made worse during the 1980s when the nature of the problems that traditionally confronted District government expanded—particularly those relative to the changing demographic composition of the city. Those changes, and the responses of the District's elected officials, contributed to the erosion of the limited home rule that had been granted to the city.

THE EVOLUTION OF HOME RULE GOVERNANCE

The home rule charter for the District of Columbia is the constitution for the national capital and dates to 1802, when citizens petitioned Congress for a municipal charter. The charter granted by Congress made Washington an incorporated city where voters had the right to elect a local legislature that could pass laws and levy a tax on real estate to pay for city services. The local government also included a mayor appointed by the president. The charter has evolved over the years to reflect congressionally mandated changes in the governance structure of the District. The history of the District of Columbia reveals seven distinct governmental periods. Indeed, the District's late twentieth-century period of home rule is not its first. In fact, since 1800, there have been numerous incarnations of local autonomy ranging from virtually none to nearly complete autonomy.

First Governing Phase: 1801 to 1871

The first period was characterized by changes in the status and form of local government. When originally configured under the Organic Act of 1801,[19] the District comprised five units of local government: the County of Washington, the City of Washington, the City of Georgetown, the County of Alexandria, and the City of Alexandria. After that point, the District's charter was amended three times in the first twenty years of its existence. First, an act passed in 1802 chartered the city of Washington with a president-appointed mayor who served a one-year term, along with a twelve-member elected City Council divided into two chambers.[20] Georgetown and Alexandria continued as independent cities. Second, in 1812, the charter was again changed to provide for an eight-member Board of Aldermen, elected biennially, and a Board of Common Council, consisting of twelve members elected annually.[21] Also under this charter change, the mayor was elected annually by a majority vote of the Aldermen and Board of Common Council. In 1820, a third charter change allowed the voters to elect both the mayor and Board of Aldermen to two-year terms.[22] The Board of Common Council continued to be elected annually.

This period also saw the retrocession to the Commonwealth of Virginia of the land it donated for the creation of the District of Columbia. Congress retroceded land to Virginia effective September 7, 1846, after protests and petitions from citizens in these areas.[23] Citizens claimed that the physical separation from the rest of the District by the Potomac River left them disconnected from important services. The act reduced the size of the District of Columbia from one hundred square miles to sixty-eight square miles.

District governance during this period also reflected the nation's concern over issues of race. The District began to face racial strife as free blacks and fugitive slaves began to enter the city in large numbers. Trafficking of slaves was terminated in the District in 1850, beginning a slow decline in the number of locally owned slaves. This rendered the District a magnet for fugitive slaves from Virginia and Maryland, as they were able to enter nation's capital and be absorbed into the city's free black population.[24]

Until the later years of this period, the District imposed "black codes" that restricted black economic, social, and political movement. These codes imposed fines, corporate punishment, and jail time on blacks who were determined to have participated in "disorderly meetings, or any other game of immoral tendency."[25] The purpose of such actions was clear:

> In addition to expecting thus to forestall possible disorders, the city fathers probably counted on the new restrictions to check the influx of free Negroes, an unwelcome element in most southern cities, if only because the mere presence of freedmen seemed likely to stir up discontent among slaves. Washington officials evidently were persuaded that if freedmen enjoyed privileges here denied them in the rest of the South, irresponsible Blacks would swarm into the city from every corner of Dixie. The Black Codes in most of the slave states were far more severe than Washington's; they forbade schooling for slaves and discouraged it among free Negroes, put heavier penalties upon them for disregarding curfew, and sometimes established restrictions on manumission or required manumitted slaves to leave the state within six months.[26]

Conversely, with the end of the Civil War and the beginning of the Great Reconstruction, home rules began to attain some stature in the community by entering government employment or teaching posts in the public schools. Black men voted for the first time in 1867; a year later, two home rule men, John Cook and Carter Stewart, were elected to the Board of Aldermen. From 1869 through 1870, eight of twenty-one Council seats were held by blacks. The local legislature introduced anti-discrimination laws, which addressed equal access of all District citizens to places of amusement or public entertainment as well as to hotels, restaurants, taverns, and saloons.[27]

This period had three important characteristics. First, it demonstrated the significance of local representation to District citizens. Debates surrounding the founding of the federal district continued the discussion begun in documents such as "Federalist No. 43," which argued that there should be local suffrage:

> As the inhabitants will find sufficient inducements of interest to become willing parties to the cession; as they will have had their voice in the election of the government which is to exercise authority over them; as a municipal legislature for local purposes, derived from their own suffrages, will of course be allowed them; and as the authority of the legislature of the State, and of the inhabitants of the ceded part of it, to concur in the cession, will be derived from the whole people of the State, in the adoption of the Constitution, every imaginable objection seems to be obviated.[28]

James Madison's statement suggests that at least some of the Federalists favored some form of home rule.

Second, it demonstrated that Congress was so concerned about exclusive jurisdiction and complete control that the principle of representative democracy was taken for granted and remained unfulfilled, leaving an important void. As one historian of the nation's capital noted, "[I]n the 1780's men concerned about the building of a stronger union had so firmly believed a federally-controlled capital a necessary part of the plan that they had incorporated the provision into the Constitution."[29]

Third, throughout this period, both the presence of the home rule community in the District of Columbia and the efforts of its members to exercise basic political rights were viewed as a challenge to the political, social, and economic status quo, resulting in a range of political and social control ordinances applicable only to home rule.

Second Governing Phase: 1871 to 1874

The second period continued local autonomy with some consolidation of separate jurisdictions. Congress created a single municipal government for the District of Columbia to replace the separate entities of Georgetown, the

City of Washington, and the County of Washington. This new government included a president-appointed governor and eleven-member Council (upper chamber), and a twenty-two-member House of Delegates (lower chamber) which was elected by the voters from twenty-two districts.[30]

In this new structure, every bill passed by the Council and House of Delegates had to be presented to the governor for approval or veto. A two-thirds vote in each chamber was required to override a veto. Any bill passed by both chambers, but not acted upon by the governor for ten days (Sundays excepted) automatically became law, "unless the legislative assembly by their adjournment prevent its return, in which case it shall not be a law."[31]

The president also appointed a secretary, whose duty was to record and preserve the laws and act for the governor in his absence, and a five-member board of health. Lastly, a provision under the reorganization allowed for the election of the first nonvoting delegate to the U.S. House of Representatives.

Congress ended this period of home rule in the wake of financial misman-agement by Alexander "Boss" Shepherd, the appointed head of the Board of Public Works. A joint select committee created to investigate the fiscal status of the District found that Shepherd overspent city budgets by millions in an effort to upgrade municipal systems such as streets and sewers. While stating that the idea of a representative body should not be precluded by abolishing the legislative assembly, the report concluded that the local government as created was unworkable.[32] The abolition of the appointed governor, bicam-eral legislature, elected delegate to Congress, secretary, and Board of Public Works initiated a ninety-four-year period in which the residents of the Dis-trict would have no elected local government. In its place was a president-appointed three-person commission to administer the local government.[33]

Third Governing Phase: 1874 to 1967

The third period began with the three-member Board of Commissioners and other appointed leaders:

> In addition, the President was authorized to select an officer from the Army Corps of Engineers to manage both the District's physical plant and the con-struction of public works under the direction of the Board of Commissioners. The District government was prohibited from contracting additional indebted-ness. The law providing for a partially elected legislative assembly and an elected non-voting delegate to Congress was repealed.[34]

The Board of Commissioners was intended to be a temporary solution. The act that abolished the locally elected government called for the creation of a joint select committee to create a framework for future District governance. The majority report, dated December 27, 1876, instead recommended making the commissioner form of government permanent, which resulted in 1878 legislation that implemented the committee's recommendation.[35]

Studies and hearings regarding District governance were conducted throughout this period. Reports issued by these bodies consistently spoke of the need to improve efficiency and management of the federally controlled District.[36] These reports help lay the foundation for bills introduced in Congress beginning in the 1940s that sought to address the question of home rule and local governance in the District. While legislatively unsuccessful, the bills were able to bring important media attention to the issue of local D.C. governance.

Between 1947 and 1973, Congress—either one chamber or both—considered legislation to grant home rule or otherwise reorganize District government on over a dozen occasions. Each bill considered increasing local autonomy in some fashion. Two bills, both introduced in 1965, were particularly notable.

Representative Abraham J. Multer introduced H.R. 4644 on February 9, 1965, to provide the District with an elected mayor, City Council, and nonvoting delegate to the House of Representatives. The bill, which had the support of President Lyndon B. Johnson, also sought to formularize the federal payment, a move designed to aid the District in its long-range budgeting. The bill was not acted upon by the House Committee on the District of Columbia, prompting a bipartisan group of home rule supporters in the House to file a petition to discharge the committee from further consideration of the bill. Upon gaining the requisite signatures, a floor vote was taken, whereupon an amended version of the bill passed. The amended version of the bill called for a citizen referendum on the question of some form of self-government. It also called for the election of a board to propose a charter vesting in a D.C. government complete legislative authority on local legislative matters then handled by Congress, save those matters which Congress chose to reserve for itself.

A second home rule bill, H.R. 10115, was reported out of the House District Committee on September 3, 1965, when the discharge petition had accrued 217 signatures. The bill offered by District Committee chairman Representative John L. McMillan was a combination of two bills sponsored by Representatives Joel T. Broyhill and B. F. Sisk, which were introduced in August 1965. Under this bill, the federal government would have retained jurisdiction over only the old federal city of Washington, as it existed from 1791 to 1871. The remaining area would have been offered for retrocession to Maryland. If Maryland rejected the area, then eligible voters of that area would then hold a referendum on the issue of establishing a board to draft a home rule charter. If approved, the charter would have been sent to Congress, subject to amendment. While this measure was reported out of the District Committee, a floor vote was not scheduled.

The McMillan bill, as well as those offered by Broyhill and Sisk, is notable in that it was authored by an avowed opponent of District home rule, with the support of other opponents. The bill was offered as a political diversion to siphon away support from Multer's bill in hopes that no meaningful measure would pass. Opponents under pressure to support home rule could vote for the McMillan bill and claim to be for local control all the while knowing the bill could never pass the House.

Fourth Governing Phase: 1967 to 1973

The fourth period emerged from President Lyndon Johnson's Reorganization Plan No. 3 of 1967, which radically changed the face of District governance. Using his authority to reorganize executive departments, Johnson ended the three-commissioner form of government that had been in place since 1874, replacing it with a single executive appointed by the president—known as the "mayor-commissioner"—and a nine-member Council also appointed by the president, and subject to confirmation by the Senate. The power of the former Board of Commissioners to organize and manage the District government was given to the mayor-commissioner and the quasi-legislative regulatory powers of the former commissioners, affecting such areas as building codes, public health services, and welfare, were transferred to the Council.[37]

According to Johnson, the plan was designed to "bring 20th century government to the capital of this nation; to strengthen and modernize the government of the District of Columbia; to make it as efficient and effective as possible."[38] The effect of Reorganization Plan No. 3 was profound: it fundamentally changed the structure of the District government by consolidating management responsibility to one commissioner and opened the door for what would come in the form of the Home Rule Act.

Congress also took steps during this period to extend electoral participation to Washingtonians. In 1968, Congress granted the District the right to elect members to its Board of Education. In 1971, the District was granted the right to elect a delegate to the House of Representatives.

Fifth Governing Phase: 1973 to 1995

The fifth period began with passage of the Home Rule Act of 1973. The Act, which allowed for an elected mayor and City Council, effective January 2,

1975, marked a watershed in District governance. For the first time in nearly a century, residents of the District of Columbia would be allowed to elect a mayor and legislature empowered with limited responsibility for managing the District government. District residents would also have an opportunity to elect uncompensated community-level representatives, known as advisory neighborhood commissioners, who would serve as conduits between citizens and the Council.

The Home Rule Act had many provisions, the most notable of which addressed the power of the mayor and City Council, and budgeting. The mayor was granted broad power to appoint officials and administer the government, while Congress retained control of how the District spent its money by subjecting the city budget to the congressional appropriations process each year. The mayor could also veto legislation passed by the City Council, though the legislative body could override such action with a two-thirds vote.

The president continued to appoint local judges instead of transferring that authority to an elected mayor. Further, Congress reserved for itself a number of powers including, but not limited to, line-item congressional control over the city's budget; confirmation of judges appointed by the mayor to the D.C. Court of Appeals and the D.C. Superior Court by the Senate (rather than the City Council), and the provision that no Council action would take effect until thirty legislative days after enactment, to give Congress an opportunity to review it.

While the Home Rule Act provided residents of the District with more autonomy than at any time during the previous century, there were structural deficiencies that would make it difficult for the District to govern itself. There are three major criticisms lodged against the Act. The first is the overarching concern that the act did not give the District enough autonomy. Critics who hold this view contend that because Congress still holds considerable authority over the District, the city is not fully able to manage its affairs.

Second, the District does not have control over the District-generated portion of its budget. As a consequence, while awaiting congressional approval of the District's annual appropriation, there have been instances when the District has been unable to spend its own funds.

Third, the District is prohibited from taxing certain entities, such as embassies and nonprofit organizations. Over time, more than 56.5 percent of the total assessed value of the property in the District was tax-exempt, including 40.3 percent owned by the federal government. The remaining tax-exempt entities include churches, universities, foreign government property, property exempt by special acts of Congress, and property exempt by executive orders of the president.[39] Similarly, the Home Rule Act prohibited the District from taxing the income of nonresidents who work in the District, popularly known as a "commuter tax."

There were two major efforts during this period to strengthen District home rule. The first step centered around the 1978 passage of the D.C. Voting Rights Amendment to the U.S. Constitution.[40] Representative Don Edwards of California introduced the proposed constitutional amendment as H.J. Res 554 in the 95th Congress on July 25, 1977. It called for the District to receive two senators and proportional representation in the House of Representatives. Although the amendment was passed by the requisite two-thirds majority of the House of Representatives (289–127) and the Senate (67–32), it fell short of the required thirty-eight states necessary for passage, and expired in September 1985, having been ratified by sixteen states.

A second effort has been the statehood movement, which has been in existence in various forms. The movement began its most vigorous push in the mid-1980s, when it became clear that the D.C. Voting Rights Amendment would not be ratified. Many city activists critical of home rule argued that statehood was the remedy for what they contended was the weakness of the Home Rule Act, the injustice of disenfranchisement, and taxation without representation.

Thirteen statehood bills were introduced between the 98th and 107th Congresses.[41] On two occasions, the bills were reported out of the committee of jurisdiction, resulting in one floor vote. The first of these two bills was introduced by District Delegate Walter E. Fauntroy in the 100th Congress in 1987 to create a state out of the federal district that would have encompassed only the non-federal land in the District of Columbia.[42] While the bill was reported out of the House District Committee, no vote was taken on the House floor, perhaps due to a promised veto from President George H. W. Bush. On the second such statehood bill introduced in the 103rd Congress, a vote was held on the floor of the House in 1993, with a vote of 277–153 against passage.

Between the 101st and 107th Congresses, seven bills that would retrocede the District to the state of Maryland were introduced.[43] The bills would have maintained exclusive legislative authority and control of Congress over the National Capital Service Area in the District of Columbia. No hearings or votes on these bills were undertaken.

Sixth Governing Phase: 1995 to 2001

Period six began when a downturn in the District's economy, questionable internal oversight of city funds, governmental inefficiency, budget deficits, increasing crime and violence, declining population, and deteriorating public schools all contributed to increased congressional scrutiny of the District, and the election of Marion Barry as mayor after one term out of office. The newly elected Republican congressional majority responded to these events with passage of the District of Columbia Financial Responsibility and Management Assistance Act of 1995.[44] The Act created the D.C. Control Board to oversee and improve District fiscal management. Congress granted this nonelected panel penultimate authority over virtually every function of District governance.

Congress determined the need for a control board based on a number of findings, including the following:

1. A combination of accumulated operating deficits, cash shortages, management inefficiencies, and deficit spending created a financial emergency in the District of Columbia.
2. A failure to provide its citizens with effective, efficient services in areas such as education, health care, crime prevention, trash collection, drug abuse treatment and prevention, human services delivery, and the supervision and training of government personnel.
3. A deleterious effect on the long-term economic health of the District of Columbia by causing the migration of residents and businesses out of the District of Columbia and the failure of new residents and businesses to move into the District of Columbia.[45]

The District's fiscal insolvency, after years of mismanagement and accumulated budget deficits, was the driving force in creating the Control Board, which was further strengthened in 1997. On August 5, 1997, Congress passed the National Capital Revitalization and Self-Government Improvement Act.[46] The Act further expanded the managerial and oversight responsibilities of the Control Board—thus reducing those of Mayor Barry and the City Council—by shifting financial responsibilities for a number of District functions to the federal government. These responsibilities include operations, financial support of the court system, road improvements and other capital projects, Internal Revenue Service technical assistance for local tax collection, and increased federal share of District Medicaid payments.

In addition, the federal government assumed financial and administrative responsibilities for one of the District's largest fiscal burdens—its unfunded pension liability for vested teachers, police, firefighters, and judges. These budget items, in the main, are those that are generally paid for by states, not cities. The legislation also granted the District tax breaks for homeowners and businesses in distressed neighborhoods.

In exchange, the Control Board assumed administrative responsibility for nine major agencies of the District government. In addition to controlling the public schools, police department, and financial management, the Control Board gained oversight and direct management responsibility of fire and emergency medical services, public works, administrative services, corrections, human services, consumer and regulatory affairs, employment services, housing and community development, personnel, and procurement. The reporting structure for department heads was shifted away from the mayor and Council to the Control Board and Chief Management Officer, a position created by the Act.

Period six concluded at the end of fiscal year 2001, when the Control Board disbanded after the District balanced four consecutive budgets. The reversal of the District's economic picture is due in part to increased tax revenues, the five-billion-dollar transfer of pension, prison, and Medicaid programs to the federal government, and increased economic growth. These factors helped the District move from a fiscal year 1996 deficit of $518.2 million to a budget surplus of $464.9 million in fiscal year 2000.[47]

Seventh Governing Phase: 2001 to Present

Period seven began at the start of fiscal year 2002 and in the wake of the terrorist attacks on the Pentagon and the World Trade Center on September 11, 2001.[48] The attacks had a significant impact on the District economy, as the city lost $750 million and twenty-four thousand jobs in the first six months following September 11. Most of the economic damage was in the hospitality industry, where numerous conferences and meetings have been canceled.

The expiration of the Control Board occurred under the mayoralty of Anthony Williams, the first chief financial officer of the District. His leadership went a long way toward calming congressional concerns about the city government. His deracialized approach to governing was seen as the antithesis of his predecessor, Marion Barry, who was largely seen as the reason why the city ended up in the fiscal crisis of the 1990s. Williams helped restore the District to fiscal health, presided over the revitalization of parts of downtown, and improved the reputation of the city with Congress. This may well have been his most important accomplishment as it may have decreased the likelihood that Congress would have micromanaged the city to the extent that it did during Barry's last term as mayor.

Adrian Fenty was elected in 2006 to succeed Williams who did not seek reelection. While still early in Fenty's term, it appears that Congress is continuing its relatively reserved approach to home rule. Fenty was elected in the same year in which Democrats regained control of Congress. This is significant in that Democrats have generally been more supportive of protecting home rule principles. Particularly notable is the work of District Congresswoman Eleanor Holmes Norton, who aggressively sought to protect and expand the District's home rule prerogatives. Norton has introduced legislation that would give the District autonomy from congressional oversight of the local budget because it is entirely derived from local sources. She also introduced a legislative autonomy bill that would eliminate congressional review of D.C. Council–passed laws.

There are still areas in which Congress, for political purposes, seeks to intercede in local issues. The most notable recent example is the recent controversy over the District's handgun ban. On June 26, 2008, the Supreme Court overturned the District's long-standing ban on handguns in homes. The Court upheld a federal district court holding "that the Second Amendment protects an individual's right to possess firearms and that the city's total ban on handguns, as well as its requirement that firearms in the home be kept nonfunctional even when necessary for self-defense, violated that right."[49]

The five to four decision was opposed by locally elected officials who have to contend with the continuing wave of gun violence. Elected officials made it clear that it would comply with the ruling, while also making it clear that it would do so in the least invasive way possible. Gun supporters in Congress have introduced legislation that would prohibit the District from writing legislation that would comply with the ruling and maintain some lower level of handgun restriction that may be allowable by the courts.[50] If passed into law, this would take out of the hands of the local government the authority to write legislation on this issue. This would represent a significant turn away from the principles of home rule.

CONCLUSION

District of Columbia home rule can best be seen as a series of political and ideological ebbs and flows. While there has been expansion and contraction of local autonomy over the decades, none of the changes have resulted in the local government having the kind of control over its affairs that we see in the relationship between many major cities and the states in which they are located. Given the political climate in which the District operates, the future of home rule in the District will continue to be uneasy, particularly if Congress is unwilling to correct the constitutional infirmity that faces this unique political structure called the District of Columbia. While the current period of home rule represents a "lull" in the back-and-forth between the District and Congress, there will come a time at some point in the future where the current structure again reveals itself to be deficient and ineffective as a governing tool and construct befitting representative democracy.

NOTES

1. The Seventeenth Amendment, passed in 1913, changed the manner of electing members of the Senate to allow for the popular election of its members. Previously, senators were elected by their respective state legislature.

2. See Lyle Schaller, "Home Rule—A Critical Appraisal," *Political Science Quarterly*, v. 76, issue 3 (September, 1961), 402–15. This study analyzes the concept of home rule relative to the concerns of its supporters and opponents. Terrance Sandalow, "The Limits of Municipal Power Under Home Rule: A Role for the Courts," 48 *Minn. L. Rev.* 643 (1964). Sandalow defines home rule in two ways: "the freedom of a local unit of government to pursue self-determined goals without interference by the legislature or other agencies of state government" and "a particular method for distributing power between state and local governments."

3. Charles Kneier, *City Government in the United States* (New York: Harper and Brothers Publishers, 1947), 85.

4. Ibid.

5. Ibid.

6. Ibid., 87.

7. Martha Hamilton and Stephen Green, "Liberals to Press for Home Rule Now," *The Washington Post*, 14 September 1972, C1.

8. Congressman Walter E. Fauntroy, interview by author, June 11, 1999 (hereafter cited as Fauntroy interview).

9. "South Carolina Runoff Results," *Congressional Quarterly*, 26 June 1970, 1643.

10. Jack Kneece, "How McMillan Lost," *The Washington Star*, 13 September 1972, B1.

11. Editorial, "The Twists in the Road to Home Rule," *The Washington Post*, 11 October 1973, A18.

12. Martha Hamilton, "Senate Gives Home Rule Final Assent," *The Washington Post*, 20 December 1973, A1.

13. Editorial, "Suffrage—At Last," *The Washington Post*, 25 December 1973, A22.

14. Eugene Meyer, "Judges Score Home Rule Bill Provision," *The Washington Post*, 19 July 1973, C1.

15. "House Passes Compromise D.C. Home Rule Bill," *Congressional Quarterly*, 13 October 1973, 2750.

16. *Congressional Quarterly*, 14 July 1973, reporting Senate roll-call vote 264.

17. "Congress Grants Nation's Capital Limited Home Rule," *Congressional Quarterly*, 22 December 1973, 3348–49, reporting House roll-call vote 514, and Senate roll-call vote 573.

18. U.S. Congress, House of Representatives, Committee on the District of Columbia, *Home Rule for the District of Columbia 1973–1974: Background and Legislative History of H.R. 9056 and H.R. 9682, and Related Bills Culminating in the District of Columbia Self-Government and Governmental Reorganization Act, Chapter 1, Subcommittee Markup Sessions*, 3051–52 (hereafter cited as 1973 home rule hearings).

19. United States Statutes at Large, "An Act Concerning the District of Columbia," February 27, 1801, 2 Stat. 103.

20. United States Statutes at Large, "An Act Additional to, and Amendatory of, 'An Act Concerning the District of Columbia," May 3, 1802, 2 Stat. 195.

21. United States Statutes at Large, "Amendment of the Charter of the City of Washington," May 4, 1812, 2 Stat. 721.

22. United States Statutes at Large, "Incorporation of the City of Washington," May 15, 1820, 3 Stat. 583. 3 Stat. 583.

23. United States Statutes at Large, "Retrocession of Alexandria to Virginia," July 9, 1846, 9 Stat. 35.

24. Constance McLaughlin Green, *The Secret City: A History of Race Relations in the Nation's Capital* (Princeton, N.J.: Princeton University Press, 1967), 46–47.

25. Ibid., 18.

26. Ibid., 18–19.

27. Nelson F. Rimensnyder, *Local Government in the District of Columbia, Congressionally Chartered Government for the Nation's Capital, 1801–1871*, U.S. House of Representatives, Committee on the District of Columbia, unpublished monograph, Washington, D.C., 1977, 3.

28. Jacob E. Cooke, ed., *The Federalist* (Middletown, Conn.: Wesleyan University Press, 1961), 289.

29. Green, Constance McLaughlin, *Washington: Village and Capital*, 1800-1878, (Princeton: Princeton University Press, 1962), p. 11.

30. U.S. Congress, House of Representatives, *Governance of the Nation's Capital: A Summary History of the Forms and Powers of Local Government for the District of Columbia, 1790–1973*, 101st Cong., 2nd Sess. (Washington: Government Printing Office, 1990), 42.

31. Congress, House of Representatives, *Governance of the Nation's Capital: A Summary History of the Forms and Powers of Local Government for the District of Columbia, 1790-1973*, 101st Cong., 2nd Sess., (Washington: Government Printing Office, 1990), p. 42.

32. U.S. Congress, House of Representatives, *Governance of the District of Columbia*, H. Rept. 647, 43rd Cong., 1st Sess., 16 June 1874. The report did not address the question of why both elected and appointed officials were abolished.

33. United States Statutes at Large, "An Act for the District of Columbia and for Other Purposes," June 20, 1874, 18 Stat. 116.

34. Jason Newman and Jacques DePuy, "Bringing Democracy to the Nation's Last Colony: The District of Columbia Self-Government Act," *The American University Law Review*, v. 24 (Spring 1975), 545–46.

35. United States Statutes at Large, "Organic Act of 1878," June 11, 1878, 20 Stat. 102.

36. *Governance of the Nation's Capital: A Summary History of the Forms and Powers of Local Government for the District of Columbia, 1790–1973*, 44–46: "the efficacy of the District government was the subject of numerous studies and hearings, within and outside the Congress during the first half of the twentieth century while its form remained the same. The government of the Nation's Capital was examined repeatedly with an eye toward reorganization or reform." The Institute for Government Research, which prepared the report *The District of Columbia: Its Government*

and Administration, was one such group to study District governance. Also, the U.S. Bureau of Efficiency conducted over one hundred studies on the administration of the District government. These were in addition to congressionally commissioned reports and District Committee hearings.

37. Newman and DePuy, 547.

38. U.S. Congress, House of Representatives, 90th Cong., 1st Sess., H. Doc. 138 (Washington, D.C.: Government Printing Office, 1967).

39. Government of the District of Columbia, Office of Policy and Evaluation, *Indices: District of Columbia Statistical Handbook, 1997–1998* (Washington, D.C.: Government of the District of Columbia, 1999), 92. According to the *Handbook,* the District has a land area of sixty square miles and a water area of nine square miles. Public rights-of-way account for 13.4 square miles of District acreage, or more than 22 percent of the land area. When these public rights-of-way are excluded, the land area is 28,898 acres, more than 56.5 percent of which is classified as tax exempt, including 40.3 percent owned by the federal government and 5.4 percent owned by the District government. See also Carol O'Cleireacain, *The Orphaned Capital: Adopting the Right Revenues for the District of Columbia* (Washington, D.C.: Brookings Institution Press, 1997), 57.

40. United States Statutes at Large, "District of Columbia Representation Amendment, August 22, 1978, 92 Stat. 3795. See also "District of Columbia Representation in Congress," *Congressional Record,* vol. 124, 2 March 1978, 5263–73.

41. In the 98th Congress, Del. Fauntroy introduced H.R. 3861 on 12 September 1983 and Sen. Edward Kennedy introduced S. 2672 on 15 May 1984. In the 99th Congress, Fauntroy introduced H.R. 325 on 3 January 1985; Kennedy introduced S. 293 on 24 January 1985. In the 100th Congress, Fauntroy introduced H.R. 51 on 6 January 1987; Kennedy introduced S. 863 on 26 March 1987. In the 101st Congress, Fauntroy introduced H.R. 51 on 3 January 1989; Kennedy introduced S. 2647 on 17 May 1990. In the 102nd Congress, Del. Norton introduced H.R. 2482 on 29 May 1991; Kennedy introduced S. 2023 on 22 November 1991. In the 103rd Congress, Norton introduced H.R. 51 on 5 January 1993; Kennedy introduced S. 898 on 5 May 1993. In the 104th Congress, Norton introduced H.R. 51 on 4 January 1995.

42. Del. Fauntroy introduced H.R. 51 on 6 January 1987. On 17 September 1987, the bill was reported to the House, with amendments, by the Committee on the District of Columbia, Rep. No. 100-305 and placed on the Union Calendar No. 188.

43. In the 101st Congress, Rep. Ralph Regula introduced H.R. 4195 on 6 March 1990. In the 102nd Congress, Regula introduced H.R. 1204 on 28 February 1991. In the 103rd Congress, Regula introduced H.R. 1205 on 3 March 1993. In the 104th Congress, Regula introduced H.R. 1028 on 23 February 1995. In the 105th Congress, Regula introduced H.R. 831 on 25 February 1997. In the 106th Congress, Regula introduced H.R. 558 on 3 February 1999. In the 107th Congress, Regula introduced H.R. 810 on 1 March 2001.

44. United States Statutes at Large, "District of Columbia Financial Responsibility and Management Assistance Act of 1995", Apr. 17, 1995, 109 Stat. 97.

45. Ibid. See also, the District of Columbia Financial Responsibility and Management Assistance Act of 1995, 2–3 (obtained via Lexis-Nexis).

46. Title XII of the Balanced Budget Act of 1997, P.L. 105-33, 11 Stat. 712.

47. Spencer S. Hsu, "District Completes Its Fiscal Comeback," *The Washington Post*, 30 January 2001, A1, citing the District of Columbia FY 2000 Comprehensive Annual Financial Report.

48. Mayor Anthony Williams, testifying before the House Subcommittee on the District of Columbia, 2 November 2001.

49. *District of Columbia et. al. v. Heller*, No. 07-290, June 26, 2008 (slip opinion).

50. Representative Mark Souder introduced H. Res. 1331 on July10, 2008.

BIBLIOGRAPHY

Green, Constance McLaughlin. *The Secret City: A History of Race Relations in the Nation's Capital*. Princeton, N.J.: Princeton University Press, 1967.

Green, Constance McLaughlin. *Washington: Village and Capital, 1800-1878*. Princeton: Princeton University Press, 1962.

Government of the District of Columbia, Office of Policy and Evaluation. *Indices: District of Columbia Statistical Handbook, 1997–1998*. Washington, D.C.: Government of the District of Columbia, 1999.

Hsu, Spencer S. "District Completes Its Fiscal Comeback." *The Washington Post*, January 30, 2001.

Kneier, Charles. *City Government in the United States* (New York: Harper and Brothers Publishers, 1947).

Meyer, Eugene. "Judges Score Home Rule Bill Provision." *The Washington Post*, July 19, 1973.

Newman, Jason, and Jacques DePuy. "Bringing Democracy to the Nation's Last Colony: The District of Columbia Self-Government Act." *The American University Law Review*, v. 24 (Spring 1975), 545–46.

O'Cleireacain, Carol. *The Orphaned Capital: Adopting the Right Revenues for the District of Columbia*. Washington, D.C.: Brookings Institution Press, 1997.

Rimensnyder, Nelson F. *Local Government in the District of Columbia, Congressionally Chartered Government for the Nation's Capital, 1801–1871*. U.S. House of Representatives, Committee on the District of Columbia, unpublished monograph, Washington, D.C., 1977.

U.S. Congress, House of Representatives, Committee on the District of Columbia. *Home Rule for the District of Columbia 1973–1974: Background and Legislative History of H.R. 9056 and H.R. 9682, and Related Bills Culminating in the District of Columbia Self-Government and Governmental Reorganization Act, Chapter 1, Subcommittee Markup Sessions*. Washington, D.C.: Government Printing Office, 1974.

U.S. Congress, House of Representatives. *Governance of the Nation's Capital: A Summary History of the Forms and Powers of Local Government for the District of Columbia, 1790–1973*, 101st Cong., 2nd Sess. Washington, D.C.: Government Printing Office, 1990.

3

Walter Washington: Mayor of the Last Colony

Toni-Michelle C. Travis

BEFORE HOME RULE

From 1874 to 1967 Washington was run by three commissioners who functioned as the executive and legislative authority over the city. The Board of Commissioners was composed of two civilian members, D.C. residents who usually had political connections or ties to the business elite, along with someone from the Army Corps of Engineers. Collectively they ran all city departments. In reality, however, the engineer commissioner was the most powerful because he was responsible for the city's infrastructure—bridges, tunnels, and the water supply. He determined the physical appearance of Washington, D.C., including decisions about urban renewal. He also decided where to site new highways which had the potential of destroying a neighborhood. These became important issues in the 1950s as the black population increased.

Washington operated under this system of governance through both world wars, while Congress assigned many of the functions of municipal government to federal agencies. The result was a hodgepodge bureaucracy where agencies such as the Bureau of the Budget and the Justice Department played a role in District affairs.

Until World War II no one gave much thought to the governance of Washington, D.C., or its peculiar government. It was a Southern, segregated city where local residents had no say in electing officials at the local or federal level. The real power running the city was Congress, with the Board of Trade playing a supporting role. After World War II, Congressman John McMillan of South Carolina became chairman of the House District Committee which traditionally included congressmen from Maryland and Virginia whose constituents were often federal employees and Southerners who had a special interest in overseeing any policy which affected African Americans. Consequently, the committee was seen as a thorn in the side of residents who wanted home rule. Essentially, Washington, D.C., was run as if it were just another bureau of the federal government.

The other base of power in the District was the Board of Trade. For years, the Board worked in conjunction with the commissioners and the House District Committee to set local policies. Congress and the Board of Trade worked together to promote business and to keep the taxes low. This unelected government working with a powerful Board of Trade did not foster citizen participation. Indeed, citizen input was heard primarily through neighborhood associations composed of mostly of white residents.

The government of Washington, D.C., was never a model of democracy. In the 1950s the unelected commissioners who supported segregation and the conservative business leaders never had the concerns of the black residents on their agenda. The urban renewal of Southwest, the abolition of substandard housing known as alley dwellings, and planning highways that would cut across neighborhoods all adversely affected the black community. There were even racial implications in the battle to build a subway system. Congressman Natcher of Kentucky made it clear that he would block funding for the subway until the highway program went forward.[1]

Natcher's plan would have destroyed black neighborhoods. After hearings, citizen protests, and compromises, Washington got subway funding only after highway money was transferred to it. Simultaneously, external factors such as demographic changes, civil rights protests, and the growth of suburbia began to have an impact on the District. As a Southern city, race relations were always a consideration in congressional oversight of D.C. In the 1950s the black population protested against segregated housing, schools, and neighborhoods as the civil rights movement gained national momentum. African Americans in many cases had government jobs, but were relegated to the lowest pay grades as clerks or messengers, with few ever rising to the professional ranks. The District government had few black employees, with only a handful of police officers or fire fighters. One issue that incensed residents was urban renewal of the southwest section of the city. This became a hotly contested policy which caused the black community to protest the massive displacement of low income blacks. Whites tended to view southwest as a complete disaster with substandard housing that could only be remedied by razing the entire area. The blacks who were against the complete demolition of southwest were advocates of community preservation, with an approach to building new low-income housing. The result was that the planners leveled the southwest section as the displaced residents moved into other areas of the city.

In 1950 Washington reached a peak population of eight hundred thousand as the white population declined and the black population steadily increased. The Maryland and Virginia suburban white population increased dramatically after the 1954 school desegregation decision. With a growing African American population, Congress did not make granting home rule to D.C. residents a priority. By 1957 Washington was the first major American city to attain a majority black population. The black population continued to increase through the 1970s to become well over 70 percent of the population.

Before home rule, blacks were not very active in the citizen associations. However, many joined the NAACP or the Urban League to voice their concerns about the community. These establishment interest groups, which had worked for years to improve the status of black people, were soon overshadowed by more militant groups such as the Southern Christian Leadership Conference (SCLC) and the Student Nonviolent Coordinating Committee (SNCC) that advocated for the rights of blacks and D.C. home rule. This brought a number of young, new people to Washington, D.C.—Sterling Tucker to head the Urban League; Rev. E. Franklin Jackson, to head the NAACP; Julius Hobson to head Congress of Racial Equality (CORE); and Marion Barry to head SNCC, along with liberals such as attorney Joseph Rauh and Democratic Party activist Polly Shackelton.

These activists questioned and challenged local rules and regulations. Newcomers saw home rule as a critical issue that must be addressed. Northern newcomers were accustomed to voting for local officials. Those from the South also highly valued the rights of D.C. residents because they had often fought for black voting rights in the South. Among the newcomers, Marion Barry from Mississippi stood out when he led a successful boycott of the D.C. transit system to protest a fare increase. He was also a critic of the police department's tactics against blacks. Julius Hobson, a native of Birmingham, Alabama, served as a PTA president, in a leadership position with the NAACP, and as vice president of the Federation of Civic Associations. It was, however, as head of the D.C. chapter of CORE that he put the most pressure on local businesses when he organized a campaign to force downtown merchants to hire black workers. Later, he focused on the tracking system in the D.C. public school system. He asserted that there was inequity between the white and black schools on the basis that the white schools had smaller classes, better teachers, and more resources than the black ones. He won his suit which forced the tracking system to be dismantled. The consequence was the implementation of busing to ease the pressure on the overcrowded black schools.

These activists fought to change the District's undemocratic government. Obtaining a vote for the president of the United States in 1961 was only a minor victory. These activists were protesting congressional control, management of the District by an appointed-commissioner system of government, and the remnants of segregation. Dissidents were well aware that John F. Kennedy's election as president in 1960 would play a role in the future status of D.C. residents. When Kennedy took office the District had a majority black population that was demanding home rule. The District was caught in its usual conflict—President Kennedy was sympathetic to home rule supporters, while Congressman McMillan of the House District Committee stonewalled any attempt to pass a home rule bill. Following Kennedy's death, President Johnson's 1964 electoral victory brought renewed hope to D.C. home rule supporters.

President Johnson, now elected in his own right, sought congressional approval of home rule legislation, only to meet the continued opposition of the chair, Congressman McMillan. The Board of Trade also opposed home rule because it thought that would diminish its power to influence Congress on local issues. The commissioner system of governance was acceptable to both parties because they were not accountable to D.C. residents. Realizing that home rule legislation was a dead issue, President Johnson continued his efforts by proposing a plan to reorganize the District government where he would appoint a mayor-commissioner and a nine-member City Council. Although this plan was opposed by Congressman McMillan and the Board of Trade, Johnson was successful in moving Washington, D.C., one step closer to an elected government. The question then was who would accept the job of running a capital city which had a hybrid bureaucracy, congressional oversight, and a black majority population.

A unique city, Washington, D.C., needed a public administrator and a politician who could answer to all of the constituencies. Previously, the citizens had had little voice in governance, but Congress, the Board of Trade, and the U.S. president were still major players in D.C. governance. The mayor-commissioner was going to face certain problems: a racially polarized declining school system, a predominantly white police force in a majority black city, and a militant segment of the population that demanded complete home rule. Since the nineteenth century, Washington had been run by the whims of Southern congressmen who wrote laws and regulations to suit their purposes. Long-standing practices were to keep alcohol and tobacco taxes low and provide patronage jobs such as Capitol Hill police positions for their constituents. Washington, D.C., was run as if it were a colony controlled by Southern congressmen. Immediate problems were:

- how to reorganize the functions of the government that had been divided among three commissioners
- how to negotiate with Congress
- how to govern a majority African American city which was the capital city

EARLY CAREER

President Johnson needed someone who would be respected on Capitol Hill and simultaneously be acceptable to the residents of Washington, D.C. He reviewed the names of a number of possible candidates, but settled on a local who was familiar with congressional influence over D.C. He selected Walter E. Washington, who grew up in Jamestown, New York, but had been in Washington, D.C., since his student days at Howard University in the 1930s. After graduating he pursued a public administration program at American University and married into a locally prominent family. Later he decided that law school was a more suitable career. After finishing his degree at Howard University School of Law he took a position with the Alley Dwelling Authority, a federal agency. He rose through the ranks of the housing department from 1941 to 1961 when he was appointed its executive director by President Kennedy. This appointment made him the first African American to hold such a position in the housing field.

During his years at National Capital Housing Authority, Washington provided for the poorest residents, while he worked to build ties to Congress "by creating confidence and goodwill."[2] Washington was open to new ideas as he worked with the architects who designed the public housing. However, aside from his official duties, Washington found time to talk with the average guy on the street. Robert Asher of the *Washington Post* praised Walter Washington's housing career by saying that because of him "new ideas are now accepted practice in public housing: day care centers, job counseling and financial advice, credit unions, and tenant councils."[3]

Walter Washington's administrative skills were noticed by New York City Mayor John V. Lindsay who invited Washington to become chairman of the New York Housing Authority in 1966. Washington immediately tackled the housing problems by settling a strike of public housing employees, introducing "scattered-site" housing, leasing and renting units, and implementing his "turn-key" concept of private constructions for public use.[4] Washington was seen as an innovator who took a personal interest in citizen demands. Although he was only in New York briefly, Walter Washington had a positive impact.

THE APPOINTMENT

In 1960s Washington, D.C., local black activists were pressing for home rule in the face of a Southern-dominated Congress, while the civil rights movement intensified on the national stage.

President Lyndon B. Johnson was a supporter of home rule for Washington, D.C., but he also had to consider objections from the House District

Committee's chairman, John McMillan, who opposed any measure of home rule. Johnson's reorganization plan allowed him to go around Congressman McMillan in order to appoint the mayor-commissioner and City Council. President Johnson considered several names of prominent African American men for the position. Washington's name had come to his attention in part because of Mrs. Johnson's Beautification Committee. Mrs. Johnson knew of Walter Washington's work with her committee and thought highly of his abilities to work with people at the community level.[5] Johnson's choice was Walter Washington, a man who "provided the leadership, the vision, the understanding and the talent to move the Capital City forward." [6]

REORGANIZATION

Upon assuming office in January 1968, Washington faced two sets of problems. On the local level he had to address problems of crime, employment, and welfare. However, because Washington, D.C., was the capital, the city had to handle the numerous anti–Vietnam War demonstrations and the riots after Martin Luther King Jr.'s death. The resolution of both of these issues garnered national interest, which was only heightened by television coverage.

Although he was appointed, the symbolism of an African American becoming mayor of the capital of the United States was clear. Washington, D.C., a unique city because of congressional power, had structural problems of changing a political culture where citizens were just being brought into the governing process. As Washington reorganized the government he also had to respond to the demands of the various constituencies: the Board of Trade, the House District Committee, the black bourgeois residents, and the young civil rights militants.

The proposed city government had to be reorganized to reflect the division of power between the executive—the mayor—and the newly established legislative component—the City Council. The new government and structure called for a city manager who was to be selected from outside of Washington, D.C. However, both the mayor and city administrator were presidential appointments. The first city manager, Thomas Fletcher, found that there had been mismanagement under federal control, minimal structure for central management, as well as a system of personal relationships among D.C. employees and congressional as well as executive branch officials. The White House was still in the background, but in continuous contact with the city manager. In addition, the government consisted of "forty departments, 120 boards and commissions, and 35,000 employees."[7] The inadequate budget, which was determined by Congress, remained a nightmare because it went through the White House, the Office of Managment and Budget (OMB), and then to the House District Committee before final approval. The District was still mired in layers of federal bureaucracy.[8]

The structural problems were only one worry for the new government. When Walter Washington took office he also found all of the typical urban problems of a rising crime rate, a deteriorating school system, and a rising number of welfare recipients. As the first mayor-commissioner, Walter Washington found that he had an integrated City Council, a white city administrator, and a predominantly white police force. Although he only accepted the job with the stipulation that the mayor would have control of the police force, Washington still had a number of underlying issues of intergovernmental power and the existing racial hierarchy to address.[9] Racial issues were often handled under the guise of congressional power. Paternalistically, Congressman McMillan would refer to the need for Congress to oversee the District's operation, when the real issue was always keeping African Americans in a subordinate position.

McMillan and his ilk did not want blacks to have any power, especially not over the police force. Maintaining power over public safety officials was just one of many thinly disguised references to race. There had always been racial issues—the slave versus free controversy; the status of newly freed slaves; providing housing, often substandard, for domestic workers; maintaining a dual school system; and enforcing segregation of government workers. African American Washingtonians had waged a long fight against segregation and for the right of self-government. Twentieth-century D.C. residents had lived under segregation and an oppressive system of government controlled by Southern Democrats who wanted to maintain segregation. Until the 1960s Washington, D.C. blacks were confined to the bottom of the District and federal government pay scale. African American residents found that they were restricted to living in just a few neighborhoods. A dual school system operated, one for the white students and one for the "colored." Yet out of the confined segregated environment a vibrant, educated black middle class had developed. The African American population was atypical because it had the opportunity to obtain an education at Dunbar High School (which had a classical curriculum for college-bound students), Miner Teachers College, or Howard University.

In addition to the daily local governance and home rule battles, Washington, D.C., had to handle the numerous anti–Vietnam War demonstrations which only increased. In 1967 the mayor was faced with two hundred thousand people who marched on the Pentagon, resulting in 681 arrests.[10] These demonstrations continued through 1971 when the D.C. police force was confronted with an estimated high of 120,000 demonstrators whose goal was to close the federal government and the city.[11] One of the most delicate issues for the mayor to address was the racial composition of the D.C. police force. Upon assuming office in 1967 Mayor Washington had a situation where "four of five officers in the D.C. police department were white, and no blacks ranked higher than lieutenant."[12] Police-community relations were best described by "tension, anger, and fear."[13] To address this problem Washington created the position of director of public safety. This allowed him to bring in Patrick V. Murphy, a former police chief of Syracuse, New York.[14] Murphy, who was now head of the fire and civil defense departments, improved the image of the police department by promoting blacks to the higher ranks and by attending community meetings.[15] This minimized the role of Chief of Police John B. Layton, who ran a 3,100-person department. In 1969, upon Murphy's recommendation, the mayor appointed a North Carolinian, Jerry V. Wilson, as police chief. The appointment of Wilson, a veteran of the D.C. police force, was appealing to Rep. John L. McMillan (D.-S.C.), the powerful conservative chair of the House District Committee. This was a shrewd move to placate McMillan who was reluctant to give blacks any authority.[16]

THE RIOTS AND THE RESPONSE

Walter Washington was clearly aware of the symbolism of his role as mayor of the national's capital, but never more acutely aware than on April 4, 1968. After the death of Dr. Martin Luther King Jr. some young rioters burned and looted entire blocks of businesses. Washington, D.C., the city where people lived, and Washington, the "Capital of the Free World," were both shown on television from April 4 onward as the city burned against a backdrop of the historic monuments. The mayor had the problems of restoring calm, commanding the white police chief of a predominantly black city, and presenting an image of authority to those outside of Washington, D.C. By walking the streets, constantly staying in touch with the chief of police and the White House, Walter Washington and his aides, along with the assistance of Army, Marine, and District of Columbia National Guard troops (thirteen thousand troops), worked to calm residents and minimize the destruction.[17]

Washington, D.C., had a public façade which focused on congressional or White House activities. But there was another Washington, D.C., composed of neighborhoods. In the city that was supposed to be riot-proof, a number of problems were simmering just below the surface. Until the riots of 1968 Washington, D.C., was perceived as a city of black and white, middle-class bureaucrats who made a decent living. Black dissidents were supposed to be satisfied because the mayor was black, there were a majority of blacks on the City Council, and the Corporation Counsel was black. At the federal level Thurgood Marshall served on the Supreme Court and Robert C. Weaver was a secretary of housing and urban development. It appeared that African Americans were economically well off and in positions of power, but this was only the outsiders' view of Washington, D.C.

The real Washington, D.C., which was not visible to the tourist, was rife with racial and class problems. Racial problems stemmed from Southern congressional control over a predominantly African American city, while class problems were evident in the black community because of income disparities. The black bourgeois residents were often professionals who were Howard University graduates. Lower-income residents frequently were Southern newcomers who lacked a college degree and had few marketable skills. There was little friction in the community until the 1960s when the middle-class blacks felt that the civil rights movement should be fought through the court system by the NAACP. They believed in and fought hard for integration. The opposition, often younger activists, felt that SNCC and Black Power advocates had the right approach to securing civil rights. Among the militant newcomers was Marion Barry, who favored black control over a black majority population.

A number of growing problems—unemployment, increasing numbers of welfare recipients, declining schools, and distrust of the police—were among the local problems facing the mayor. In the Washington, D.C., that tourists did not see there were rat-infested slums, a school system with decaying buildings where a majority of students did not read at grade level, an infant mortality rate second only to Mississippi, an unemployment rate at 4 percent by official figures, and a system of public transportation that did not adequately serve certain sections of the city.[18] The creation of a new position, the director of public safety, improved police-community relations. However, there were always congressional naysayers who thought that the police authority should be held by a higher authority. Congress, always reluctant to grant powers to D.C., even considered legislation to remove the police force from the control of the city. Under that plan, Congress would have run the D.C. police force.[19]

When the underlying problems of District residents exploded in a riot by angry youth, Walter Washington responded with a calm, measured approach. Now it was crucial that he was in charge of the police force. The riots pitted Walter Washington's integrationist philosophy against the militant position of Stokely Carmichael and Marion Barry, who were proponents of Black Power. By age and temperament Walter Washington did not view the white power structure as an enemy to be destroyed. He felt that he had to work with all parties to solve D.C.'s problems. As he walked the streets of Washington, D.C., in an attempt to calm angry rioters, he took the position that neither he nor his police force would be responsible for blood being spilled in Washington, D.C. Washington, in contrast to other mayors, ordered the police *not* to shoot looters. While this position may have been acceptable to D.C. residents, he immediately put himself at odds with Southern congressmen, J. Edgar Hoover, and white District business owners. Approximately 16,600 participated in the riots which resulted in 900 fires, 1,097 injuries, 10 deaths (primarily from fire), and 6,124 arrests.[20] While Washington, D.C., was only one of more than one hundred cities to sustain rioting, it received considerable media attention because it was thought that D.C. residents were too middle class to engage in violence.

Walter Washington knew that his police powers were under scrutiny, yet he ordered restraint. He also understood that the situation tested his ability to respond to widespread civil disorder in a predominantly black city. From an integrationist perspective, he took the long view of considering how he was going to govern and rebuild the city after the fires were extinguished. He looked ahead to ponder how blacks and whites were going to live and work in Washington, D.C., the capital city, after this wrenching experience where primarily property and businesses owned by whites were destroyed. Racial relations were severely strained after King's death. Tension remained high as residents tried to return to daily activities.

Following the restoration of order another problem immediately caused the media to again focus on Washington, D.C. Prior to Martin Luther King Jr.'s death a demonstration focusing on economic disparities was planned on the Mall. The tents pitched on the Mall were another reminder that the civil rights movement was not over. After King's death, Rev. Ralph Abernathy carried out the plan to build a tent city to house the demonstrators on the Mall. Unfortunately, the project was mired in continuous rainstorms. From the mayor's perspective it was just one more demonstration that required public safety resources. After Resurrection City collapsed, Walter Washington had to return to the day-to-day problems of delivering city services, answering to Congress, and negotiating with local business owners who wanted to abandon their Washington, D.C., locations after the April riots.

Between 1967 and 1974, Walter Washington focused on trying to reorganize the District's government, bargain with Congress for more resources, and encourage the residents to become involved in civic activities through elections for the school board beginning in 1967 and for a delegate to Congress in 1971. While the problems of Washington, D.C., looked familiar, the solutions were more complex than in any other city. As Walter Washington tried to demonstrate managerial capability to Congress he did so in an atmosphere of protesters agitating to "Free D.C." Protesters were seeking to promote statehood for Washington, D.C. Creating the position of a mayor-commissioner was a step forward, but not true home rule. Marion Barry and Julius Hobson, two of the members of the elected school board in 1967, were constant critics of congressional influence. The 1971 election of Walter Fauntroy as D.C.'s nonvoting delegate to the U.S. House was a congressional gesture at granting District residents full representation in the U.S. Congress. This made District residents hopeful that home rule, without congressional oversight, was a possibility.

1974 RACE FOR MAYOR

In the 1974 race, D.C. residents were finally given an opportunity to elect a mayor. Walter Washington handily won the first election for mayor in the twentieth century because he was popular throughout the heavily Democratic District, well known among voters, and acceptable to Congress. But the civil rights activists were critical, especially of his slow pace and consensus-building style in handling the local problems. His style was considered too slow, too deferential to Congress.

In 1978 Marion Barry emerged as one of the activists who was moving from protest to electoral politics. The mayor faced serious competition from Marion Barry, who had gathered media attention over the years when he was with Pride, Inc., a federally funded job training program, and in his elected positions on the school board and City Council.

Barry, the neighborhood organizer and gregarious politician, won, helped in part by an endorsement from the *Washington Post*. Although Walter Washington had strong ties to communities throughout the city, many voters were looking for change and a more progressive mayor. Marion Barry beat Washington in a three-way primary race. Barry came in first with 32,841 votes to Sterling Tucker's 31,277 and Washington's 29,881.[21] In his elected and appointed role as mayor, Washington proved to be an able public administrator, but he lacked the political drive and organization needed to win a three-way race.

LEGACY

Walter Washington's background in public administration and his skills in public relations proved to be invaluable in managing an orderly transition to an elected mayor and city council form of government. His publicly easygoing personality facilitated working with local residents, members of Congress, and the business community to promote a more democratically governed capital city. He provided optimism for a new, more participatory era in D.C.

politics, while, without rancor, he simultaneously confronted racial and managerial issues remaining from a commissioner form of government.

Washington occupied a unique position unlike any other U.S. mayor. While other mayors could look to a governor and the federal government for assistance, Washington could only look to Congress for assistance. He had to run Washington, D.C., a jurisdiction with both city and state functions. Simultaneously, he had to meet congressional expectations on managing programs, especially crime prevention, and had to seek congressional approval for his budget. An initial success was the reorganization of government aided by the appointment of lawyers familiar with local politics. In a time of racial transition he appointed men such as Julian Dugas, John Risher, and Charles Duncan, which signaled that his advisers would be experienced, respected African Americans.

The riots after Dr. Martin Luther King's death placed a heavy burden on Walter Washington and his government. There had been an immediate threat not only to life and property, but also to the long-term status of race relations in the nation's capital. Walter Washington's calm demeanor, his visibility in the community, and his restraint of the police powers helped to restore order. His philosophy of valuing life over property set a framework for better race relations. Extinguishing fires and jailing looters was the first concern, but in the long run he was worried about repairing relations with the business community. There were numerous cases where the owners of longstanding clothing stores, auto dealerships, and record stores which were burned or looted did not plan to reopen. Owners decided that they were either going to retire or relocate in the suburbs. Walter Washington had successfully prevented police officers from killing young black males, now he had to persuade white business owners to help rebuild Washington, D.C. He was persuasive in convincing key stakeholders to remain in the District, but the revitalization of the 14th and 7th Street business corridors took over twenty years to accomplish.

Walter Washington certainly deserves credit for setting a tone and atmosphere for future economic development and racial understanding in the District. His relationship with Congress and the business community spurred the renewal of downtown Washington. His emphasis on sound management facilitated the transition to an elected government. Although he was always aware of congressional oversight, Walter Washington guided the residents to a new level of civic awareness and inspired electoral participation. By looking beyond the racial dimensions of problems to long-term public policy outcomes, he set Washington, D.C., on the course to greater self-government. By not making race an issue, but instead focusing on applying standard public administration procedures to budgeting and personnel issues, he demonstrated that Washington residents could run the city.

Walter Washington was once asked how he would like to be remembered. He replied,

> What I would like to be remembered for is that Walter Washington changed the spirit of the people of this city, that he came in as mayor when there was hate and greed and misunderstanding among our people and the races were polarized . . . and in the span of just a little over a decade he had brought people together through love and compassion, had helped bring about home rule . . . and had helped people have more meaningful, satisfying and enjoyable lives.[22]

In retrospect, Walter Washington was an architect and advocate for a community that was learning how democracy worked on the local level.

As the first African American mayor of a major U.S. city, Walter Washington did not follow the course of most big city mayors by crafting his role as a popular politician. He was not a visionary, civil rights crusader, nor a power broker who sought to enhance his resume. In the long run, he was an able manager and politician in the context of Washington, D.C. Walter Washington understood the riots as a form of communication. He knew that many local black residents felt that civil rights had never been fully achieved by Washington, D.C.'s lowliest residents.

Intractable problems such as crime, budgetary battles, and declining schools have bedeviled every subsequent mayor because home rule remains structurally flawed.[23] Under the U.S. Constitution, Congress still has exclusive jurisdiction over Washington, D.C. Consequently, democracy in Washington, D.C., operates with constraints not imposed on U.S. citizens in any of the fifty states.

Washington was a pragmatist who successfully served under three presidents, including Richard Nixon, one of his critics. From his early experiences with the National Capital Housing Authority, he knew that Congress would always be looking over his shoulder. He understood that the District of Columbia as the capital city had a higher visibility than any other U.S. city coupled with the fact that the president and Congress could influence District policies at any time. He did not aggressively try to reorganize a dysfunctional, segregated bureaucracy, although he made personnel changes. He realized that the District would never be run as efficiently as other major cities because its budget was dependent on Congress, the limited tax base could not be expanded, and that race was going to remain an issue no matter what course the civil rights movement took. Yet his tangible accomplishments include securing approval to build the convention center, which was expected to boost downtown retail activity, and striking the deal with Congress to get funding to build the subway system.

The riots following Dr. Martin Luther King's death posed a major challenge for the mayor because it tested his powers versus those of the executive
branch, namely the FBI. As the 7th Street, 14th Street, and H Street N.E. corridors began to burn and looters were plundering the businesses, the mayor
walked the streets of Washington, D.C., to restore calm. He fully realized the
symbolism of how television would depict the burning of the capital city run
by a black mayor. In contrast to other mayors facing rioters he gave the order
to his police chief not to shoot looters. While this position was later praised
by many, Walter Washington stood up to J. Edgar Hoover and displeased
many local business owners.

Walter Washington's legacy is that he successfully presided over a transition to a limited home rule after Washington, D.C., had not elected a government for over one hundred years. In the roles of mayor-commissioner
and then mayor he set the tone of governance of Washington, D.C. As he
presided over the shift from a triumvirate to a single person executive, Walter
Washington sent the signal that he wished to serve all the citizens, not just the
wealthier wards, that he wanted to work with the business community, and
that he was respectful of congressional priorities, but that he now presided
over a city where residents had a voice in governance.

Reflecting on the Walter Washington years shows that he exemplified
only one type of leader among those who have now governed under limited
home rule. The basic mayoral duty of delivering services was just one of his
problems. While delivery of services is a primary job of mayors, this is not a
straightforward task in Washington, D.C., because of congressional funding
and congressional approval power over the D.C. budget. Washington's record
on delivery of services is far better in terms of getting money from Congress
than at the consumer end. A 1969 Carl Bernstein article notes that the first
sixteen months of Mayor Washington's administration faced "11 strikes from
sanitation, to transit to taxis."[24] Obtaining funding was no small matter, but
delivering services was a challenge in a city heavily dependent on federal
money and with limited options for raising taxes.

As the first black mayor he felt race issues were a priority. In many cases
Washington acted as the conciliator by trying to get black and white, Jew and
Gentile to work together to advance the city. He did not see his job as being
the chief cheerleader for home rule. Taking that position would have merely
cost him credibility with congressional overseers of Washington, D.C.

In retrospect one of Walter Washington's strengths—building relations
with Congress and all branches of the federal government—proved to be
transitory. Congressional responses to Mayor Marion Barry were not always
as favorable as they had been to Walter Washington. Barry's style, which promoted black power, did not advance home rule efforts to reach a minimum

goal of voting representation in Congress or the maximum goal of D.C. state-hood.

Washington holds a singular position because he managed the transition from the commissioner to the elected system. As the mayor he set a positive tone for government and business collaboration. His administration proved the ability of blacks to govern a structural hodgepodge inherited from the commissioner form of government. However, he did not pursue the more ambitious task of creating a framework to empower D.C. residents, which was the desire of the ardent home rule advocates. Walter Washington shaped the role of mayor by establishing the supremacy of the mayor over the police chief and over executive branch officials, especially in a time of crisis. Under his administration the promise of true democracy for D.C. residents remained unfulfilled.

NOTES

1. Howard Gillette Jr., *Between Justice and Beauty*, Baltimore: Johns Hopkins University Press, 1995: 167–69.

2. Marie Garrett, "Walter E. Washington—Mayor, Lawyer, Housing Administra-tor," 2 (typed statement).

3. Robert E. Asher, "Walter Washington: Back Home," *Washington Post*, September 7, 1967: A16.

4. "Due for Post in Capital," *New York Times*, August 25, 1967.

5. Asher, A16.

6. Peter Milius, "Washington Named D.C. Mayor," *Washington Post*, September 7, 1967.

7. Steve Diner and Helen Young, eds., *Managing the Nation's Capital*, Center for Applied Research and Urban Policy, University of the District of Columbia, 1986: 2–6.

8. Ibid.

9. Conversation with Walter Washington, June 1998.

10. Milton Coleman, "Walter Washington Dies at 88," *Washington Post*, October 27, 2003.

11. Ibid.

12. Ibid.

13. Ibid.

14. Ben W. Gilbert and the staff of the *Washington Post*, *Ten Blocks from the White House*, New York: Frederick A. Praeger, 1968: 8.

15. Ibid.

16. Coleman.

17. Ibid.

18. Ibid.

19. Ibid.

20. Coleman (n.p.) and Gilbert, 224.

21. Paul W. Valentine, "Mayor Says Barry Won D.C. Vote; Mayor Concedes Barry Victorious in District Voting," *Washington Post*, September 28, 1978.

22. Paul W. Valentine, "Mayor Recalls Era of Tumult," *Washington Post*, December 31, 1978.

23. Sharon Taylor, "Denial of Democracy," BIS paper, George Mason University, 2003.

24. Carl Bernstein, "The Mayor Speaks His Mind," *Washington Post*, February 16, 1969.

BIBLIOGRAPHY

Asher, Robert L., "Walter Washington: Back Home," *Washington Post*, September 7, 1967.

Bernstein, Carl. "The Mayor Speaks His Mind," *Washington Post*, February 16, 1969.

Coleman, Milton, "Walter Washington Dies at 88," *Washington Post*, October 27, 2003.

"Due for Post in Capital," *New York Times*, August 25, 1967.

Diner, Steve, and Helen Young, eds., *Managing the Nation's Capital*, Center for Applied Research and Urban Policy, University of the District of Columbia, 1986.

Garrett, Marie, "Walter E. Washington—Mayor, Lawyer, Housing Administrator," typed statement, 2.

Gilbert, Ben W., and the staff of the *Washington Post*, *Ten Blocks from the White House*, New York: Frederick A. Praeger, 1968.

Gillette, Howard, Jr. *Between Justice and Beauty*, Baltimore: Johns Hopkins University Press, 1995.

Milius, Peter, "Washington Named D.C. Mayor," *Washington Post*, September 7, 1967.

Taylor, Sharon, "Denial of Democracy," BIS paper, George Mason University, 2003.

Valentine, Paul W., "Mayor Says Barry Won D.C. Vote: Mayor Concedes Barry Victorious in District Voting," *Washington Post*, September 28, 1978.

Valentine, Paul W. "Mayor Recalls Era of Tumult," *Washington Post*, December 31, 1978.

4

Marion Barry, Jr.: A Politician for the Times

Wilmer J. Leon III

INTRODUCTION

A 1998 *Washington Post* article stated, "To understand the District of Columbia, one must understand Marion Barry." Councilmember Barry has been involved in District politics since he came to the city in 1965 as a fundraiser for the Student Nonviolent Coordinating Committee (SNCC).

How does a person born to sharecropping parents in Itta Bena, a town in Leflore County, Mississippi, in the late 1930s become the mayor of and one of the most influential politicians in the history of the District of Columbia? How does an activist translate his activism in the civil rights movement into institutionalized politics in city government? How does the mayor of a major American city establish effective governmental practices and provide fundamental services to his constituents, while struggling to implement the missing elements of democracy to those who need them most?

These are the issues that will be examined in this chapter in an attempt to explore the ongoing struggle of District of Columbia residents to achieve both fair representation and effective government. One of the solutions that District of Columbia residents have employed in an attempt to address these issues is to elect Marion Barry Jr. to the school board, City Council, and then as their mayor multiple times.

BACKGROUND

Marion Barry Jr. served as the second elected mayor of the District of Columbia from 1979 to 1991 and as the District's fourth mayor from 1995 to 1999.

He was elected to the first District school board that held elections in 1971 and served as its president until he won a seat on the first elected District of Columbia City Council in 1974. He has served five terms on the city council from 1974 to 1978, 1992 to 1994, and 2004 to the present.

Marion Barry Jr. was born at a very important time and in a very important place as it relates to the struggle for civil and voting rights. He was born on a Mississippi cotton plantation in Itta Bena in Leflore County on March 6, 1936. Itta Bena is in the heart of the Delta not far from a town called Money where in 1955 Emit Till, a teenager visiting from Chicago, was lynched for talking to a white woman.

His parents, Marion Barry Sr. and Mattie Barry, like many in the Mississippi Delta, were sharecroppers. As a child, Marion Barry picked cotton alongside of his mother. According to a 1987 *Washington Post* article, one of the lingering images of his childhood in Itta Bena is "riding the tail of a cotton sack down a dark furrow at picking time."[1]

His birth in 1936 allowed him to come of age as the civil rights movement was in its infancy. This was almost thirty years before the beginning of the national civil rights struggle but a time when a number of factors were in play that contributed to its development. During the 1930s large numbers of blacks migrated from the South to the North, enabling many to enjoy the franchise for the first time as well as being free from the repressive sharecropping system. Also, as a result of the Supreme Court's 1938 *Gaines* decision, many Southern states increased funding for black colleges in an attempt to head off anticipated court-ordered integration decrees. Black colleges used this funding to increase programs and improve facilities, resulting in a sharp increase in black college enrollment, particularly after 1940, as well as an increase in black organizations such as the NAACP.[2]

Marion Barry's birth on a cotton plantation in the Mississippi Delta provided him with a similar background to Mrs. Fannie Lou Hamer and the Reverend James Bevel, both of whom would later play instrumental roles along with Barry in developing the Student Nonviolent Coordinating Committee (SNCC) and other civil rights organizations.

In 1940 at the age of four, after the death of his father, Barry's mother moved the family to the Foot Hill public housing project in Memphis, Tenn. Growing up in the segregated public housing complexes of Memphis played an important role in the development and sensibilities of Marion Barry as evidenced by his becoming one of the first African American Eagle Scouts in Memphis. The drive and determination that it would take to earn the merit badges of an Eagle Scout as well as the understanding it would take to navigate a racist, segregated Memphis would serve Barry well in his political pursuits later in life.

Marion Barry would graduate with a bachelor's degree from Le Moyne College (now LeMoyne-Owen College), a small commuter HBCU (historically black colleges and university), in 1958. It was here during his senior year that Marion Barry's life of activism and struggle for civil rights would begin.

While reading the *Commercial Appeal*, a Memphis, Tennessee, newspaper, Barry saw a story about patronizing and bigoted statements made by the chairman of LeMoyne's board of trustees, Walter Chandler. During a trial in federal court contesting segregation, Chandler, a former mayor of Memphis and congressman, was reported to have said,

> The problems of the Negro will not be eliminated by permitting him to be seated alongside of white passengers on the busses in the city. I have heard it said that the Negro is a second-class citizen. If he is a second-class citizen, it is just because he wants to be, and has applied the label to himself. . . . The Negro is our brother, but he should be treated as a younger brother, and not as an adult.[3]

As the president of the LeMoyne College chapter of the NAACP, Barry co-authored a letter to the LeMoyne College president, Dr. Hollis Price, calling for the removal of Chandler from the Lemoyne board of trustees, stating, "We feel that it is humiliating and embarrassing that such an obvious demagogue should have direct connection with our college, especially when this institution stresses to its students the importance of fighting for equal rights."[4]

Threatened with dismissal from school two weeks before graduation for his activism, the community came to his defense and Barry was allowed to graduate. One of those speaking the loudest in support of Barry was Roy Wilkins, who would later become the head of the NAACP.

His unprecedented challenge to a powerful white city father had made him an overnight celebrity—not only at Lemoyne but in Memphis's larger black community, which was stirring to the drumbeat of the civil rights movement spreading throughout the South.[5]

Marion Barry furthered his education at Fisk University in Nashville, Tennessee, earning a master's degree in organic chemistry in 1960. He participated in the lunch counter sit-ins in Nashville and other cities on the heels of the sit-ins in Greensboro, North Carolina, as black students tried to integrate a Woolworth's lunch counter. Early in the spring of 1960, Marion Barry and a number of other students were invited by Dr. Martin Luther King Jr. and Ms. Ella Baker to attend a meeting in Raleigh, North Carolina. At this meeting the Student Nonviolent Coordinating Committee SNCC) was formed with Marion Barry as its first chairman.

This same year Marion Barry took his activism to the national level, speaking before the platform committees of the 1960 Democratic and Republican parties, along with Dr. Martin Luther King and other civil rights leaders, urging support for the Southern sit-in movement. In this address Barry called for a "community in which a man can realize the full meaning of self, which demands an open relationship with others." In a nine-page statement, Barry said that Southern students wanted an end to racial discrimination in housing, education, employment, and voting.

According to Jonathan Agronsky,

> Apparently the party elders on the Democratic Platform Committee paid attention to Barry and other civil rights leaders. In what the *Congressional Quarterly* later described as the "strongest civil rights plank in the history of the [Democratic] party," the Democrats called for federal aid to the desegregated school districts, strong federal backing for civil rights lawsuits, and the creation of a federal Fair Employment Practices Commission.[6]

This was the beginning of Marion Barry integrating the politics of direct action and conventional party politics.

Barry completed three years of the doctoral program in chemistry at the University of Tennessee before abandoning the program to become a full-time participant in the civil rights movement. He honed his organizing skills in the South and worked as a SNCC fundraiser in New York. When James Forman, SNCC's executive field secretary, needed an experienced organizer in Washington in 1965, as the civil rights movement was in full swing, Barry moved to Washington, D.C., to continue the work of the SNCC.

THE EARLY WASHINGTON, D.C., YEARS

With his skills being honed by working to help organize an NAACP chapter at Fisk University, being involved in the Memphis bus desegregation case, integrating lunch counters with John Lewis and others in Nashville, desegregating public libraries in Memphis, organizing voter registration drives and establishing workshops on nonviolence for teenagers in Pike County, Mississippi, Barry was sent to Washington, D.C., as an organizer, where he became the head of the SNCC office.

Washington, D.C., was a city of contrasts in 1965. According to the 1960 U.S. Census of Population, Washington, D.C., had a population of almost 764,000 residents of which 54 percent were Negro. The largest percentage of Negroes living in any metropolitan area lived in Washington, D.C. Just below the Mason-Dixon Line, Washington, D.C., for all intents and purposes, from a social perspective, had the characteristics of a Southern city, in terms of its sultry climate, its slow-moving pace of life, its conservatism, and its large black population, which was in fact, if not by law, segregated.[7] Historically, even though Washington, D.C., had very few "Jim Crow" laws, segregation and the vestiges of racism existed in the city. Through the 1950s and 1960s segregated schools, housing, and social accommodations were a reality for black residents in the city.

> The problem of the American Negro, once predominantly Southern, has gradu-
> ally over the past few decades become predominantly a Northern problem.
> Millions of Negroes have come North seeking escape from the miasma of the
> South, where poverty and oppression kept the Negro in an inferior caste. . . . A
> million and a half left the South in the years 1950–1960.[8]

There were other social and civil rights groups in Washington, D.C., at that time raising money and organizing. The United Planning Organization (UPO) was established in 1962 as a local human services organization that plans, coordinates, and implements social services for the Washington, D.C., area. Using federal and private grant monies, UPO implemented a Neighbor-hood Youth Corps, funded a Model School System, and inaugurated a pilot Head Start program. The NAACP is a national civil rights organization that was founded in 1909 to ensure political, education, and social equality rights for all people on a national level. The National Urban League is a national organization that was founded in 1910 as a community-based organization that focuses on empowering African Americans to enter the economic and social mainstream by securing economic self-reliance, parity, and power. The Congress of Racial Equality (CORE) was founded in Chicago in 1942 as a civil rights organization that used the principals of nonviolence as a tactic against segregation. In 1963 CORE helped to organize the March on Wash-ington and through CORE, the Student Nonviolent Coordinating Committee (SNCC) and the National Association for the Advancement of Colored Peo-ple (NAACP) organized their Freedom Summer campaign. Its main objective was to attempt to end the political disenfranchisement of African Americans in the Deep South.

James Forman saw Washington, D.C., as a great opportunity to apply the Southern SNCC strategy of political reform in a Northern city that bordered the South and had many Southern customs. Forman sent Barry to Washing-ton to manage the SNCC office. This was the nation's capital, with a black population of 54 percent, that did not have voting representation in the U.S. House of Representatives and the U.S. Senate and was unable to vote for the U.S. president or elect its own mayor, City Council, or school board.

Marion Barry wanted to do more than just raise money; he wanted to in-crease the visibility of SNCC in Washington, D.C. He felt that SNCC was loosing some of its appeal and a shift in the civil rights movement was in the making. The traditional channels and coalitions were not going to give Marion Barry the foundation and momentum he wanted: "He also believed that he could exploit the city's volatile ingredients: a white economic power structure; a political system controlled by racists on Capitol Hill; a black community that was spoiled and docile at the top, and sick and frustrated at the bottom. The traditional civil rights groups with middle-class emphasis couldn't or wouldn't reach the poorest blacks, but Barry was uniquely pre-pared."[9] Barry was ready to use his skills in community organizing to have a positive impact on the poorest in the community. Mukusa Dada, then known as Willie Ricks, worked with Marion Barry in SNCC and is credited with coining the phrase "Black Power"; Dada described Barry as "a strong young man . . . somebody that was speaking out for African people, speaking out for our people and standing up against the odds, standing up against the police, going to jail."[10]

THE D.C. TRANSIT STRIKE

Marion Barry's first effort at organized protest in Washington, D.C., began in January 1966 in response to O. Roy Chalk, the owner of D.C. Transit, the company that operated Washington's bus company, when he decided to raise bus fares from twenty to twenty-five cents.

Barry saw this as an opportunity to coordinate a citywide boycott, or "man-cott," as it was called. After some research it was decided to focus on the Ben-ning Road bus line since those passengers were mostly African American, working class, and would be disproportionately affected by the fair increase. This one day "mancott" was set for January 24, 1966. Barry worked with full-time staff and volunteers to provide rides for the protesting passengers, telephone banks to get the word out, and post notices through out the city.

It is estimated that at least seventy-five thousand people responded to Barry's call to "mancott" the Benning Road bus line, costing O. Roy Chalk more than $27,000. Two days after the protest, the transit commission, in a unanimous de-cision, denied Chalk his fare hike. However, that decision was later overturned. What makes this effort significant is not its impact on Chalk but Barry's ability to organize and mobilize the poor and African American citizens of the nation's capitol in the mid-1960s. Barry told the *Washington Post*'s Richard Prince, "Washington was always a difficult town to mobilize. . . . To organize—that was considered a radical move. It's basically a government town, and there was always the feeling that you shouldn't be active in the community."[11]

There was also another social dynamic at play that made the Benning Road bus line protest significant. It reflected a subtle change in activism tactics from a Northern-based strategy to a Southern-based strategy. Historian Dr. Clayborne Carson discusses the problems that SNCC activists encountered as they attempted to use their tried-and-tested Southern tactics to mobilize poor, Northern, urban African Americans who had not grown up and experienced "Jim Crow." Carson writes that the poor urban blacks were angry, antisocial, and more alienated than their Southern counterparts. Without being able to clearly define the "enemy" as those raised in the South could, it was harder to galvanize the energy and direct it towards a common cause.

This sense was true in Washington, D.C. It was not that African Americans in Washington had not experienced prejudice and discrimination; they had plenty. Even though slavery and segregation played a major role in the social and political dynamics of Washington, D.C., the city has a unique history of progress and success for the African American community. As far back as 1862, Congress passed the District of Columbia Emancipation Act, freeing enslaved Washingtonians nine months before President Lincoln's Emancipation Proclamation of 1863. Four years later Congress passed the Reconstruction Act of 1867 granting black male Washingtonians the right to vote three years before the passage of the Fifteenth Amendment.

African Americans have played a significant role in the development of Washington, D.C.'s civic life and politics since the city was first declared the nation's capital in 1791. The size of the African American population (one of the largest urban populations in the country), the number of academic institutions in the city, the availability of federal jobs, and other cultural support mechanisms created a viable African American middle class and upper class in the city. In 1921 the *Washington Bee*, the city's largest black paper, editorialized that the growth of black business in Washington, "more than anything else, marks real and prominent racial progress." The thriving business district was a symbol of what blacks could achieve.[12] These factors contributed to the racial lines not being as clearly defined in Washington, D.C., as in Southern cities.

The difference, as Richard Wright discovered, was that in the South the racial lines were clearly drawn and were not to be crossed. From a fear of lynching and other reprisals a "latent sense of violence" controlled the social dynamics between the races and those lines were rarely crossed. In the North there was a sense of "emotional safety" that made the racial dynamics in the North different than those in the South.

Up until 1960, most of the leaders of the African American struggle came from the North: "It used to be that Northern Negro leaders, often from the NAACP, would make forays into the South as a kind of uncharted battleground where bridgeheads of freedom might be won by legal battles."[13] For years, African Americans from the South were looked upon by their Northern brethren as passive, docile, and less ambitious.

From the mid-1950s forward there was a shift in leadership as ministers from Southern churches and college students from the South began to play a more significant role in the civil rights movement. Organizations such as the Southern Christian Leadership Council (SCLC), CORE, and SNCC took on a much greater role in the liberation of African Americans. Marion Barry, as a student organizer from the South, was a prime example of this shift in tactics. His ability to utilize the Southern SNCC strategies in Washington, D.C., was an important accomplishment.

FREE D.C.

Based upon his success with the D.C. Transit protest, Marion Barry looked for the next political challenge. He decided to take on the issues of home rule for the residents of the District and creating an independent political system.

From 1874 to 1974, the District of Columbia was governed under the exclusive jurisdiction principle, with the U.S. Congress acting as the direct legislative body for the federal district. This meant (according to the U.S. Constituion, art. I, sec. 8, clause 17) that Congress had the power to "exercise exclusive legislation in all cases whatsoever" relating to the District. This power was exercised by a number of congressional oversight committees and appointed commissioners who ran the city.

In 1965 Congress was considering a home rule bill that would have allowed the citizens of the District to implement their own independent political system, their own government. This home rule bill was supported by President Lyndon Baines Johnson. He believed that a city with a majority African American population that was run by Euro-American congressmen was a grave injustice and considered the home rule bill to be part of his civil rights agenda.

As the home rule bill reached the floor of Congress for a vote, the Metropolitan Washington Board of Trade launched a national publicity campaign aimed at Congress to convince it that "a great many Washingtonians—including an overwhelming majority of local professionals and business leaders—were opposed to pending Home Rule legislation."[14] This was the continuation of the Board of Trade's decade-long campaign against home rule.

This national ad campaign was a success. People from all over the country wrote their congressional representatives and the bill was defeated. Even President Johnson saw this as a personal defeat. One day at the White House, President Johnson ran into Charles Horsky, his aide in charge of the legislation, and said "You really screwed up. . . . This was one of the most bitter defeats for me."[15]

President Johnson's bitter defeat proved to be a moment of political opportunity for Marion Barry. District residents, both African American and

Euro-American, were furious with the Board of Trade's tactic and the outcome. Marion Barry worked with L. D. Pratt, Rev. Walter Fauntroy and other religious leaders, the NAACP, and other community organizations, and on February 21, 1966, he called a press conference where he launched the "Free D.C. Movement." The objective was to rally support for self-government in the District. Barry said,

> We want to free D.C. from our enemies: the people who make it impossible for us to do anything about lousy schools, brutal cops, slumlords, welfare investigators who go on midnight raids, employers who discriminate in hiring, and a host of other ills that run rampant through our city.

Barry's tactic was simple and right out of the SNCC playbook; hit the Board of Trade in the pocketbook. As sit-ins and boycotts were used to desegregate lunch counters, transportation, and other businesses in the South, boycotts and pickets would be used in Washington, D.C. The Free D.C. Movement developed bright orange window stickers and signs that read "Free D.C." and local merchants would place them in the windows of their stores. If the sign was visible, local residents would support the business; if there was no sign or sticker, local residents would take their business elsewhere.

Marion Barry clearly understood the power of the race and class dynamic in a city that was 63 percent African American. It was a city that was segregated inter- as well as intra-racially, white vs. black, as well as lighter-skinned blacks vs. darker-skinned blacks. Barry was championing issues and developing a grassroots power base among the less educated, un- and under-employed African Americans: "Barry was a radically new kind of politician. Raised in poverty, he built a political base from Anacostia rather than through the traditional black power-brokers on 16th Street's Gold Coast."[16]

PRIDE, INC.

In January 1967, Marion Barry officially resigned from SNCC in order to focus his attention and efforts on developing a political base in Washington, D.C. As a result of his work with the bus boycott and the Free D.C. Movement, Barry saw a link between economic empowerment and political activism in the inner city. He felt that it was difficult to talk with people about the abstract benefits of democracy when they were faced with the everyday realities of substandard education, unemployment, poor housing, and police brutality. Also, Barry believed that many of the Washington, D.C., residents had come to the city from small cities and towns in North or South Carolina, Virginia, or other places in the South. They, like many of the longer-term city residents, were not used to participating in the political process and it would take a lot of convincing to get them involved.

Barry's timing was also fortuitous in that it coincided with President Lyndon Johnson's efforts to bring home rule or some form of independent government structure to the District of Columbia. As Marion Barry was becoming more involved in District politics, President Johnson was creating the environment for District politics to expand.

Having been a resident of Washington since the 1930s, Johnson saw self-governance in the District to be a part of his civil rights agenda.[17] In 1965 President Johnson tried in vain to get a home rule bill through Congress. The bill met stiff resistance from the very powerful Washington, D.C., Board of Trade and died on the floor of the House and a similar bill died in the Senate as well.

In 1967 President Johnson tried again, and this time he revised his plan and proposed creating an appointed City Council and an appointed mayor-commissioner. He left budget and legislative oversight with Congress but saw this as a real first step toward home rule. This time, in spite of opposition from the Board of Trade, President Johnson got his legislation passed. After much discussion, Walter Washington was appointed as Washington, D.C.'s first mayor-commissioner and the City Council was formed as well.

The summer of 1967 was a difficult one for the nation's inner cities. Riots in Detroit, Michigan, and Newark, New Jersey, threatened to spread to other urban centers. This proved to be an opportune time for Marion Barry.

Labor Secretary Willard Wirtz and others within the Johnson administration were looking for programs to fund under Johnson's War on Poverty program that would improve education, housing, and employment for those in the inner cities. Wirtz was especially concerned about riots breaking out in Washington, D.C. If the nation's capital went up in flames, it would have a devastating impact on the Johnson administration.

In order for any program to work in the inner city it was going to take a combined effort between the government and those who were in tune with the sentiments of the community. Barry had been working since May 1967 to organize the community around the shooting death of Clarence T. Booker. On May 1, 1967, Booker was killed by police during a confrontation outside of a convenience store in northeast Washington.

Barry teamed with a friend of Booker's, Rufus "Catfish" Mayfield, and together they began to work the streets of Washington, protesting and holding press conferences to call the public's attention to the shooting and to hold the police accountable. In the end, the grand jury believed the police account of the shooting and failed to return an indictment against any of the officers.

The outcome of the grand jury process was not a failure for Barry. Through these efforts, as well as his bus boycott and Free D.C. campaign, Barry connected with the black youth and the dispossessed of Washington who were victimized by the system.

Labor Secretary Willard Wirtz, who had been following the Booker case as well, was concerned that this incident could be the spark or catalyst to set the city ablaze. He ordered his aides to develop a program and secure funding for a summer job-training program for Washington, D.C., youth. Wirtz was willing to try anything he could to prevent riots in Washington, D.C.

Wirtz invited Barry, Mayfield, and others to his office to discuss a possible summer jobs program. Barry's concern was that a program was needed to reach the hard-core unemployed. What also set Barry's program apart from other proposals that were submitted was the element of self-sufficiency. It was always the intention of Barry and the other Pride, Inc. creators to use the federal funding as seed money to create a for-profit, self-sustaining company that would be able to pay employees from its own profits. From this discussion, Pride, Inc. was born.

Pride, Inc. started in August 1967 as a private company, funded by the government, created to hire teenagers to clean their neighborhood streets. They employed five hundred people for five weeks at a cost of $250,000. Based upon this initial success the program was extended for forty additional weeks at $1.2 million and before it was closed three years later, Pride, Inc. received nearly $9 million from the federal government for job training of Washington, D.C., youth and related business development. At its height, Pride, Inc. and its subsidiary Youth Pride Economic Enterprises operated gas stations, a landscaping company, a printing company, an apartment building, and other service-related companies. For Secretary Wirtz, this was a good investment to keep peace on the streets of Washington, D.C. For Marion Barry, this became his bridge between the grassroots politics of the inner city and mainstream establishment politics. Barry would walk back and forth across this bridge for many years to come.

WASHINGTON BURNS

On April 4, 1968, at 8:05 p.m., ironically in Memphis, the city where Marion Barry spent his formative years, Dr. Martin Luther King Jr. was assassinated. Initially, local officials as well as many in the White House believed that Washington, D.C., was riot-proof. Many felt that the African American middle class in Washington, D.C., would never resort to violence and if they did, the requisite military response could happen in such short order that any disturbance would be quelled before it took hold. Even the founders of Pride, Inc.—Barry, Tredwell, and Harvey—did not think the city would burn. They believed "if the black teenagers hadn't burned the city into cinders in the summer of 1967, it would never burn."[18] They were sadly mistaken.

Stokely Carmichael, a twenty-six-year-old, Trinidad-born social activist and revolutionary, was in Washington, D.C., to head an organization called the Black United Front. When word of Dr. King's assassination reached Carmichael, he went into the streets around 14th and U demanding that merchants, out of respect for Dr. King, close their business and not open until Dr. King was laid to rest.

As Carmichael went from storefront to storefront a crowd gathered with him and grew larger and larger. Eventually, this group became an angry mob that Carmichael could no longer control. By 11:00 p.m. the looting began. By 12:30 p.m. the next day, smoke was on the horizon, the city was ablaze. "It was about 3:00 p.m., and the riot was reaching its wildest period. The police were hopelessly outnumbered and outmaneuvered."[19] Hundreds of fires were burning in the city. By 4:00 p.m. the National Guard was on the way.

Mayor Walter Washington, City Council Chairman John Hechinger, and Assistant Chair Walter Fauntroy called upon Marion Barry to help them design a plan to quell the violence. As the National Guard gained control of the city block by block, Barry worked in the neighborhoods to convince the "looters" to go home. He and others from Pride, Inc. worked with Joseph Danzansky from Giant Foods, Inc. to set up food distribution centers and delivered food to those living in burned-out sections of the city. Days later the city was quiet, but never the same.

Later that summer the Black Panthers tried to establish a presence in the city by forcibly trying to take control of the local SNCC office. The director of the office, Lester McKinnie, appealed to Marion Barry for help and Barry and Tredwell sent workers from Pride, Inc. to defend him. "Barry and his allies carried the day and established Barry as the leader of the activist movement in Washington."[20]

As a result of these actions Barry's stature in the eyes of those within the establishment who worked to rebuild the city grew as well. "The activist sat with the city's business elite and tried to find venture capital for black-owned business and guided federal funds coming to the city after the riots."[21] The activist was translating his activism into institutionalized politics in city government.

THE DEMISE OF PRIDE, INC.

Eventually, Pride, Inc. and its related companies would come to exemplify what many believed to be a chronic problem for Marion Barry, lack of attention to detail. According to Carroll Harvey, Pride, Inc.'s former director of operations, Barry did not deal with the mundane operational matters: "Marion is not attentive to details, so he needs a detail man around him. He realizes he doesn't have capabilities across the board."[22]

Pride, Inc. and its subsidiaries did help a lot of the District's youth find a purpose, go to college, and learn valuable life skills. "Thousands of District residents were trained as automobile mechanics, landscapers, house painters, and became positive tax paying members of their communities."[23]

The lack of attention to detail would lead to the financial collapse of Pride, Inc. and some it its employees being indicted for crimes ranging from misappropriating federal funds to burglary, robbery, and murder. Eventually one of the cofounders, Barry's second wife, Mary Tredwell, was convicted of diverting Pride, Inc. funds for her personal use. By this time Marion Barry had left the organization to pursue his political interests full-time and was able to move beyond the negative publicity that centered on the organization that he helped to create.

FROM PROTEST TO POLITICS

As more people focused on the success stories, Marion Barry became recognized as an expert on inner city youth and was frequently asked by then-mayor Walter Washington to assist in developing programs for the city. "Even Barry's rivals conceded that he had made a significant impact on the city's Black community by creating Pride."[24] His early days with the SNCC office in Washington, D.C., his leadership of Pride, Inc., his efforts to defuse tensions during the riots, and his many other community activities would serve Barry well as he moved into what would become his life's calling: city politics.

Marion Barry's shift from protest organizer to power broker came at a time when a substantive shift in black politics was taking place as well. According to Katherine Tate, "As a direct result of the 1965 Voting Rights Act, a new stage in Black Politics has been reached."[25] The gains that were being made by the increase in black voter registration and the increase in black elected officials came to symbolize what political analysts have called the shift from protest tactics to electoral politics.

This shift was being felt in cities such as Gary, Indiana, with the election of Richard Hatcher as mayor; in Cleveland, Ohio, with Carl Stokes; and in other cities across the country. Washington, D.C., was different. The residents of the District were not allowed to elect a mayor or a City Council. It was not until 1973 that Congress passed the District of Columbia Home Rule Act, allowing the residents of the city to elect its legislative and governing branches.

In 1971 Marion Barry decided to change his focus and his politics. By his own assessment, the circumstances within Washington, D.C., were changing and he was going to change along with them. Since the only elective office in District government at the time was a seat on the Board of Education, Barry set his sights on one of the eleven seats (one seat was at large and the other ten were held by members of the eight wards).

Barry was correct; Washington, D.C., was beginning to change like Gary, Indiana, and Cleveland, Ohio, as more college-educated, activist-minded blacks moved into the city. Barry was convinced by Marty Swaim, a white liberal member of the school board, that he could unseat the sitting school board president Anita Allen. According to Jaffe and Sherwood, Barry was backed by the "liberal integrated organization" of businessmen and former civil rights leaders in the city. Barry was able to defeat Allen with 93 percent of the vote in a four-way race. Even though only 9.3 percent of the registered voters participated in the election, "Barry proved he could attract middle-class black voters where Allen was expected to dominate."[26]

By supporting a slate of four other board members who also won for the first time or retained their seats, Barry convinced them to elect him board president. This election proved to be a key for Marion Barry for two reasons. First, he used his position to develop his list of future political supporters, and second, his election demonstrated a shift away from political independence, a persistent theme in black politics, to a coalition-based politics. According to Katherine Tate, this debate "complicated almost every Black policy issue, leading to such questions as whether Blacks should work to integrate public schools or concentrate their efforts on improving Black community schools, and whether Blacks should work within the Democratic Party or form an all-Black political organization."[27] Barry's ability to form a coalition with white and black business leaders and politicians against a sitting, black, elected official demonstrated a shift away from the independent black politics that he had helped to shape during the civil rights era to a coalition-based process. This brought change to the city and supported Barry's own interests as well.

Barry stayed on the school board for three years. During his tenure "he tamed the fractious board and moved decisively to put the school system's finances in order. But he did little to improve the curriculum, buy new books, or repair broken down classrooms, according to Dwight Cropp, Barry's executive assistant at the time."[28]

HOME RULE IN WASHINGTON, D.C.

After the home rule bill passed the House, the final hurdles had been crossed. President Richard Nixon signed the legislation on December 24, 1973, and on May 7, 1974, the citizens of the District were able to vote for their own mayor. There was still considerable congressional oversight. The Justice Department retained prosecutorial power, Congress retained control over the budget and all city laws, and the District was unable to tax the income of people who worked in the District, but lived in neighboring states. The District would finally be able to elect its own mayor and City Council after nearly one hundred years. Limited home rule was better than nothing.

The first election for the Washington, D.C., City Council was held in November 1974. It was Barry's initial intention to run for the seat of Council chair but the business leader coalition that had helped him win his school board seat supported Sterling Tucker for that position. Marion Barry ran at large and was elected overwhelmingly. While serving as a councilmember he became chair of the District of Columbia Committee on Finance and Revenue. "For the next four years, Barry used his committee as a club against Tucker and Mayor Washington on the one hand, while with the other he began to woo white business interests."[29]

As Mayor Washington proposed budgets that called for tax increases, Barry and his staff proposed tax cuts and other measures to increase revenues. Barry introduced a bill that required all District employees to live in the District along with a commuter tax. The home rule charter prohibited taxing the salaries of nonresidents and many Districts residents felt that "suburbanites" were taking their jobs and exploiting the District by taking their paychecks and payroll taxes back to the suburbs. The residency requirement and the commuter tax failed but Barry was viewed as a champion of the "average" resident. He proposed a requirement that the District government invest millions of dollars into local banks that pledged to loan monies to minorities and minority-owned business; again the measure failed, but Barry won the hearts of local residents.

Marion Barry won his 1976 bid for reelection. This time he not only campaigned among the African American middle-class and poorer voters in Anacostia, he expanded his efforts into the affluent white wards west of Rock Creek Park. Before Rev. Jackson's attempts on the national level with his presidential bids in 1984 and 1988, L. Douglas Wilder's state-level success as governor of Virginia in 1990, and David Dinkins' city-level success as mayor of New York in 1990, Barry was walking a very fine line and challenging the traditions of coalition politics.

> Throughout most of the history of African American voting, these interracial coalitions have been in support of white candidates at all levels of government. Thus, the great bulk of the African American experience in electoral politics is made up of African Americans voting for the "lesser of two evils" white candidate. And these coalitions were rarely concerned with rights for African Americans.[30]

In this instance, not only were African Americans in the District able to vote for an African American candidate, white voters in the District were also being courted, while their economic interests were being championed by the same candidate.

On March 9, 1977, Councilmember Marion Barry became a local hero. At 11:00 a.m. that morning, a group of Hanafi Muslims took over the B'nai B'rith and District government buildings in response to what they felt was a slight when Jewish judges failed to sentence five men to death for murdering members of their sect in 1973. As Barry stepped off of the elevator on the fifth floor of the District building, one of the gunman fired a shotgun round, killing a WHUR reporter, Maurice Williams. Barry was struck in the chest by a shotgun pellet that lodged two inches from his heart. Doctors called it a flesh wound, but Barry was very fortunate that it was not worse.

While recovering at the Washington Hospital Center, Barry took an accounting of his life and his political future. The second mayoral race of the home rule era was only eight months away. Barry saw this as his time. His official quest for the highest office in District government politics would begin.

MAYOR MARION BARRY

Walter Washington was the incumbent mayor with a problem. During his ten years in office he had managed the city well, but the citizens were looking for stronger leadership, a new direction. Mayor Washington was viewed by many as an effective manager who was beholden to Congress and not the people of the city. "He'd replaced the lower-level officials with well-connected blacks, but he left whites in supervisory posts, and he never sank political roots into the community."[31] The perception in the city was that Mayor Washington's influence came from his relationships with the Johnson administration and members of Congress, not with his constituents in the city.

Sterling Tucker was chairman of the City Council and the presumptive heir apparent to Mayor Washington. As with the election for Council chair in 1974, Tucker expected Barry to step aside again, allowing Tucker to run against Washington for mayor and Barry to run for Tucker's vacated chairman's seat. Barry would have none of that.

He based his platform on inclusion and progressive reform. Barry saw the ability to rekindle the old liberal white and young black SNCC coalition from the civil rights movement and combine that with a growing gay voting block and senior citizens. If he could hold those groups together and allow Washington and Tucker to split the upper-class black and conservative white vote, Barry could slip in as the Democratic nominee.

Barry was also able to tap into a group of "young lions" from the business community who saw a short-term gamble of backing Barry as a long-term investment in their financial future if he won. Most of these individuals were white and Jewish restaurateurs, real estate developers, and bar owners who saw Mayor Washington as "old guard" and did not see any real vision with Sterling Tucker. "Vision" of the future Washington, D.C., became the issue.

What put Marion Barry over the top in the 1978 election was the endorsement of the *Washington Post* newspaper. This was and still is the most powerful newspaper in Washington, especially for local politics. The *Post*'s editorial dismissed Mayor Washington as old-fashioned, not progressive, and needing to be replaced, and framed the election as between City Council Chairman Sterling Tucker and Councilmember Marion Barry. According to the *Post*, "Our strong belief is that it should be Marion Barry." They saw Tucker as old wine in new bottles. Tucker would merely bring in new faces to continue Washington's old ways. They saw Barry, on the other hand, bringing in professional city administrators while he as mayor would set the tone and direction for the city. "What Mr. Barry seems to value . . . is . . . leadership—energy, nerve, initiative, imagination, toughness of mind, an active concern for people in distress, command presence if you will."[32] They saw Marion Barry as a visionary with the leadership qualities and initiative to get it done.

When the votes were tallied it was Barry, 31,265; Tucker, 29,909; and Washington, 28,286. Barry won by 1,396 votes. Just as he had figured, Tucker and Washington split the majority and Barry's coalition carried the day. On January 2, 1979, Marion Barry was sworn into office by U.S. Supreme Court Justice Thurgood Marshall.

Marion Barry, only the second person to be elected to the office of mayor of Washington, D.C., post–home rule, served three consecutive terms. He proved then and continues to be a viable and formidable political opponent.

By most accounts his first term in office was his most effective. His challenges were many. Barry inherited a $100 million deficit, a bloated city government, and a U.S. Congress with the authority to veto any decision by the D.C. City Council.

In spite of these problems during his first and second terms, the Barry administration balanced the budget, conducted the first audit of the District government in one hundred years, and reduced the city's debt. He also oversaw expansion of downtown Washington, D.C., and provided thousands of jobs to District residents.

For his second term in 1982 the *Washington Post* again gave Mayor Barry a strong endorsement: "We think Marion Barry should be re-nominated for mayor—and reelected. He has earned the right to a second term in office."

They did cite the need for improvement in the areas of crime prevention, debt reduction, and rehabilitating the housing stock. Overall, the *Post* felt that he had the right people in the right positions and he "brought a degree of order out that (financial) chaos as well as asserted a much-needed degree of control over the city's financial affairs." They hailed his summer youth jobs program a success as it employed sixteen thousand youngsters for nine weeks. They also complimented him on attracting new business to the city but felt more work in that area could be done. In November 1982 Barry was reelected with 80 percent of the vote.

During his second term, Barry achieved real fiscal success. In October of 1984 the city received the highest creditworthiness rating for short-term borrowing from Moody's Investors Service and Standard & Poor's. This rating enabled the District to enter the bond market and raise funds independently of the federal government for the first time.

Also in 1984, alcohol, drug, and legal problems surfaced for Barry as well as his inner circle. In June of that year a close associate, Karen Johnson, pled guilty to drug conspiracy charges and later in that year, Ivanhoe Donaldson, the former deputy mayor, was charged with misuse of city funds. He later pled guilty to the charges.

In 1986, Mayor Barry was up for this third term. Again, he was endorsed by the *Washington Post*. This time the endorsement was not as optimistic or uncritical as the previous two. In spite of the *Post*'s misgivings and reservations, it still believed that Mayor Barry should prevail. This endorsement seemed based as much upon the shortcomings of the challengers as with their concerns with the mayor and "about the atmosphere inside city hall and the stagnant state of political affairs that can so easily breed executive boredom, casual management—and worse." In November Barry was reelected with 61 percent of the vote.

Unfortunately for the citizens of the District, the *Post*'s concerns were proving to be true. At this point, alcohol, drugs, and women were impairing Barry's ability to manage himself and his city. In January of 1987, while the mayor was attending the Super Bowl in Los Angeles, two blizzards dumped twenty-six inches of snow. Washington, D.C. was paralyzed. The city could not manage the snow removal while its leader was sunning in California.

The city workforce was bloated with workers hired as a result of patronage. The mayor exchanged jobs for votes. "The 1988 census and an independent commission on budget and financial priorities put the count at forty-eight thousand—one worker for every thirteen residents—more government workers per capita than any other city or state government, including New York, Chicago, Houston."[33]

The sheer number of employees was not as much of a problem as the fact that more people did not translate into better services. Even the most serious and critical social services were in shambles. Social service recipients could not get assistance in a timely manner, child support was not being collected, the city's ambulance service could not find the people in need of life-saving support, and the city's infant mortality rate was on the rise at an alarming rate. According to the *Washington Post*, "The District's infant mortality rate, already among the highest in the country, increased by nearly 50 percent in the first half of the year because of a surge in babies born to cocaine-addicted women . . . babies are dying in the District at a rate more than triple the national average of 9.9 deaths per 1,000 in 1988."[34] It was the poorest in the city, those who had supported the mayor from the beginning of his political career, who were suffering the most.

As bad as things were in the city, life for Marion Barry was about to take a dramatic turn. In 1988, crack cocaine devastated the city and rival drug gangs drove up the murder rate to a record 372. On February 14, 1989 (Valentine's Day), thirteen people were shot in one twenty-four-hour period. On January 18, 1990, the FBI arrested Barry in room 727 of the Vista Hotel in Washington, D.C. He instantly became the highest-ranking African American elected leader to be arrested on drug charges.

On August 10, 1990, a jury rendered the verdict in the case *U.S. v. Barry.* He was convicted of only one of the fourteen charges pending against him. It was a misdemeanor charge of possession of cocaine in 1989. He was acquitted on one other charge, while the jury was deadlocked on the other twelve charges. On October 26, 1990, Marion Barry was sentenced to six months in prison, yet he continued to run for political office. On November 8, 1990, Marion Barry lost the only election of his life. After bowing out of the mayor's race on June 13 and entering the City Council race for an at-large seat as an Independent, he lost. Hilda Mason, a Council veteran, and Linda Cropp, a former school board president, won the two at-large seats. On January 2, 1991, Sharon Pratt Dixon was sworn in as mayor of Washington, D.C. She became the first African American woman to serve as mayor of a major American city.

OUT OF THE ASHES

On April 23, 1992, after serving his six-month sentence in a Pennsylvania prison, Marion Barry returned to Washington. He was escorted back into the city by five buses filled with his supporters and well-wishers.

He relocated into a small apartment in Ward 8, east of the Anacostia River, still one of the poorest sections of the city. The "Mayor for Life" had returned to his political roots. There are small clusters of middle-class neighborhoods in this ward but most of the residents are working class or poor. It was here that Marion Barry would begin his political resurrection.

He focused his attention on rallying the poorer residents of Ward 8, those who felt disenfranchised or had never voted before. He pledged to bring power to the powerless, hope to the hopeless, and resources to an impoverished, forgotten section of the city. It worked. On September 15, 1992, Marion Barry defeated the incumbent councilmember, Wilhelmina Rolark, by a three-to-one margin. This was the beginning of one of the most amazing political comebacks in history.

Even though Mrs. Rolark had raised more money than he had and was supported by the Washington establishment, Marion Barry outworked her. He went right to the grassroots politics and campaign tactics that had worked for him throughout his political career. He registered more than 2,500 new voters in the ward. He set up transportation to get the voters to the polls. As an ex-convict and former alcohol and drug abuser, he played to the sentiments of his constituents. He was now "one of them." Barry's campaign slogan was "He May Not Be Perfect, But He's Perfect for D.C."

In 1994 Marion Barry defeated Sharon Pratt Kelly and was reelected mayor. In her initial campaign for mayor, Sharon Pratt Dixon (later Sharon Pratt Kelly) ran as a political outsider. She had not held public office and ran as the fresh voice not beholden to political interests. As a native Washingtonian she ran a grassroots, reform-focused campaign, and committed to slash the bloated city government payroll.

"Dixon simply couldn't make the transition from the candidate—whose candor and passion thrilled people . . . to the empathetic politician who could manage a city."[35] She blamed the District's financial problems on the fact that it was not a state and made enemies in Congress in the process. In her efforts to "clean house" she dismissed a number of individuals with the historical knowledge of how the city worked and alienated many others. She proved to be a weak and ineffective administrator who never gained the trust of the citizens of the District or Congress.

These weaknesses and many others enabled Marion Barry to regain control, but the times had changed, the city had changed, and Barry had changed. In 1995, as the city nearly became insolvent, it lost much of its home rule authority to the congressionally created D.C. Financial Control Board. The District of Columbia Financial Control Board (officially the District of Columbia Financial Responsibility and Management Assistance Authority) was a five-member body established by Congress to oversee the finances of the District. Created through the District of Columbia Financial Responsibility and Management Assistance Act of 1995, the board had the power to override decisions by Washington's mayor and City Council.

Even though many blamed Barry, many of the District's problems were a result of a dysfunctional government, a decreasing tax base, and a structural imbalance in the relationship between Congress and the District government. Even though Barry had been calling for the federal government to assume a greater share of its financial responsibility such as the unfunded pension liability, federal control of the District prisons and courts, and the District's inability to tax income earned in the District, he was criticized, but not aided by Congress. In spite of these problems, Mayor Barry presided over the revitalization of downtown Washington, and laid the foundation for a new convention center.

As old habits die hard, new allegations surfaced about the mayor's personal life and health concerns. In 2002 U.S. Park Police reported that they found a trace of marijuana and $5 worth of crack cocaine in Barry's Jaguar while he was parked at Buzzard Point in southwest Washington. He also battled high blood pressure, diabetes, and cancer. Mayor Barry did not seek reelection to a fifth term.

On June 12, 2004, former mayor Barry announced that he would once again seek the Democratic nomination for the Ward 8 City Council seat. In the primary election he defeated the incumbent with 58 percent of the vote. On September 14, 2004, Barry received 95 percent of the vote in the general election, giving him a victory in the race to represent Ward 8 on the City Council where he continues to serve.

His current tenure on the City Council has been much like his past—politically active and personally turbulent. Barry currently serves on a number of City Council committees. His committee assignments include the Committee on Housing and Workforce Development—chairperson; the Committee on Economic Development; the Committee on Finance and Revenue; the Committee on Health; and the Committee on Human Services.

Since his return to the Council, Barry has sponsored/cosponsored and passed a number of pieces of legislation dealing with a wide range of issues from evictions to mortgage disclosure. The Evictions with Dignity Amendment Act ensures that tenants who are evicted are provided the option of having their personal possessions placed in storage for up to ninety days at the expense of the government of the District of Columbia. The Student Access to Treatment Act permits a student with a diagnosis of asthma or anaphylaxis to possess and self-administer inhaled asthma medications or auto-injectable epinephrine while on school property. The Homestead Housing Preservation Amendment Act allows for proposals to develop Homestead properties submitted by for-profit developers to be considered provided that 100 percent of the units are affordable to low- and moderate-income households. The Mortgage Disclosure Amendment Act requires mortgage lenders to provide full and complete information to District consumers for all non-conforming mortgage loans. The Jobs for D.C. Residents Amendment Act provides that all subordinate agencies give a five-point preference to all qualified District resident applicants for any position over qualified non-District resident applicants.

In 2005, with the help of local businesses and volunteer agencies, Councilmember Barry started a program to give away two thousand turkeys to needy Ward 8 residents during the holidays. In 2006 Councilmember Barry was selected by the National Black Caucus of State Legislators (NBCSL) to receive the 2006 Nation Builder Award. This award recognized his exemplary service as a leader and civil rights activist.

Councilmember Barry's personal life has been as turbulent as ever. In 2006 Barry was given three years probation after pleading guilty to misdemeanor charges for failing to file his tax returns from 1999 to 2004. In February of 2009, while preparing to enter the hospital for a kidney transplant, prosecutors were seeking to have Barry jailed for failing to file his 2007 federal and local tax returns. In May of 2009 his probation was extended for an additional two years.

Beyond health and personal financial problems, in July of 2009 Councilmember Barry was arrested by the U.S. Park Police and charged with stalking a female acquaintance. These charges were dropped but this incident has led to other problems for the councilmember. The female acquaintance has turned out to be political consultant Donna Watts-Brighthaupt, a former girlfriend of the councilmember, and, according to city records, the recipient of a $20,000 contract from Barry. This revelation has led to a preliminary public corruption investigation by the FBI amidst allegations he steered city grant money to nonprofit organizations that appeared to be run by members of his staff. Federal authorities are not sure any crime has been committed but believe they would be remiss if they did not examine the allegations.

Again, Councilmember Marion Barry's current tenure on the City Council has been much like his past. Only time will tell how the most current chapter will end and whether or not Barry will prevail. This time it may not be left up to the electorate.

When the final chapter is written, Marion Barry will be considered one of the most astute politicians of his generation and our time. When Barry was first elected mayor in November of 1978, the District of Columbia faced challenges unlike any other city in America. The District's unique relationship with the federal government has made it difficult if not impossible for the locally elected District government to function as a true representative democracy.

The U.S. Constitution granted Congress complete control over the District of Columbia, its government, and local affairs. Even though Congress ceded some its power to the District in 1973 via the Home Rule Act, allowing the residents of the District to directly elect their mayor, City Council, school board, and other representatives, residents have never been free to totally manage their own legislative and financial affairs. Congress retained the authority to retract home rule as it did in 1995 by creating the D.C. Financial Control Board to oversee the finances of the District.

Even as Congress has retained ultimate legislative authority through its power to veto any of the district's legislation, District residents have never had an equal voice in how those decisions are made on the floor of Congress or implemented. The District delegate is entitled to sit in the House of Representatives and vote in committee (including the Committee of the Whole), but is not allowed to take part in legislative floor votes. District residents have no national voice and their local voice can be stymied. District residents can serve in war and loose their lives in war, but are unable to express their support, or lack thereof for war on the floor of Congress. District residents are taxed like every other American citizen but are unable to have their voices heard as it relates to how those taxes are levied and tax dollars are distributed. District residents are not empowered through the vote as other American citizens are.

These limitations have inhibited the ability of every mayor of the District to govern effectively. By exercising the "power of the purse," Congress has been able stifle the democratic process and manipulate and control the will of the voters in the District by withholding funding and placing stipulations on how funding can be spent and how individuals can be taxed. In spite of the congressional restrictions placed upon the District and the historical context in which Marion Barry Jr. governed, as mayor, he governed Washington, D.C., on his terms. As a City Council and school board member he wielded and continues to wield considerable influence. In the words of the British poet William Ernest Henley, people will say what Barry has said of himself: "It matters not how straight the gate; How charged with punishments the scroll; I am the master of my fate; I am the captain of my soul."

NOTES

1. *Washington Post*, 26 April 1987.

2. Tate, Katherine. *From Protest to Politics: The New Black Voters in American Elections* (Cambridge, Mass.: Harvard University Press, 1994), 55.

3. Agronsky, Jonathan I. Z. *Marion Barry: The Politics of Race* (Latham, N.Y.: British American Publishing, 1991), 90.

4. Ibid., 91.

5. Ibid., 93.

6. Ibid., 104.

7. Ibid., 120.

8. Clark, Kenneth B. *Dark Ghetto: Dilemmas of Social Power* (New York: Harper & Row, 1965), 22.

9. Jaffee, Harry S., and Sherwood, Tom, *Dream City: Race, Power, and the Decline of Washington, D.C.* (New York: Simon & Schuster, 1994), 43.

10. Interview with Mukusa Dada, Silver Spring, Maryland, 15 May 2008.

11. Agronsky, Jonathan I. Z., *Marion Barry: The Politics of Race* (Latham, N.Y.: British American Publishing, 1991), p. 123.

12. Tucker, Carlson, "Washington's Lost Black Aristocracy," *City Journal* (Autumn 1996).

13. Brink, William, and Harris, Louis. *The Negro Revolution in America.* (New York: Simon and Schuster, 1964), 113.

14. Agronsky, Jonathan I. Z., *Marion Barry: The Politics of Race* (Latham, N.Y.: British American Publishing, 1991), p. 124.

15. Jaffee, Harry S., and Sherwood, Tom, *Dream City: Race, Power, and the Decline of Washington, D.C.* (New York: Simon & Schuster, 1994), 45.

16. *Washington Post*, 21 May 1998.

17. Jaffee, Harry S., and Sherwood, Tom, *Dream City: Race, Power, and the Decline of Washington, D.C.* (New York: Simon & Schuster, 1994), 44.

18. Ibid., 70.

19. Ibid., 77.

20. Ibid., 85

21. Ibid., 87.

22. Agronsky, Jonathan I. Z. *Marion Barry: The Politics of Race* (Latham, Md.: British American Publishing, 1991), 138.

23. Ibid., 147.

24. Ibid., 147.

25. Tate, Katherine, *From Protest to Politics: The New Black Voters in American Elections* (Cambridge, Mass.: Harvard University Press, 1994), 1.

26. Jaffee, Harry S., and Sherwood, Tom, *Dream City: Race, Power, and the Decline of Washington, D.C.* (New York: Simon & Schuster, 1994), 99.

27. Tate, Katherine. *From Protest to Politics: The New Black Voters in American Elections* (Cambridge, Mass.: Harvard University Press, 1994), 151.

28. Jaffee, Harry S., and Sherwood, Tom, *Dream City: Race, Power, and the Decline of Washington, D.C.* (New York: Simon & Schuster, 1994), 99.

29. Ibid., 106.

30. Gomes, Ralph C. and Williams Linda Fay, eds., *From Exclusion to Inclusion: The Long Struggle for African American Political Power* (Westport, Conn.: Praeger, 1995), 144

31. Jaffee, Harry S., and Sherwood, Tom, *Dream City: Race, Power, and the Decline of Washington, D.C.* (New York: Simon & Schuster, 1994), 112.

32. *Washington Post Editorial*, 30 August 1978.

33. Ibid., 186

34. *Washington Post*, 30 September 1989.

35. Jaffee, Harry S., and Sherwood, Tom, *Dream City: Race, Power, and the Decline of Washington, D.C.* (New York: Simon & Schuster, 1994), 312.

BIBLIOGRAPHY

Agronsky, Jonathan I. Z. *Marion Barry: The Politics of Race.* Latham, Md..: British American Publishing, 1991.

Brink, William, and Harris, Louis. *The Negro Revolution in America.* New York: Simon and Schuster, 1964.

Clark, Kenneth B. *Dark Ghetto: Dilemmas of Social Power.* New York: Harper & Row, 1965

Gomes, Ralph C., and Williams Linda Fay, eds. *From Exclusion to Inclusion: The Long Struggle for African American Political Power.* Westport, Conn.: Praeger, 1995.

Jaffee, Harry S., and Sherwood, Tom. *Dream City: Race, Power, and the Decline of Washington, D.C.* New York: Simon & Schuster, 1994.

Tate, Katherine. *From Protest to Politics: The New Black Voters in American Elections.* Cambridge, Mass.: Harvard University Press, 1994.

5

Sharon Pratt Kelly*: The Reform Mayor

Toni-Michelle C. Travis

INTRODUCTION

In 1990 Marion Barry was in his third term as mayor of Washington, D.C. In the entire twentieth century, Washington, D.C., had only elected two mayors—Walter Washington and Marion Barry. Compared to any other city, Washington, D.C. voters had had limited experience in electing officials. The District had made the transition from an appointed mayor to an elected mayor in 1974, but the ultimate goal of statehood was still elusive. The popular Marion Barry was mayor in 1990 when the image of Washington, D.C., the nation's capital, was shattered by television coverage of his arrest while he was smoking crack. His conviction and subsequent six-month imprisonment only highlighted questions of managerial competence and the ability of African Americans to govern cities. For months the press had questioned Barry's conduct. Simultaneously, congressional members who controlled funding for the District questioned Barry's management. Consequently, Congress was not disposed to grant the District's requests for supplemental funds to run the city. To many residents this situation was an embarrassment, including Sharon Pratt Kelly. She and others wondered how D.C. could ever attain statehood if Congress and the press had no respect for Mayor Marion Barry.

In this unfavorable atmosphere where city administrators were not held in high esteem, Sharon Pratt Kelly (Sharon Pratt Dixon was her name at the time) decided to become a mayoral candidate.

---

* Sharon Pratt Dixon married Arrington Dixon in 1967. They divorced in 1982. In December 1991 she married James R. Kelly III. They subsequently divorced.

Mayor Barry's conduct raised questions about the quality of his leadership and the image of the mayor in the nation's capital. But in Washington, D.C., now a majority black city, race had always been an underlying issue. Before home rule the city was run on the Southern principles of segregation where blacks were confined and limited to only subordinate positions. Under a segregated school system, blacks could attend one of three high schools. The upwardly mobile went from Dunbar High School, with its classical curriculum, to elite East Coast colleges or locally to Howard University. When these college-educated blacks returned to Washington, D.C., they formed the core of a black middle class. As an educated group they believed in democratic values and home rule for the District of Columbia. After the 1954 *Brown v. Board of Education* decision, along with subsequent federal legislation, the barriers of segregation began to break down, except for one major sticking point. Washington, D.C., with a majority African American population, was still under congressional control by white Southerners on the House District Committee. The colonial attitude that Capitol Hill had toward the District irked residents who felt that they could run their own affairs. Mayor Walter Washington's administration answered many of the doubts about the competence of blacks to govern. Marion Barry's administration, however, raised doubts about good governance, questions about the possible extent of corruption, and the future of the sullied image of Washington, D.C.

When Kelly became a mayoral candidate in this murky political atmosphere, the pressing issues were appointing competent administrators and handling a budget deficit. Less obvious were the issues of race and gender in terms of governing Washington, D.C. No longer were questions raised about whether a black could govern because Walter Washington had proved that blacks could run D.C. Now the question was, could a female manage to run the D.C. government?

The electorate found Kelly to be an appealing candidate because she was a native who was familiar with the local problems. Since race was not the overriding issue, attention was focused on gender. She was a female candidate when no major American city had a female mayor. Kelly appeared to be an audacious political newcomer because she had not even served on the school board before jumping into the mayor's race.

As a female, Kelly was not one of the typical candidates who came from the ranks of the City Council or the school board, nor did she have credentials as a civil rights activist. Yet, she made the bold move to challenge Marion Barry who had been in office since 1980. With Kelly's candidacy race took on a different dimension. In previous elections Barry had used race as a way to garner support among African Americans. Now it was just assumed that an African American would become mayor. It was a matter of what kind of black candidate would become mayor. Barry represented those who had come out of the civil rights movement—those men who saw issues in black or white. He fought for the downtrodden who asserted that race was a major barrier to their achieving success. On the other hand, Walter Washington, the first elected mayor, represented a different kind of candidate. Although not a native, Walter Washington had become very much a part of the black elite because he was a Howard University graduate and had achieved a high position in the government. Kelly's candidacy illuminated the intra-class differences between the black bourgeoisie, who were graduates of Dunbar High School and Howard University, and other black Washingtonians. Kelly faced criticisms that she was too middle class, aloof, and, as a corporate executive, was too out-of-touch. Detractors portrayed her as an elitist with fair skin who could not identify with the low-income blacks of Washington, D.C. Media critics focused on Kelly's middle-class background and lack of experience in public office.

As the first native of Washington, D.C., to seek the mayor's office, Kelly lifted the spirits of residents, who again felt pride in their city. Her campaign and election raised high expectations with the press, Congress, and residents who wanted D.C. to have a well-run government free of scandal. Morale was at an all-time low point, but especially among city workers, when Barry left office in disgrace. As a middle-class Washingtonian, Kelly had the image of being the respectable candidate who might be able to set Washington, D.C., back on the path to attaining complete home rule. With a clear message of a new political style and the endorsement of the *Washington Post*, she was swept into office as the reformer who would restore a tarnished public image.

PERSONAL BACKGROUND

Born in Washington in 1944, Sharon Pratt Kelly was the first of two daughters of Carlisle and Mildred Pratt, who died when Kelly was only four. Her father, a lawyer and later superior court judge, helped shape and guide her toward a legal career. A product of the D.C. public schools, she was a graduate of Howard University and its law school. Prior to running for office she worked in her father's law firm and taught at the Antioch School of Law. Subsequently, she worked for the Potomac Electric Power Company (PEPCO), where she became the first woman and African American vice president of public policy.

In 1966 she married Washingtonian Arrington Dixon, who was active in city politics as a city councilman, while she was active at the national level in the Democratic Party. Locally she was a political wife, but nationally she was known among the inner circle of the Democratic Party. Although knowledgeable about Democratic Party politics, Kelly had not previously sought nor served in public office.

Her only political experience was within the Democratic Party, where she held several positions from 1977 to 1989. From 1977 to 1980 she represented D.C. on the Democratic National Committee, and from 1985 to 1989 she was treasurer of the Democratic National Committee, the first female to do so. Her only electoral experience had been as campaign manager in the unsuccessful 1982 mayoral campaign of Patricia Roberts Harris against Marion Barry. As a former cabinet member under President Lyndon B. Johnson, Pat Harris was considered a national figure. District voters, however, did not see her as relating to local issues and the needs of Washingtonians. Barry handily won that race.

When Kelly announced that she would run for mayor she became the longshot candidate because of her inexperience. The political landscape changed completely when Marion Barry withdrew from the race before the primary election. With her main adversary out of the way, she prepared to run in the primary election against three councilmen with greater name recognition.

THE ELECTION CAMPAIGN

Although she was inexperienced in electoral politics, Kelly proved to be a tough campaigner. The press noted that she was focused, driven, and eloquent in contrast to Marion Barry.[1] Kelly ran as a reformer who was going to sweep the city clean after Barry's conviction for crack cocaine possession and use. Barry's withdrawal from the race left her to face councilmen whom she labeled "the three blind mice." In passionate speeches she made ambitious campaign promises. She asserted that she would "clean house with a shovel, not a broom," reduce the very high murder rate in D.C., and eliminate the bloat of approximately two thousand jobs in D.C. government. Her policy proposals directly attacked Marion Barry's administration. There were many skeptics who wondered how such an inexperienced candidate could win and how she would govern with such pressing financial and bureaucratic problems. As of August 1990, Kelly was seen as a serious candidate, but not a winner. The *Washington Post* editorial endorsing her for mayor noted:

> Mrs. Dixon has guts. She was the first major city figure to call for Mayor Barry's resignation, and she was right. She was the first candidate to say that thousands of local government jobs must be trimmed, and she was (and is) right about that too. The next mayor faced with critical financial trouble, will have

to make painful and sometimes unpopular choices. Why not vote for someone whose campaign has shown she can do so.

Can Mrs. Dixon win? The polls still say no. The situation is odd: more and more people who are turning out for candidate forums are saying that her message strikes the right note—but that it's "too bad she can't win" or that maybe it all just words. Still you keep hearing that what Mrs. Dixon is saying about returning local government to prouder days is sweet music, that the three council members and one House delegate all have been in office a long time and must share some responsibility for the state of city hall today.[2]

KELLY'S CAMPAIGN

Kelly's campaign did not have an auspicious beginning. She was running on sheer energy and her message of change. Initially, her campaign events were so small that they were primarily family affairs with her daughters, her sister, a few believers, and a young, dedicated follower, David Byrd. The public perception was that these "campaign events" were a joke.[3] Yet she and the twenty-nine-year-old Byrd, who was not a professional campaign manager, went on to win. She crafted her image as the outsider. However, it should be noted that for sixteen years she had been the wife of Arrington Dixon who became chairman of the City Council. Therefore, she would have had some firsthand knowledge of issues before the City Council. It was often said that she was truly the political brains in the Dixon household.[4] Neither the press nor the political insiders bet on Kelly when Councilman John Ray seemed the likely successor to Marion Barry. Ray had the support of the traditional money sources: developers, realtors, labor leaders, and clergy.[5]

After winning the nomination she went on to face Republican convert Maurice T. Turner, a former D.C. police chief. As a mayoral candidate, Turner, a police veteran of thirty-two years, was in the difficult position of having to defend his record as police chief when the homicide rate had climbed on his watch because crack cocaine use escalated and the homicide rate went from 197 deaths in 1986 to 438 in 1989.[6] Those were years when Turner worked for the Barry administration. Even with questions about his record as police chief, Turner was considered a viable candidate.

Sharon Pratt Kelly was able to ride the wave of an overwhelming desire for change in Washington, D.C., in the early 1990s. As the election drew near Kelly found that she could capture the mayor's office. Despite Turner's charges that she was out of touch with the common people, especially the low-income residents in the District of Columbia, in the end she was able to appeal across color and class lines, as well as age groups, to defeat Turner.

Kelly also had a broad base of support through Democratic and personal connections which extended her fundraising efforts to California. Consequently,
she had very little difficulty raising money. Polls found that she was appealing to both black and white voters, especially those who were "economically
comfortable."[7] "With all 140 precincts reporting, . . . Sharon Pratt Dixon
defeated Republican rival Maurice T. Turner, Jr. with 86 percent of the vote,
the largest winning share of any mayor candidate in the District's modern
political history."[8]

KELLY'S ADMINISTRATION

Since Kelly had no track record in politics, the press was eager to follow her
initial moves: negotiating with Congress, working with the City Council, and
making key appointments. Her initial round of appointments was a signal
regarding her managerial style, especially in the selection of a city administrator and her chief of staff. When Kelly came into office she relied on a
small circle of friends from law school and her campaign workers for advice.
The mayor's appointments favored females, which raised the attention of the
press. Kelly created a stir by appointing women to "a majority of the top positions—believing that women [are] generally better team players than men."[9]

One of many controversial appointments was the selection of law school
classmate Patricia Worthy as chief of staff. She immediately clashed with
the newly appointed city administrator, a seasoned public administrator, Jack
Bond, who had left his position as county manager of Durham, North Carolina, for what he thought was a position paying more than his $96,000 salary.
He had been led to believe that he would be paid $108,000 per year.[10] Later,
Bond was informed that his salary was not to be more than $90,705 because
District law stated that his salary could not exceed the mayor's.[11] Bond and
Patricia Worthy had disagreements because Worthy's personal friendship
with the mayor dictated that all paperwork go through her before going to
the mayor. In Bond's opinion this was not the appropriate chain of command
because it undermined his authority. Bond resigned in November 1991, while
Worthy went on medical leave shortly thereafter.

Bond's replacement was a thirty-four-year-old lawyer who did not inspire
confidence because he lacked prior experience in municipal administration. This left Mayor Kelly with two key vacancies, along with a number of
unfilled positions, in addition to cases where a nominee's name had to be
withdrawn. Without a smooth transition to a staff that could hit the ground
running, doubts were raised about the ability of Kelly and key appointees to
manage the government. These missteps did not bode well for Kelly because

critics had hoped for a professionally managed District government after Marion Barry's ten years in office.

The problem of making qualified appointments was not limited to just the mayor's office. There was considerable opposition to Mayor Kelly's choice to run the Department of Finance and Revenue. District City Council chairman John A. Wilson, along with the spokesman for the D.C. Federation of Civic Association, opposed the appointment of Sharon Morrow on the grounds that she had not exhibited "management ability and technical competence required of the director."[12] The spokeswoman of the Palisades Citizens Association joined the opponents by noting that Morrow had experience in "working on property tax issues for three years during the Barry administration." Therefore her appointment was not considered a sign of reform.[13] Two nominations, one for the Convention Center Board and another for the D.C. Taxicab Commission, were withdrawn because of prior criminal convictions.[14]

Working with the City Council was a challenge for the mayor. Once Kelly was in office she had to deal with the City Council and Congress, in addition to the voters. Upon assuming her first public office, Kelly had to face a steep learning curve to maneuver between the City Council and Congress. She was confronted with a bureaucracy that was unresponsive and very slow to change in a political climate where federal and local political objectives often collided. Under the home rule provisions, all District legislation that had been passed by the City Council and signed by the mayor was still subject to congressional review. This situation could create an impasse because the mayor, City Council, and Congress often had different perspectives on any issue. To get all three parties to agree to any controversial legislation was a daunting task. An additional obstacle was that the City Council had to get used to Kelly's style of governance.

Every metropolitan city mayor faces challenges and uphill battles. However, the mayor of Washington, D.C., is inevitably placed in a unique political and bureaucratic bind unlike any other urban area. Any mayor of Washington, D.C., faces intractable problems because of the congressional oversight of the District mandated by the U.S. Constitution. It is imperative that a mayor faced with this type of political situation make allies with federal officials whenever possible. However, this is no easy task because sometimes the creation of amicable relationships with Congress can cause alienation of local officials. Kelly needed to build relationships with both congressmen and councilmembers because she was not a member of either "club."

Trying to implement campaign promises became "mission impossible." Kelly had vowed to reduce the homicide rate within six months of taking office, eliminate the boards of all city-owned housing within eighteen months, and commit the government to reduce spending without curbing vital city services.[15] Tackling these issues was overwhelming when she found that the infrastructure for daily operations was inadequate.

Kelly had an ambitious agenda, although she had no experience in electoral office on which to draw. Upon taking office she found that the problems she had to face were formidable—a budget deficit, an entrenched and often inept bureaucracy, a growing Latino community, and a high crime rate. Kelly and her "merry band of reformers," as she called them, found that the city government was in shambles. Her estimate of the deficit was about $100 million. What she found was a more than $300 million deficit. It was a government that did not function because of the disarray left by Marion Barry's administration left, with

> contracts and personnel records missing or misfiled; huge agencies running on file card and papers scattered all over town; the few computers in evidence often unable to communicate with one another, no-show employees, layer upon layer of unnecessary city workers, and good workers who were demoralized; not to mention the rats that were roaming the basement of the District building.[16]

What became the most contentious issue was the plan to cut two thousand mid-management-level jobs. This appeared to be a direct attack on District employees who had been hired during Mayor Barry's years in office, when the District government was referred to as the employer of last resort. Kelly's idea was to follow the federal policy of streamlining public service jobs by following the principles of reinventing government. The goal was for government to do more with less by privatizing local services. The principles of reinventing government were a popular governing philosophy during the Clinton-Gore administration.

Moving from a campaign promise to actually laying off two thousand District managers from a bloated bureaucracy of forty-eight thousand workers set the stage for a battle.[17] While the objective had merit because it was an effort to remove inefficient workers from the government, the problem became complicated. Among the issues were a projected budget deficit, opposition from council members, especially from John Wilson, and opposition from the press which was pointing out the benefits of sustaining a black middle class.[18] The attempt to reduce the District's workforce hit a nerve because it seemed to target the employment of black middle-class workers who had always looked to government—city or federal—for job security. Mayor Kelly was attacking this longstanding assumption of always being able to get government employment in a town where there were few employment options outside of government. Sharp criticisms against Kelly continued to claim that she was out to remove all Barry supporters from the government.

The objective to streamline government in light of a projected $25 million deficit may have been the best management approach, but it immediately put the mayor in a political minefield. What started out as an appealing campaign promise to rid the city of unnecessary workers became a nightmare to implement. Good government seemed to have met its limits when the alternative was increasing unemployment and probably the number of welfare recipients in the District. It was acceptable as an abstract idea, but when it came to putting people out of work, Mayor Kelly was accused of being politically motivated and of infringing on the rights of workers. Kelly did not accomplish her objective because the bureaucracy was too entrenched and the opposition for such a massive removal of civil service employees was intense.

Five months into her administration Kelly had to respond to her first major public safety crisis. In May of 1991 a street incident in Mt. Pleasant, a Latino neighborhood, erupted into violence. On Sunday May 5, 1991, during a Cinco de Mayo street celebration, a black female police officer attempted to arrest a Latino male for disorderly conduct. It is unclear whether the man was drunk or approached her with a hunting knife, but the officer responded by shooting the man who was wounded as a result. The situation quickly escalated to the point where there was looting of businesses, damage to city transit buses, and destruction of police vehicles. The mayor instructed the police not to make arrests for looting because of the fear of creating more violence. Although over one thousand riot police were on the streets, violence broke out on a second night. At this point Mayor Kelly declared a state of emergency along with a curfew for the three neighborhoods of Mt. Pleasant, Adams Morgan, and Columbia Heights. After two nights of violence the neighborhood began to calm down because most residents feared arrest if they did not observe the curfew. Washington, D.C., had not had riots since 1968 when Mayor Washington had to use the National Guard to restore order.[19]

Now Mayor Kelly was faced with a civil disturbance that required restoring order in a Latino neighborhood primarily composed of El Salvadorans. Unlike the 1968 riot, the Mt. Pleasant incident was confined to only one neighborhood of the city, which made it manageable for D.C. police officers without outside assistance. However, one of the biggest complications was that only a handful of D.C. police officers could speak Spanish. There were over two hundred arrests, but most of the injuries were sustained by the police. This riot, in which over sixty police vehicles were damaged or destroyed along with some twenty city buses, private property, and approximately thirty-five businesses, highlighted the lack of communication between the black governing structure and a heavily Latino community.[20] No subsequent riots have occurred, but relations between the black and Latino communities have continued to demand attention.

If riots are seen as a form of communication, then residents of the Mt. Pleasant community were trying to communicate their frustration with city officials who had not provided for bilingual city services, especially calls to 911. Since one of the city's problems was crime, any assistance with crime prevention was helpful to the police. One outcome was that city officials agreed to hire more bilingual officers and 911 operators to better serve the Latino community.[21] Mayor Kelly found this to be an abrupt wake-up call to the needs of Washington residents, who now lived in a multicultural community. The issues were no longer just black or white, but more culturally nuanced. This was also a signal that the heterogeneous Latino community could not be ignored.

The daily administrative problems never ceased. Raising sufficient revenue to run the District usually ended up with a plea to Congress for additional funds. Crime continued to be a problem as teenage gangs emerged. The bureaucracy did not shrink in meaningful numbers because it had a number of advocates supporting employment of District residents, even though workers were not performing satisfactorily. In short, the mayor could never get ahead or move beyond the next crisis.

1994 ELECTION

Sharon Pratt Kelly sought a second term in office, but first had to face a primary election against the rehabilitated Marion Barry. Out of federal prison for just a few months, Barry beat Kelly in the primary which was the key to making a comeback. Barry had a core of faithful voters, especially in Ward 8, who supported him as he went to prison and celebrated his release. The general election was an easy victory for Barry because his longtime supporters across the city rallied once again to elect him mayor. Over the years Barry, the former community organizer, had built a successful organization that had political operatives in every ward. As Jonetta Barras noted:

> He retained on the government payroll a prostrating cadre of precinct captains and "coordinators" in each of the city's eight wards. . . . [T]he office of Constituent Services "built the fires, put out the fires, and organized programs other departments were mandated to do." . . . [T]hese were the loyalists who, until Barry was caught on tape sucking a crack pipe, vehemently protested accusations of the mayor's drug use. They faced down the allegations even when reports from their colleagues were filled with descriptive language of the mayor's incoherence at cabinet-level meetings, of profuse sweating, and of long absences from his office.[22]

ASSESSMENT OF KELLY

Kelly's election to office was facilitated by not having to compete with Marion Barry's political organization. She did not have the organization, widespread base of support, or the political experience to run against a seasoned politician such as Marion Barry. His arrest heightened the contrast between a swaggering politician with a civil rights philosophy and a non-politician seeking the restoration of good government. Taking the position of being an outsider and a reformer, Kelly garnered support across the city and received the key endorsement from the *Washington Post*. She was such a contrast to Marion Barry that for her first year in office the *Washington Post* was very supportive with what was termed "cozy coverage."[23]

Kelly's style and demeanor were acceptable to Capital Hill and the press. This smoothed her way in improving relations with Congress. To the surprise of residents and her critics, in her first days in office she persuaded Congress to appropriate $100 million in emergency funding for D.C. to increase federal funding by $200 million.[24] This was an unexpected triumph for a D.C. mayor who had no previous rapport with congressional members.

Kelly's personality and temperament were factors in her relations with constituents and the press. Although she was successful with Congress, she was often criticized by the press and the City Council for being aloof. Indeed, it was said of her appointments that she seemed to attract others of the same ilk. In interviews she would even characterize herself as shy and not a public person.[25] However, according to Perl, in some cases Kelly appeared boastful and haughty. In talks with a banker who was appealing to her for assistance because banks outside of Washington were "pulling loans on healthy local companies," she replied, "I'm going to make Washington the entertainment and recording capital of the world." This claim was never realized. Because Kelly was a first-time officeholder, the press was keen on scrutinizing her appeal to voters. Although Kelly won the election, she appeared detached from the average voter. Essentially, she was a shy person with a flair for the theatrical who sought center stage. Yet, once she achieved her goal of becoming mayor, everyone focused on her. The constant attention to every aspect of her public and private life came as quite a surprise to Kelly.[26]

Kelly ran as an outsider against a group of candidates who had served on the City Council. She was going to reform D.C. government, yet she had not taken the steps to build allies on the City Council. There was an especially contentious relationship with Councilman John Ray, a Barry supporter who served on the City Council from 1979 to 1996. One clash was over electing a new chairman after the death of John Wilson in 1993. In that election Kelly backed Councilwoman Linda Cropp rather than John

Ray. Her major battles were clearly with the City Council, rather than with Congress.

Another touchy point that received considerable media coverage during the Kelly administration was how often the mayor took trips. This was an issue that had carried over from Marion Barry's administration because he had been in California during a Washington snowstorm. The press duly noted that in one year Kelly went to Cancun, Palo Alto, Los Angeles, Atlanta, Martha's Vineyard, Boston, South Carolina, New York, and Florida.[27] However, taking frequent trips has been a pattern for other D.C. mayors.

Not an outgoing, gregarious politician in the Barry style or a seasoned administrator in the Walter Washington mold, Kelly proved not to be the mayor the neighborhoods needed or that the press expected. Unfortunately, Kelly did not follow either as a model in crafting her role as mayor. Although Kelly's style was in sharp contrast to Barry, she began to encounter criticism of her managerial style and her ability to govern before her first year in office ended.[28]

Kelly had little chance of being reelected once she had to face Barry in the primary. Having spent her time on the day-to-day governance problems, she had not developed a long-term strategy, nor built a broad constituency base. Barry's return to the electoral arena with an appeal to his base of the working class, churchgoers, and city employees cut Kelly's public career short. With Kelly leaving center stage the press had to cover Barry again. Now the press was likely to attack Barry because he raised the level of uncertainty about how well the city would be run. Reporters now wondered to what extent the mayor had reformed his personal lifestyle or his style of cronyism governance.

LEGACY

Because she presented a clear contrast to Marion Barry in style, personal background, and governing priorities, the press and residents met Kelly's election with high expectations. As an advocate for statehood, Kelly was the great hope of these advocates and residents who felt that Washington, D.C.'s image needed restoration. However, there was a huge gap between her hopes for full D.C. home rule and the sorry state of the District government following Barry's administration.

Funding services for D.C. residents was a central problem. However, to get D.C. government on the road to recovery would take more than just a massive infusion of money. Yes, there was a deficit of $316 million she was facing in December of 1992, which grew to one billion dollars by January 1993.[29] However, this pointed to her bigger structural problem of needing a much larger tax base to adequately fund the District's services. Kelly then linked the issue of statehood to a possible commuter tax, which created tensions with Delegate Eleanor Holmes Norton, an ardent supporter of statehood and suburban residents. Kelly knew that only 43 percent of the land in D.C. was taxable and that "fully 60 percent of the income earned in the city, however, [was] exempt from taxation by the D.C. government."[30] This longstanding issue always evoked a passionate response from Maryland and Virginia residents who only worked in D.C. Norton felt that pushing the issue would jeopardize statehood efforts for D.C.[31] She told the press that Kelly's position that the District should wean itself entirely from federal political control and financial dependence would "raise severe problems in the Congress."[32] Norton quickly amended her legislation for statehood to ensure that the District would still get an annual federal payment of $600 million even if it became a state. She certainly had reservations about Kelly's haughtiness that the District did not need federal assistance.[33]

Kelly's campaign had made lofty predictions about sweeping the District building clean. Removing the bloat in personnel was far more difficult than Kelly imagined. Lacking a public sector background, Kelly was shocked at the condition of the District government after Barry's administration. Not only did Kelly have to address the deficit issues, but she also had to continue to deliver services to constituents with a crippled bureaucracy. There were several administrative blunders: the cabinet-level officials were not experienced administrators, boards and commissions could not function because vacancies remained for months, and there were multiple personnel changes in Kelly's inner circle.

Kelly's one term has pluses and minuses. She was unique because she was the first female mayor of the nation's capital which still lacks true home rule or voting representation in Congress. As the first African American female to become mayor of Washington, D.C., she opened the door for other women to consider running for mayor. Her unconventional route to the office of mayor showed that a female did not have to serve first on the PTA then the school board and the City Council before running for mayor. She represented a new role model of a career woman who had a family, but was not a politician before becoming mayor.

Kelly was an effective antidote to the Marion Barry years because she gave Washington, D.C., a fresh, respectable image. Although Kelly was not successful in managerial terms, her strengths were in restoring respectability to Washington, D.C., and in improving congressional relations. She was seen as a no-nonsense mayor who would confront Congress. In immediately tackling the deficit issue she acted decisively to present the District's case to Congress to appropriate emergency funds.

Kelly's term met with limited success if measured against her campaign promises. The urban problems along with structural impediments made it very difficult for Mayor Kelly to make much progress on running a lean bureaucracy within budget. Indeed, her inept management style was costly and did not help the case for statehood.

Kelly fell far short of the mark of being an effective reformer, especially in restructuring government. Even her best intentions could not compensate for her lack of experience in running a public bureaucracy or installing appropriate administrators. However, the question could be raised: Can anyone effectively run Washington, D.C., given the nature of congressional oversight, City Council input, and citizen priorities for increased municipal employment over bureaucratic efficiency?

Mayor Kelly and a few strong supporters came to office with a reformer's zeal, which was admirable. She plunged into the race to improve local government and its service delivery system without a cost/benefit assessment. For Kelly, running for office was seen as a civic duty, not as a route to personal gain, nor her only possible source of employment, nor a way to make her friends rich. However, the problems she confronted—a deficit, crime, an unwieldy bureaucracy—remain because the District continues to be an administered government.

NOTES

1. Mark Plotkin, "The Mayor's Withering Base, Fading Identity," *Legal Times*, October 18, 1993.

2. "Clean house—Dixon for Mayor," *Washington Post*, August 30, 1990.

3. Peter Perl, "The Struggles of Sharon Pratt Kelly," *Washington Post*, January 31, 1993: 14.

4. Ibid.

5. Ibid.

6. Ibid.

7. Plotkin.

8. Vincent McCraw, "Her Honor, Sharon Pratt Dixon," *The Washington Times*, November 7, 1990.

9. Perl, 15.

10. James Ragland, "Departing D.C. Administrator Leaves Speculation Behind Him," *Washington Post*, November 7, 1991.

11. Ragland, "D.C.'s City Administrator Said to Be Resigning Post," *Washington Post*, November 5, 1991; and "It Came Down to Money," *Washington Post*, November 6, 1991.

12. Nell Henderson, "Citizen Groups Oppose D.C. Revenue Nominee," *Washington Post*, May 30, 1991.

13. Ibid.

14. Pamela McClintock, "Dixon Nomineee Arrested in '73" (*Washington Post*, June 25, 1991), and "Dixon Withdraws 2nd Nomination" (*Washington Post*, June 29, 1991).

15. Mary Ann French, "Victory Won, Dixon Faces Hard Road," *Washington Post*, November 7, 1990

16. Perl, 14.

17. Vincent McCraw, "Bond's Bear Hug Grips 'Bloated Bureaucracy,'" *Washington Times*, March 25, 1991.

18. Courtland Milloy, "The Honeymoon Is Over," *Washington Post*, July 4, 1991.

19. *Washington Post*, May 6–12, 1991.

20. Ibid.

21. Ibid.

22. Jonetta Rose Barras, *The Last of the Black Emperors*, Baltimore: Bancroft Press, 1998:25.

23. Harry Jaffee, "Running on Empty," *The Washingtonian,* January 1992:137.

24. Perl, 14.

25. Ibid., 24.

26. Ibid., 29.

27. Jaffee, 137.

28. Ibid.

29. Vincent McCraw, "Kelly Sweeps Dirt, Struggles with Mess," *The Washington Times*, January 3, 1993.

30. Rudolph A. Pyatt Jr., "Fairer Federal Payment Would End D.C.'s Need to Tax Suburbanites," *Washington Post*, February 18, 1993.

31. James Ragland, "Budget Woes Put Kelly on Political Tightrope," *Washington Post*, December 25, 1992.

32. Ibid.

33. Ibid.

BIBLIOGRAPHY

Barras, Jonetta Rose, *The Last of the Black Emperors*, Baltimore: Bancroft Press, 1998.

French, Mary Ann, "Victory Won, Dixon Faces Hard Road," *Washington Post*, November 7, 1990.

Henderson, Nell, "Citizen Groups Oppose D.C. Revenue Nominee," *Washington Post*, May 30, 1991.

Jaffee, Harry, "Running on Empty," *The Washingtonian*, January 1992.

McClintock, Pamela, "Dixon Nominee Arrested in '73," *Washington Post*, June 25, 1991, and "Dixon Withdraws 2nd Nomination," *Washington Post*, June 29, 1991.

McCraw, Vincent. "Kelly Sweeps Dirt, Struggles with Mess," *Washington Times*, January 3, 1993.

McCraw, Vincent, "Bond's Bear Hug Grips 'Bloated Bureaucracy,'" *Washington Times*, March 25, 1991.

Melton, R. H., and Sari Horwitz, "Ex-chief As Mayoral Candidate," *Washington Post*, November 1, 1990.

Milloy, Courtland, "The Honeymoon Is Over," *Washington Post*, July 4, 1991.

Perl, Peter, "The Struggles of Sharon Pratt Kelly," *Washington Post*, January 31, 1993.

Plotkin, Mark, "The Mayor's Withering Base, Fading Identity," *Legal Times*, October 18, 1993.

Pyatt, Rudolph A. "Fairer Federal Payment Would End D.C.'s Need to Tax Suburbanites," *Washington Post*, February 18, 1993.

Ragland, James, "D.C.'s City Administrator Said to Be Resigning Post," *Washington Post*, November 5, 1991.

Ragland, James, "It Came Down to Money," *Washington Post*, November 6, 1991.

Ragland, James, "Departing D.C. Administrator Leaves Speculation Behind Him," *Washington Post*, November 7, 1991.

Ragland, James, "Budget Woes Put Kelly on Political Tightrope," *Washington Post*, December 25, 1992.

Washington Post, May 6–12, 1991.

Washington Times.

6

The High Tide of Pragmatic Black Politics: Mayor Anthony Williams and the Suppression of Black Interests

Daryl B. Harris

In a real sense, Washington, D.C.'s 1998 mayoral election helped magnify a chasm in the style and substance of black electoral politics that had been widening and simmering with increasing intensity over the previous two decades. Beginning roughly in the late 1980s (and continuing into the present), more and more black mayoral candidates have self-consciously espoused a brand of politics that plays down or disregards the racialized realities and dynamics of their cities. This shift arguably dulled or cheapened their sensitivities to the point where black and brown peoples' policy interests were given short shrift. Of particular interest in this regard was the Washington, D.C., mayoral contest of 1998 because, as a signifying event, it vividly contrasted the discord and discontinuities in black political motivation, technique, and purpose. Most noticeable to some election observers was that it seemed to presage the demise of insurgent, transformative black mayoral leadership personified in Marion Barry and the ascension of technocratic, managerial black mayoral leadership exemplified by Anthony Williams. Barry, of course, was not on the 1998 mayoral ballot, but his ghost—the by-product of his long-standing and formidable presence in Washington, D.C., first as insurgent and community organizer then as councilman and mayor—enveloped and agitated the entire city.

For better or worse, Barry almost certainly came to be reviled by just as many people as adored him. Whereas substantial numbers of black Washingtonians praised Barry for extending substantial employment and business opportunities to the black community, others, especially white media but also some of the District's black bourgeoisie, openly heaped scorn on him and belittled his political prowess. The *Washington Post*, for instance, opined that on the whole Barry's mayoral tenure was disastrous for the city and that

Barry was especially to blame for ruining the city's ability to govern itself.[1] It should be noted, however, that the *Post*'s disapproval of Barry's reign as mayor contrasts sharply with the favorable read it gave him at the dawn of his assuming the helm in 1978; indeed, in endorsing Barry's first mayoral bid in 1978, the *Washington Post* helped propel him to a Democratic Party primary victory over Walter Washington, the District's first black mayor. Of course, winning the Democratic mayoral primary in Washington, D.C., customarily translates into victory over any and all general election opponents.

Some critics of Barry have even gone to great lengths to proffer their rebukes. The blows they meted out came with two edges, one aimed explicitly at Barry, while the other focused on cutting deep into and mortally wounding if possible the insurgent, transformative tradition of black politics. This is the angle journalist Jonetta Rose Barras took in *The Last of the Black Emperors*, where she lambasts both Barry's mayoral tenure and insurgency black politics, and labels them as dated, unsettling, and ineffective.[2] Barras is among those who believe that the age of black pragmatism has dawned, but that for it to blossom the age of black insurgency must be laid to rest so that it never again is permitted to grace the staid halls of government. In a sense Barry's undoing as mayor prefigured just what Barras wished for—a shifting of the guard—although we should point out that his downfall came to pass for more consequential reasons than just his copious personal flaws and failings. As it were, intense congressional consternation with Washington, D.C.'s budgetary crisis and with Barry (the personal and the political) in the first half of the 1990s stirred the august body to circumvent the city's governing privileges as established in the home rule charter, thereby paving the way for the ascension of technocrat Anthony Williams.

Our objective in this chapter is to consider some of the critical issues during Williams's mayoral tenure, which we believe provide an interesting backdrop for pondering the reach and prospects for democratic governance in the nation's federal city and for gauging the general status of black empowerment and black policy interests. Invariably, the situational context of cities in the urban and federal milieu figures prominently in how the issues of democratic governance and black empowerment are worked out. Therefore, it is imperative that we take into account the structural and systemic location of the American city. Doing so will certainly augment our understandings of the kinds of forces that shape urban governance. But before exploring these concerns, we recognize and appreciate that the District of Columbia cannot be placed among the ordinary register of American cities without specifying its uniqueness.

Officially established in 1800, Washington, D.C.'s distinctiveness stems from the fact that it is constitutionally chartered as the federal district or capital. Then as now, Congress stands as its ultimate arbiter of law and policy, even though since the early 1970s District officials and residents have accrued some democratic prerogatives via home rule legislation. Even with Congress overreaching, the rights accrued still allow for District officials to establish their own policy priorities, although Congress still can override District legislation.[3] Notwithstanding that none of the concerns enumerated by Dillon's Rule (see below) apply directly to the District—meaning, neither its legal standing nor its allotted powers derive from state sanction—the question of democratic governance or lack thereof is particularly relevant for the District and its residents because of Congress's utmost position in the American hierarchy of power. Whereas governing officials of the typical American city petition mainly their respective state legislatures for various allowances and enhancements, District officials, in contrast, prostrate annually before congressional committees for similar benefits. On a range of programs and issues, especially those that are hotly contested in the public sphere (such as gun control and needle exchange), members of Congress as far away as Wyoming and Montana use congressional committees as a means to browbeat District officials and residents into policy conformance. We will revisit this concern more directly when we explore the mayoral tenure of Anthony Williams. For now, however, let us consider more generally some important theoretical issues that inform urban governance.

BETWEEN A ROCK AND A HARD PLACE: THE NATURE OF URBAN GOVERNANCE

Chief among the complex of issues that any mayor, but especially black mayors, confronts in her or his governance of an American city is the structural (or societal) context of the urban environment. To begin with, in the hierarchal arrangement of American federalism, cities have the distinction of being the administrative units closest to the people. Being nearest to the people, however, does not automatically, if ever, confer a sense of calm for city mayors. Except perhaps for mayors of small hamlets or villages, mayors aspiring to satisfy the needs and demands of their constituents can expect a steady dose of anxiety due to, among other things, the constraints that inhere in the city's place in the federal system. That is to say, municipalities (excepting Washington, D.C., of course) are juridical creations of state legislatures. In so being, their official powers, too, are by-products of state actions. Accordingly, the states use a particular kind of charter—(a) specific or special, (b) general or classified, or (c) home rule—to specify the scope of powers allotted to their respective municipalities. This does not mean, however, that the states have appropriated all power unto themselves. Even though the formal trappings of federalism denote that state powers supersede local powers, practically all municipalities possess some measure of local autonomy.

Over the past century and a half, the scope of municipal powers has evolved in response to a legal philosophy known as Dillon's Rule. The rule is named after Judge John Forest Dillon, chief justice in 1868 of the Iowa Supreme Court. Dillon's philosophy interprets grants of power to local governments very narrowly, holding that municipalities have no powers except those conferred on them by state constitution or law. Per Dillon's Rule, local governments have only three types of powers: (a) those granted in express words, (b) those necessarily or fairly implied in or incident to the powers expressly granted, and (c) those essential to the declared objects and purposes of the corporation. Of Dillon's reach over the country, thirty-nine states either apply the rule selectively to some of their municipalities or universally to all of them. Ten states have opted not to use the rule at all.[4]

Apart from the structural constraints that inhere in American federalism, one can, as political scientist Clarence Stone does in *Regime Politics*, quarrel with Paul Peterson for describing "city politics in which, within each policy arena, the type of policy (the independent variable) molds the form of political participation and the character of politics (the dependent variable)"[5] and still concede Peterson's point that cities have limits that circumscribe the politics and policy choices cities make. Of these limits, Peterson contends,

> The place of the city within the larger political economy of the nation fundamentally affects the policy choices that cities make. In making these decisions, cities select those policies which are in the interests of the city, taken as a whole. It is these city interests, not the internal struggles for power within cities that limit city policies and conditions what local governments do.[6]

Peterson's thesis goes far beyond merely marking out the city's limits. It advocates that city officials adopt a market-centered ideological attitude which would then facilitate their espousal and implementation of policies that satisfy what he deems as "the interests of cities." Here, it is worth quoting Peterson at length so as to capture the fullness of his argument.

> The interests of cities are neither a summation of individual interests nor the pursuit of optimum size. Instead, policies and programs can be said to be in the interest of cities whenever the policies maintain or enhance the economic position, social prestige, or political power of the city, taken as a whole.
>
> Cities have these interests because cities consist of a set of social interactions structured by their location in a particular territorial space. Any time that social interactions come to be structured into recurring patterns, the structure thus formed develops an interest in its own maintenance and enhancement. It is in

that sense that we speak of the interests of an organization, the interests of the system, and the like. To be sure, within cities, as within any other structure, one can find diverse social roles, each with its own set of interests. But these varying role interests, as divergent and competing as they may be, do not distract us from speaking of the overall interests of the larger structural entity.[7]

Peterson delineates what is worthy of pursuit in policy terms for a city. His demarcation, however, suggests that some policy demands—the ones made by the indigent, for instance—ought not be part of the policy discourse for city officials because they "fall outside the limited sphere of local politics."[8] There can be no doubt that such a view, were it to triumph and become the dominant mode of black political expression, would practically spell doom for promoting and securing the interests of the black masses. As we have noted already, even with the federalism structure of the American political system, it is precisely at the local level where the rubber meets the road, so to speak. City governments or, more precisely, Peterson's role interests that do not vie for black interests or indigent persons' interests (these Peterson categorizes as redistributive policies) cannot possibly hope to satisfactorily attend to them.

In contradistinction to the rigidity intimated in Peterson's market-oriented construct of urban governance, Stone suggests that the governance process is in fact more nuanced and dynamic. With this in mind, he developed the urban regime concept, which he defines thusly:

The informal arrangements by which public bodies and private interests function together in order to be able to make and carry out governing decisions. . . . [T]hey are driven by two needs: (1) institutional scope (that is, the need to encompass a wide enough scope of institutions to mobilize the resources required to make and implement governing decisions) and (2) cooperation (that is, the need to promote enough cooperation and coordination for the diverse participants to reach decisions and sustain action in support of those decisions).[9]

Stone may dissent from Peterson's doctrinaire theory of market exclusivity all right, but what both he and Peterson (and others) hold in common about city governance is the relative primacy of the corporate or business sector. Never is the corporate sector absent from the policy debates and decisions of city governments. Usually the corporate class is in the know about the more consequential policy choices that are at play. And their interests, more often than not, trump all other interests, or at least shape the contours within which they are determined and meted out.

In what follows, we argue that during Anthony Williams's stewardship of the District its issue agenda and concomitant policies were driven in large part by corporate interests. Indeed, one might say that the entirety of the Anthony Williams/control board governance of the District reflects the dominance of corporate interests.

To be sure, corporatist concerns and the structural limits of American federalism such as we have highlighted do not necessarily prescribe in a dictatorial sense the policy choices a mayor makes, but they certainly do shape and heavily influence them. There is, however, a certain degree of fixedness, as well as flexibility, presented by these constraints, such that they allow for the variance of choices one might observe from one mayor to the next. And then on top of the structural context (or alongside it, depending on one's vantage point) there is the critical and sensitive question of ideological disposition. Even as the structural limits weigh heavily on mayoral decisions, her or his ideological bent (which evolves out of and reinforces one's value orientation) affects the vigor with which she or he articulates interests associated with said value orientation. A transformative mayor who places a premium on social justice, for example, might be more inclined than a pragmatist mayor to push for affirmative action programs in the city bureaucracy, summer jobs for teens, racial and ethnic parity in the allocation of city contracts, or increased expenditures for homeless shelters. In this sense, then, Barry's mayoral rise and fall, in all of its astonishments and incongruities, and Williams's mayoral ascension underscore what has been transpiring and troubling in black urban and electoral politics over the past two decades.

THE STATE OF BLACK EMPOWERMENT AND POLICY INTERESTS DURING ANTHONY WILLIAMS'S STEWARDSHIP

Duly noting some of the contextual themes at play in city politics, we are left wondering what they portend for black empowerment and black policy interests in Washington, D.C., during Anthony Williams's mayoral tenure. Here, again, our reflections are heavily weighted by the reality that among American cities, Washington, D.C., truly is in a league unto itself. Not only are black empowerment and policy issues wedded to the rock that is the corporate-driven U.S. political economy, but they are also circumscribed by the hard place that is the strong arm of Congress. Washington, D.C., differs from other American cities in that its ultimate political and fiscal authority resides with Congress, although Congress has ceded some basic elements of home rule to the District of Columbia. Via the Home Rule Act of 1973, residents of Washington, D.C., acquired the right to elect a mayor and City Council. Before then, however, District of Columbia residents were governed for much of the city's history by a three-member appointed commission. The commission form of government was followed in the late 1960s by a government comprised of an appointed mayor and City Council. Of these developments, however, we need to emphasize that the limited democratic prerogatives Washingtonians now enjoy and practice—the right to elect a mayor, City Council, board of education, and a nonvoting delegate to the U.S. House of Representatives—are by-products of furious political struggle in the 1960s and 1970s. No heavenly light pricked Congress's conscience to put it on a course to enlarge the democratic idea. To be sure, it was the general black movement (with its local, interconnecting tributaries) that brought about the eventual expansion of democratic principles.

But, as Congress demonstrated in 1995, when as an interim measure it nullified some democratic rights in the District of Columbia, often what is given with one hand can be easily taken away by the other.[10] Congressional action to impose a control board (and other forms of meddling) on the federal city bears out what is inherently problematic about democratic governance in Washington, D.C. Indeed, the very structure of District of Columbia government itself, with Congress ever lurking as arbiter and overseer, inhibits the full blossoming of democracy and of the District determining its own policies. Structurally hemmed in by constitutional fiat, even after the extension of home rule, the District's policy actions invariably have to be teased out in the rough and tumble of congressional hearings and sanctions, some of which are petulant and patently colonialist. Such was the case in 1995 when Congress passed the Control Act.

The occasion of Washington, D.C.'s fiscal woes in the early 1990s presented Congress with both a pretext and subtext to usurp the reins of city government. In the name of restoring fiscal and managerial responsibility, Congress enacted the Control Act, which created the District of Columbia Financial Responsibility and Management Assistance Authority (the control board); the Office of Chief Financial Officer (through which Anthony Williams made his entry into District politics); and the Office of Inspector General. In retrospect, one might say that Williams's foray into electoral politics was fortuitous because prior to doing so he really only distinguished himself as a technocrat. Before his appointment as chief financial officer for the District, Williams held various other administrative and management positions, the most significant one was as chief financial officer for the U.S. Department of Agriculture during the early years of Bill Clinton's presidency. He held lesser management posts before coming to Washington, D.C. In Connecticut he served as the deputy state comptroller, where he managed 250 separate funds and the state's budget and accounting services. In St. Louis, Missouri, he served as executive director of the Community Development Agency. And in Massachusetts, he was assistant director of the Boston Redevelopment Authority.

Born in Los Angeles, California, Williams is an adopted son of Virginia and Louis Williams. In addition to doing a stint in the U.S. Air Force, Williams attended two of the nation's elite educational institutions: Yale College, where he graduated magna cum laude with a bachelor of arts in political science, and Harvard University, where he earned a master of public policy from the Kennedy School of Government. While at Harvard he also earned a J.D. degree from its law school.

By virtue of historic timing and his position as the District's chief financial officer, however, Williams became the perfect emblem of a purported black politics in transition that was supposedly moving steadily but surely away from race consciousness and confrontation to a stoic, perhaps even detached, managerialism. Here, Williams's educational and employment experiences, particularly the administrative portion, appear to have cast a long shadow over how he imagined his role and contribution. Plainly put, unlike Marion Barry, Williams was not cut from a race-conscious mold. Rather, by training and force of habit, his sensitivities were more attuned to the technical aspects of officialdom. After all, as chief financial officer Williams terminated large numbers of municipal workers as a way to streamline the District's budget; many blacks, of course, were on the short end of these actions. To top things off, Williams's managerial style and substantive positions in addressing the District's fiscal health resulted in him being hailed by antagonists of blackness (and the agenda it implies) as the antidote to Barry (read: his style and substantive positions).

With an emasculated Mayor Barry—Congress had all but stripped him of his governing powers in 1995, leaving only to his charge the libraries, the Department of Recreation, and other similar agencies—Williams seized the moment and tossed his hat into the 1998 mayoral contest, having served three years as chief financial officer. His subsequent general election victory over Republican Carol Schwartz was lauded by Congress and white media as a victory for efficiency and good government. The *Washington Post*, for instance, regarded the election as a statement by voters "to trade charisma and clubbiness for a chief executive with the skills, experience and professional stature to bring credibility, order and much-needed direction to the D.C. government."[11] Just a few months into the newly elected Williams administration when the mayor presented his fiscal year 2000 budget and financial proposal, the *Washington Post*, extending its praise of Williams, envisioned his administration doing "big and bold things" on several policy issues, including education, health care, and small businesses.[12]

In all, Williams wound up serving two terms as mayor. As a techno-manager, he arguably joined an emergent class of techno-managerial black mayors comprised of Mike White of Cleveland, Dennis Archer of Detroit, and Bill Campbell of Atlanta. By and large their modus operandi arguably revolved around creating favorable climates for corporate adventurers to flex their capitalist muscles. This is as Paul Peterson would have it, since to do otherwise (that is, to pursue redistributive policies) in his view would likely be going against the best interests of cities. Whereas for Peterson "[d]evelopmental policies enhance the local economy because their positive effects are greater than their cost to community residents," redistributive policies, by contrast, "are not only unproductive but actually damage the city's economic position."[13]

The pressure on big city mayors (barring none on account of race, ethnicity, or ideological disposition) to emphasize developmental policies is undoubtedly intense. The first wave of big-city black mayors in the late 1960s through the 1970s, their inclinations tilted toward redistribution, discovered how difficult it is to govern without the blessings of the corporate sector. The District's Marion Barry did not escape this conundrum. Writing on the limits of protest politics, Howard Gillette explains how Barry, while expanding a range of opportunities for Washington, D.C.'s black masses, nonetheless engaged in significant outreach to the corporate sector. Big-city mayors simply cannot afford to totally alienate key business entities of their cities for fear that they may either do business elsewhere or support opposing campaigns. Indeed, in Barry's case, Gillette contends that in his first term developmental policies were his "most visible achievement."[14] It is quite sensible in the rough-and-tumble of electoral politics for incumbent mayors to cater to more powerful interests of their cities. But the danger in doing so is that the policy demands of the black masses can easily be minimized. Corporate executives whose policy wishes are disregarded by the political leadership of their cities can easily relocate their respective industries to other locales. Still, one can make a distinction between the first wave of big-city black mayors like Barry who pushed and implemented policies and programs for the black community and the techno-managerial mayors like Anthony Williams who are averse to pointed advocacy on behalf of the black community. Even as all big-city mayors experience and respond to some corporate pressure, still it is the techno-managerial mayors, more so than others, who genuinely fit the developmental policy mold. They are in this sense already inclined to give the corporate class what it wants. Being predisposed in this way, however, arguably means that they are relatively deaf to the redistributive policy calls of the black masses, and are more or less content to accord benefits to the masses to the extent that the corporatist class prospers and grows.

In regards to Williams's mayoral tenure, several issues—Major League Baseball, neighborhood gentrification, and the fate of D.C. General Hospital, among others—highlighted the schisms between the corporatists' developmental interests and the redistributive interests of the black masses. Of these issues, none generated more discord than the city's policy decision that determined the fate of D.C. General Hospital.

Health care services and the lack thereof easily rank among the most pressing and persistent challenges for black Washingtonians. In the District alone, there are approximately eighty thousand residents who are uninsured, which means that they cannot avail themselves of regular checkups and other preventative measures. Emergency medical situations are what drive them to seek out medical services, the overwhelming bulk of which are provided by Howard University Hospital and, when it was fully operating, by D.C. General Hospital. D.C. General Hospital, which serviced much of the southeast quadrant of the city, was put on the chopping block in June 2001.

At the behest of Mayor Williams and the control board, the city sought to transition inpatient services at D.C. General to the privately owned Greater Southeast Community Hospital to be managed by a group of private firms under the leadership of Greater Southeast. The wave of privatization engulfing the public domains of urban governance was now encroaching on one of the District's most cherished and trusted public spaces: D.C. General Hospital. Although the privatization policy was enacted, there was intense resistance from many circles of Washingtonians. Echoing a sentiment about the policy felt broadly in the city, one resident contended that the democratic process was circumvented when the control board met: "I came out to support D.C. General Hospital. I can't believe we have been shut out of this meeting."[15] Indeed, public outrage and its concomitant resistance at the control board's first meeting were so ardent that a second meeting had to be called. Fearing more public outrage and resistance, the control board held a clandestine meeting, barring the public from participating in or witnessing any of its deliberations and actions. Secreted away from public scrutiny, the control board voted unanimously for privatizing D.C. General. Of the control board's proceedings, Vanessa Dixon of Health Care Now Coalition, one of the organizations in resistance to the privatization policy, put an asterisk on the anti-democratic, corporatist slant of the Williams/control board regime: "This was a disgrace. They literally ran from the public. Democracy has been trampled on. We are not giving up. The [City] Council and the people were never part of this process."[16]

Aside from the curbing of community and City Council (meaning, democratic) voices, shutting down inpatient services at D.C. General neither addressed nor resolved the issue of health care for indigent Washingtonians living in the southeast quadrant. In fact, the early proposals proffered by the private firm that assumed command of indigent health care included reestablishing (with the for-profit proviso, of course) some of the same inpatient services at the same D.C. General location. This seemingly contradictory development led Health Care Now's Vanessa Dixon to say: "Greater Southeast is basically admitting that the mayor's plan makes no sense, that the D.C. General location requires hospital inpatient services, and so they are re-creating D.C. General. . . . They're taking public space and using it for a for-profit purpose."[17] Vanessa Dixon's sentiments on the hospital issue, widely held by black Washingtonians, meant that the hospital issue came to be perceived, rightly or wrongly, as primarily a budgetary or fiscal concern and not so much as a human concern. It also came off as an imposition insensitive to those most in need.

And there was and is, despite all of the denials, evasions, and equivocations, a definite racial dimension to the way policy decisions are made in Washington, D.C., as well as in other big cities with substantial black and brown populations. But insofar as there are technocratic black mayors trending toward dodging the racialized fissures of their cities, J. Phillip Thompson warns that as a method of governance it is certainly difficult, and probably untenable, because the public space in which these mayors operate "is itself highly racially polarized."[18] And when pragmatic black technocrats like Williams self-consciously opt out of using race consciousness as a political asset, their value to the black masses on matters related to empowerment and policy is reduced all the more to mere symbolism provided by their phenotype. Such a stance obviously puts him in a terrible conundrum. That is to say, as long as race awareness is not part of the issue agenda of policymakers, it is highly improbable that the empowerment and policy interests of the unserved and underserved will be fully met.

Fanning the flames of this challenge even more is the merciless conservative political environment of our day. All big-city mayors, but especially black ones, have to grapple with what conservatism portends for not only black policy interests but also with the day-to-day damage it inflicts on black communities. Indeed, the entirety of the post-1960s period is littered with assaults by conservative political activists, ideologues, and organizations on the liberal social welfare and diversity programs of that era and earlier.[19] One of the consequences of the conservative assault has been that technocratic black mayors have had to contend with a shrinking pool of federal dollars from which to draw aid, which in itself has limited their effectiveness in empowering black people. Still, considering the aversion black pragmatists have to race consciousness, one must wonder: How can critical segments of black elected leadership remain relatively mute when black people and their particular interests are the targets of neglect on the one hand and ruthless and unremitting attack on the other? Could it simply be old-fashioned self-interest, wherein ambition compels one to self-consciously deny one's peoplehood in exchange for career advancement?[20]

A query of this sort, of course, does not lend itself to easy answers. Nor does it help us to make definitive assessments of a mayor's tenure. Just as Marion Barry provoked contrasting views of his stewardship of Washington, D.C., so has Anthony Williams. In fairness, both played both the developmental and redistributive sides of the policy development. But of the two, Barry clearly is the one a great many black Washingtonians regard with affection. He comes from the people. He fought for the people. Williams, on the other hand, could never quite shake his outsider image. He was goaded on and subsequently supported by the mortal enemies of Barry and the aura of black assertion he personified. In one sense, Williams was imposed on the people, even though he won his mayoral contests fair and square. These are matters that seemed to color some of the appraisals of Williams throughout his tenure, and especially in 2006 when he decided not to seek a third term.

That Williams never truly bonded with the black community throughout the entirety of his tenure is not an invention aimed at disparaging him; it is real. Perhaps his discomfort and disconnect with blacks stemmed from his avoidance of dealing thoughtfully and caringly with black interests. Instead, he continued to do as mayor what he did prior to becoming mayor: manage as opposed to lead. Consequently, many black Washingtonians came to view him as efficient in matters having to do with the budget but insensitive in matters having to do with the day-to-day realities of black life in the District. Echoing this point of view is Reverend Willie Wilson, pastor of Union Temple Baptist Church in southeast Washington, D.C., who said, "Balancing the budget is crucial, but the government should not crush its citizens' spirit in the process." Rev. Wilson added a specific public policy perspective to highlight his discontent with Williams's rulership: "The rush of new residential units will increase the property tax base. But the high cost of housing is forcing long-term residents out of the city. The District must create affordable homeownership and rental opportunities for low-and moderate-income residents."[21] An elderly resident of the Mount Vernon Square neighborhood, which is one of the areas undergoing redevelopment, agreed wholeheartedly with Rev. Wilson, when she says: "You know what he was telling the city with all this development? He was telling the poor people to get out because none of them can afford to live in the Washington, D.C. he was creating."[22]

In contrast to what low- and moderate-income District residents experience in relationship to the city's developmental/revitalization frenzy, its beneficiaries obviously have a great deal to be happy about. In a real sense, Anthony Williams's Washington, D.C., reads as a tale of two cities (no pun intended to Charles Dickens and his *Tale of Two Cities*), one flourishing in opulence, and the other floundering in privation. Of course, the same observation is applicable to other cities, big and small, in the United States. So Williams is not particularly unique for helping to perpetuate this schism. To be brutally honest, it is one of the features logically produced when the American political economy functions the way it is supposed to. That is to say, to have obscene wealth at one end of the spectrum and abject poverty at the other end is neither accidental nor problematic.

In the larger scheme of things, excluding his appointed positions, Anthony Williams's political career was a relatively short eight years. If you will, he took the grand stage of politics like a lion but exited it like a lamb. The in-between years were spent prioritizing and servicing corporatist interests. But he was never able to gain his footing, particularly among black Washingtonians, not to mention address their most pressing policy concerns. The quintessential pragmatist black politician, Williams could practically be taken as one devoid of ideological affiliation. But this is most improbable because there is always the default affixation of the dominant culture. Whenever and wherever one claims innocence on ideological grounds, count that person as a purveyor of the dominant culture's ideas, positions, and interests. The black pragmatist, like the white moderate and liberal Dr. Martin Luther King Jr. wearied of in his "Letter from a Birmingham Jail," often plays the tragic role of obstructer, as opposed to way-opener, of black interests. Way too often he and she relegate black interests to the back burner, not to be lifted up until the more powerful factions in American society consent to doing so. But then again this is the very argument Paul Peterson makes about urban governance: that there are powerful countervailing forces pushing and urging for the suppression of black and indigent persons' interests.

THE STATE OF DEMOCRACY UNDER MAYOR ANTHONY WILLIAMS: A SUMMARY

The fortuitous political ascension of Anthony Williams in Washington, D.C., politics in the mid-1990s coincides with the diminution of some of the democratic prerogatives District officials and residents had enjoyed for two decades. Via the Control Act of 1995, Congress, in its colonialist/overseer role, imposed on the District a governing regime (known as the control board), which set out to repair the city's fiscal crisis. Anthony Williams was a direct by-product of Congress's interventionist actions. A proven techno-manager at the Department of Agriculture as its first chief financial officer, he was given the same title in 1995 with the charge to right and steady a wobbly and nearly sunken District.

Three years into his position as the District's chief financial officer, he was tapped to run for mayor. Actually, the confluence of several forces really set the stage for the ascension of a techno-manager: several years of staggering deficits; an embattled incumbent mayor entangled in a web of personal failings; and aggressive and merciless conservative politicos intent on halting the policy advance of black interests. Williams was the perfect antidote, so to speak. He was a proven administrator. He carried none of the personal behavior baggage that hovered over Marion Barry. And, most significant, he embodied the traits of the deracial politician; that is, he expressed no interest whatsoever in projecting blackness and black interests as a part of his political posture. In this sense, he was, pejoratively speaking, "not black enough." In other words, with respect to value orientation and interest articulation, not phenotype, Williams was practically estranged from the black community. Although he won his electoral contests outright and was widely supported across the spectrum, he did not emerge out of the black community. It was practically imposed by anti-democratic forces: members of Congress whose stance is to rule from without.

Like all mayors of the District of Columbia, Williams, too, expressed support for enhanced democratic prerogatives, but his managerial inclinations probably got the better of him. Perhaps this may help explain why he never quite warmed up to being a politician. Being a techno-manager by training most likely contributed to his awkwardness among the people. Williams's strength was hacking numbers, not moving people, as Marion Barry could, to big causes. And, along with the control board, Williams did hack numbers. This strength of his also easily translates into him tilting more toward the developmental policy side. Thus, on issues such as D.C. General Hospital and gentrification, one can appreciate his embrace of the corporatists. Of course, all mayors favor the corporate sector to some extent. But in Williams one never sensed that he would go to bat for the "little people."

Notwithstanding who is the mayor of Washington, D.C., the challenge of democracy remains. Democracy in the District took a battering in the 1990s not because of who was mayor, although Barry did not help matters, but because of colonialist tendencies in the Congress. There still is the problem of members of Congress, notwithstanding constitutional rules, desirous of usurping democratic rights from District officials and residents and dictating the shape and substance of the city's programs and policies. Truly, it is a sad commentary on the limits of democracy in what is the political capital of the world.

NOTES

1. "Marion Barry: A Summing Up," *Washington Post*, December 31, 1998, A26.
2. Jonetta Rose Barras, *The Last of the Black Emperors: The Hollow Comeback of Marion Barry in the Age of New Black Leaders* (Baltimore: Bancroft, 1998).

3. Howard Gillette Jr., *Between Justice and Beauty: Race, Planning, and the Failure of Urban Policy in Washington, D.C.* (Baltimore: The Johns Hopkins University Press, 1995), 191.

4. Clay L. Writ, "Dillon's Rule," *Virginia Town and City*, Vol. 24, No. 8 (August 1989), retrieved September 2008 from www.fairfaxcounty.gov/dmb/fcpos/dillon.pdf; Jesse J. Richardson and Meghan Zimmerman Gough, "Is Home Rule The Answer? Clarifying The Influence Of Dillon's Rule On Growth Management," retrieved September 2008 from www.brookings.edu/reports/2003/01metropolitanpolicy_richardson.aspx.

5. Clarence N. Stone, *Regime Politics: Governing Atlanta, 1946–1988* (Lawrence: University Press of Kansas, 1989), 164.

6. Paul E. Peterson, *City Limits* (Chicago: University of Chicago Press, 1981), 4.

7. Ibid., 20–21.

8. Ibid., 6.

9. Stone, *Regime Politics*, 6.

10. Robert Benedetto, Jane Donovan, and Kathleen Duvall, *Historical Dictionary of Washington, D.C.* (Lanham, Md.: Scarecrow Press, 2003), 112–13; Keith Melder, *City of Magnificent Intentions: A History of Washington, District of Columbia* (Washington, D.C.: Intac, 1997), 292.

11. "District Voters Speak," *Washington Post*, November 5, 1998, A22.

12. "New Mayor, New Directions," *Washington Post*, March 16, 1999, A20.

13. Peterson, *City Limits*, 42–43.

14. Gillette, *Between Justice and Beauty*, 197.

15. Azure Thompson, "Mayor, Control Board Enacts Privatization of D.C. General," *Washington Afro-American*, May 5, 2001, A1.

16. Ibid., 2

17. Paul Offner, "D.C. General Is Everyone's Problem," *Washington Post*, August 27, 2000, B8.

18. J. Phillip Thompson III, *Double Trouble: Black Mayors, Black Communities, and the Call for a Deep Democracy* (New York: Oxford University Press, 2006), 13.

19. Lee Cokorinos, *The Assault on Diversity: An Organized Challenge to Racial and Gender Justice* (Lanham, Md.: Rowman & Littlefield, 2003); Ronald Walters, *White Nationalism, Black Interests: Conservative Public Policy and the Black Community* (Detroit: Wayne State University Press, 2003).

20. Joseph P. McCormick II and Charles E. Jones, "The Conceptualization of Deracialization: Thinking Through the Dilemma," in Georgia A. Persons (ed.), *Dilemmas of Black Politics: Issues of Leadership and Strategy* (New York: Harper Collins, 1993), 66–84.

21. Willie Wilson, "Willie Wilson Responds," *Washington Post*, September 7, 2002, A16.

22. Lori Montgomery and Eric M. Weiss, "For Williams, A Contested Legacy—Some Residents Grateful for City's Transformation, Others Feel Left Behind," *Washington Post*, September 30, 2005, A1.

PUBLIC POLICY

7

The Mayor as the Head School Master

ReShone L. Moore

The public educational system in the United States has for many years been reviewed, analyzed, debated, and reformed—all in hopes of creating a better system that would result in increased test scores and graduation rates, a decrease in the achievement gap, smaller class sizes, and ultimately more students attending and completing postsecondary education. According to Dr. Floretta Dukes McKenzie, education by its very nature is future-oriented. "Teacher preparation," "pre-service experience," and "curriculum planning" are all terms that drive the education industry and have been the topic of debate concerning how they should be effectively implemented to better prepare students in rural, urban, and suburban school districts.[1]

Periodically during U.S. history, an initiative ignites a groundswell of support in an effort to improve the public school systems. A number of the challenges are unique to a particular region, socioeconomic status, or race. Although many of the issues and concerns have been prevalent for several decades and have grown in terms of their detriment to society, the quest continues regarding a proven strategy for improving education. Nonetheless, the abysmal performance of many urban and rural public school districts has remained on course. Critical education reform efforts in recent times have focused on racial integration, busing, affirmative action, school choice, and outcome-based education, none of which have yielded the intended results. Because these issues continue to persist, the education community, including teachers, administrators, politicians, business leaders, interest groups, and parents, continues to search for proven methods to improve the delivery of education in this country.

For the District of Columbia, each of the previous mayors has made education a major platform issue; unfortunately, the system has continued to decline for the past several decades. However, each mayor put forth various reform initiatives attempting to make a positive impact on the lives of the students. On April 19, 2007, the District of Columbia City Council gave final approval to Mayor Adrian Fenty's District of Columbia Public Education Reform Amendment Act of 2007.[2] This ambitious reform initiative shifted the governing infrastructure to the office of the mayor. According to Mayor Fenty in a January 4, 2007, press release, "we have a crisis on our hands. Over the past two decades, study after study has spelled out the same problems and made nearly the same recommendations. My proposal changes a critical piece of the puzzle—increased accountability and action. I am asking for that responsibility to be placed squarely on my shoulders."[3] The mayor's ambitious plan for the District of Columbia Public School System (DCPS) was bold, ambitious, and challenging. Some of the major priorities of Mayor Fenty's educational initiative included the following:

- Ensure that all children start school ready to learn;
- Improve transparency of and accountability for public education performance to ensure equal access to excellent public education;
- Centralize State Education Agency functions;
- Support the implementation of the research-based education reforms included in the Master Education Plan (MEP);
- Create an interagency, outcome-driven strategy for delivery of youth-related services in support of education;
- Increase retention of quality principals and teachers;
- Ensure that all public school students have access to appropriate facilities;
- Improve access to and quality of special education services;
- Ensure the continued success of District-based institutions of higher education; and
- Ensure school, university, employer, and community alignment in support of a seamless transition from the education environment to the workforce.[4]

This list of priorities covered grades K–16. It called for a more holistic approach for providing educational services to the city and allowed all involved in the learning process to play a more participatory role for ensuring success. The mayor's plan had massive appeal because it offered a fundamental approach for reform. This approach would include streamlining responsibility. All of the decision-making authority would be held by the mayor and the chancellor. Under this new reform initiative, parents would be empowered. The Office of the Ombudsman for Public Education would serve as a customer-service center. Parents would be allowed to express issues and concerns impacting the schools and students. They also would be able to track progress after reporting had been completed. Some of the other major reform initiatives included plans for faster renovations, controlled spending, and consolidated functions.

The last two issues dealt with governance reform. The State Board of Education replaced the Board of Education as the entity responsible for overseeing state-level decisions for education including approval of state education standards and the District's accountability plan under the federal No Child Left Behind Act. The last central nucleus of the reform package included how all of the pieces would function together. The Interagency Collaboration and Services Integration Commission will gather the leaders of District government agencies who impact the lives of our youth. This component is a major milestone for the District. For the first time, it promised to bring together all those involved in protecting and providing for the quality of life for the students that they serve. This level of accountability directly impacts student achievement, retention, and safety.[5]

Another major component of this legislation included the creation of a Department of Education. The person mandated with managing this entity would be appointed directly by the mayor. This cabinet-level position would report directly to the mayor and provide oversight for all aspects of education. Another critical component of the mayor's reform initiative included the roles and responsibilities of its frontline professionals—the teachers. Teachers must have the tools, support, infrastructure, and resources needed in order for students to succeed. Teacher support would include collective bargaining, focused attention on positive student behavior, clean and well-maintained facilities, professional development and support, respect and rewards, and the Office of the Ombudsman. During interviews with District teachers, they expressed mixed emotions that ranged from frustration, apprehension about change, depression, excitement, and optimism regarding this new approach for managing the public school system. This wide range of emotions highlighted their deep desire to see quick and drastic improvements for the students in the District. Many teachers expressed feelings of isolation and a lack of support from those in senior management. Some reported a disconnect between those charged with running the District and the frontline professionals who are charged with working daily with the students.

Many of the teachers with tenure who were interviewed mentioned that they had witnessed various types of reform proposals, but none had alleviated the ailments of the system. The predicaments of District public schools have been diagnosed and analyzed for more than twenty years. In December 2006, the Parthenon Group released a fact-based executive summary and final report calling for DCPS reform. This entity is considered a leading advisor to the education industry. According to the summary, the group was engaged to conduct a privately funded assessment of the DCPS system. The Parthenon Group sought to achieve the following objectives with its assessments:

1. outline a fact-based rationale for reform;
2. identify leading reform levers; and
3. assess different school district governance options within the context of reform prioritization needs.

The report documents a timeline of the major studies that have examined the state of DCPS:

1989	COPE Report "Our Children, Our Future"
1995	"Our Children Are Still Waiting" (COPE)
2001	DCPS Business Plan for Strategic Reform
2005	Restoring Excellence to DCPS
2006	DCPS Master Education Plan[6]

This continued diagnosis of the problem has manifested very little in the form of improved educational conditions for the students. The study concluded by strongly arguing for the need for a change in structural accountability. Some of the major advantages mentioned in the report offered a strong rationale for moving to a mayor-controlled educational system. Shifting control to the mayor would undoubtedly accelerate the pace of reform, and its visibility on the city's agenda would provide direct accountability for decisions implemented and offer stability in leadership.[7]

The challenges facing this particular school system in the nation's capital are indicative of the situation at various other urban as well as rural school districts around the country. America must address the crisis in the public school system in order for this country to remain competitive in the global arena. It is said that education is considered the "great equalizer" in this country—unfortunately, the country has been struggling with successfully addressing this public policy issue. In 1983, the *National Commission on Excellence in Education* postulated that "the education foundations of our society are presently being eroded by a rising tide of mediocrity that threatens our very survival as a nation and as a people."[8] The erosion has swelled into a massive divide between the haves and the have-nots that is further complicated by race and socioeconomic status.

Parents, practitioners, administrators, business leaders, and politicians all agree that reform is needed around the country within our educational system; however, deciding which approach is most beneficial and/or most applicable to a particular school district will be judged best by history and documented results.

This latest iteration of public school reform has been labeled "mayor-centric." This approach grants the mayor of the city autonomy over the public school system. In many instances, this approach has been used primarily by districts with predominately black students and school leadership.[9] The District of Columbia is the latest city to adopt this reform method. It has been utilized in Boston, Chicago, Cleveland, Detroit, and New York City. Mayor Fenty has met with numerous mayors, particularly the mayor of New York City, as well as business leaders regarding the future of D.C. public schools. Each meeting confirmed for the mayor the real need for radical and aggressive change in the District's educational system.

Granting the mayor greater control over the public school district proposes to have a great impact on district governance in the following areas: centralized accountability, a broadened constituency concerned with education, and reduced micro-management.[10] This level of oversight by the mayor is designed to address major deficiencies in the overall productivity of the public school system. This great departure in how public school systems have operated is very different from past reforms that either allowed school districts to operate in isolation or be governed by grassroots interest boards and administrators.

A number of factors have led to this latest cycle of reform initiatives that are guided by city mayors. Many urban school districts have been dealing with gross mismanagement of funds, low standardized test scores, increased dropout rates, and growing discontent of parents and civic organizations with student performance. This restructuring by shifting operational responsibility to the office of the mayor has been met with mixed reactions. There are those advocates who see this as political posturing and are unsure if the mayor can galvanize the support needed to adequately address the schools, when in many instances the city as a whole is grappling with sufficiently handling other major public policy areas.

Yet others see this as a positive step towards revitalizing America's public school systems. This whole notion depends heavily upon the mayor's commitment toward reform. The mayor must be willing to provide the time, talent, and resources needed to radically redirect how schools have conducted business. Each decision must be based solely upon improving the quality of education for the students in that city.

When a new person enters office, he or she has an opportunity to present a platform on how reform will be implemented and formulate solutions to improve overall delivery of public service initiatives without suffering back-lash from any failed attempts by previous administrations. A new leader, whether at the local, state, or national level, is able to capitalize on his or her position because they are new and offer a new perspective in dealing with an old policy issue. President George W. Bush was able to capitalize on his new position in implementing the No Child Left Behind Act of 2002 (NCLB).[11] Upon entering office as president, he was able to leverage bipartisan support from the 107th Congress for an important issue that impacts the country as a whole.

This legislation was designed to improve student achievement and close the achievement gap between racial groups. This legislation, which passed with great fanfare because of the overall need to improve education for students in grades K–12, clearly articulates a need for dramatic changes in the delivery of our educational system. The foundation of NCLB was built around four basic critical need areas: accountability for results, an emphasis on doing what works based on scientific research, expanded parental options, and expanded local control and flexibility.

When this legislation was enacted, the U.S. Department of Education noted that since 1965, when the Elementary and Secondary Education Act was passed in Congress, the federal government had spent more than $267.4 billion to assist states in educating disadvantaged children. However, according to data released in the *National Assessment of Educational Progress* on reading in 2002, only 31 percent of fourth graders could read at a proficient or advanced level.[12] This statistic reiterates the need for radical change in how we support students within the educational system.

The momentum that President Bush was able to build on, and the aggressive implementation that was coordinated by former secretary of education Rod Paige, started a national dialogue on the state of K–12 education around the country. This discussion targeted all stakeholders in order to make sweeping changes in educational systems nationwide. As a new leader, making education a national priority set the stage for governors and mayors to build a platform around this important public policy issue. The road toward achieving the best results has long been debated, but education and the needs of the students were now being discussed at the highest level.

A LOOK AT NEW YORK CITY

The New York City Public School System has been characterized by myriad struggles, challenges, and neglect over the past few decades. This downward spiral led the New York legislature to grant approval for Mayor Michael

Bloomberg to take over the local school system. The New York reform initiative is called Children First, a bold, commonsense plan to create great schools for all New York City children.[13]

Mayor Bloomberg noted that implementing this aggressive reform initiative is the moral responsibility of each of the more than 140,000 employees in the New York City school system. This can only be achieved by keeping "the main thing the main thing." The mayor describes how all decisions must be guided by the way in which they will improve the quality of life for the student population they are mandated to serve. This need to put "children first" must be a priority at all levels of the school system in order for tangible results to be achieved.

The foundation of this Children First initiative is built around leadership, empowerment, and accountability. According to an historical overview of the Children First initiative, there had been little standardization or coordination of services, while generations of students were leaving the New York school system without the skills and knowledge they needed to succeed.[14] This lack of cohesion did not serve the students, teachers, or community well. Some of the early steps initiated by Chancellor Joel Klein were to develop and implement a two-step process that included introducing stability and coherence system wide. This would prevent the lack of continuity that would end the practice of ad-hoc systems within the city that failed to make the placement of children a priority.

The Children First initiative began with the reorganization and streamlining of the Department of Education's management structure. As a result of this shift, Chancellor Klein was able to reallocate those resources to better assist with meeting the needs of the students. Another major highlight of this initiative emphasized greater continuity with the adoption of a single, coherent, system-wide approach for instruction in how reading, writing, and math are taught. Other major urban areas began to review the strategies being implemented in New York City. Mayor Fenty took notes and met on several occasions with the leadership to craft a plan of action for moving DCPS forward.

Chancellor Klein also led the way for the development of a partnership with the United Federation of Teachers. This new union, with an incentive package, was considered a win-win initiative for teachers, principals, and students and paved the way for the successful recruitment and retention of highly qualified teachers. The contract included incentives such as increased pay and a $15,000 housing incentive for the recruitment of teachers in science, math, and special education who agreed to teach for three years in an area that had been identified as high-need. New York City's high-need targeted areas are considered a critical need areas all across the country, and school districts must continue to do a better job in recruiting in these areas.

Implementing sweeping reform in one of this country's largest public school systems is a major undertaking because the renovation included approximately 92,000 teachers overseeing 1,300 schools with about 1.1 million students. This comprehensive reform movement will be reviewed and analyzed for years to come. Preliminary findings indicate that Children First has been a successful urban reform initiative. Some of the major areas of success are less waste, targeted spending, less crime among students, and an increase in attendance, graduation rates, and test scores. This urban reform model also will be reviewed to determine how and/or if it will be sustained in the face of leadership change.

POLITICAL CULTURE

The nation's capital is the most political city in this country. It is imperative that the role of this political culture be discussed within the context of improving the District's educational system and how this has shaped, stifled, or promoted educational reform for students in this area. Many issues impacting DCPS are magnified in many instances because they are played out against the backdrop of the legislative, judicial, and executive branches of government. Alexis de Tocqueville's *Democracy in America* is a commentary on a wide variety of social and political aspects of early America. Tocqueville left America in 1832 in hopes of defining a new political science.[15] The object of the new political science was to clarify the forces shaping the modern world and to provide "those who now direct society" with the knowledge to meet its greatest challenge of reconciling liberty and democracy.

Tocqueville was also one of the first writers to discuss political culture. He viewed *moeurs*, or political culture, as "the sum of the moral and intellectual dispositions of men in society . . . the habits of heart . . . and the sum of ideas that shape mental habits."[16] This work laid the foundation for further study regarding the role of political culture and its impact on public policymaking in various communities. For a politically driven city like Washington, D.C., education has for many years been used as a political slogan and not the primary focus of those in power who could have made a major difference in the lives of the students. An often-used political slogan relative to urban school reform is "Take the schools out of politics and politics out of the schools." Sol Cohen postulates that the widespread acceptance of this slogan has simply resulted in making the operations of school decision-makers less visible, to the detriment of accountability and responsibility.[17] In *Politics and Policies in State and Communities*, John J. Harrigan states that political culture is citizens' attitudes, beliefs, and expectations about what governments should do, who should participate, and what rules should govern the political game.[18]

Walter A. Rosenbaum, in *Political Culture*, defines it in two ways. When focusing on the individual, political culture has a basically psychological focus and entails all the important ways in which a person is subjectively oriented toward the essential elements in his political system. The second definition highlighted by Rosenbaum refers to the collective orientation of people toward the basic elements in their political systems.[19]

The author notes that although a citizen's perspective may be held subconsciously, their beliefs and attitudes govern civic behavior, help shape the governmental order, and, for many people, define political reality. Residents of the District have been told for several decades of the problems impacting student achievement, yet substantive change has not been fully manifested. In many instances, the results of several studies regarding the state of DCPS were outlined in the media, reviewed by representatives within the walls of Congress, and created spirited debates among District councilmembers regarding the best approach for instituting change to improve education for its children. Yet measurable positive outcomes were not achieved.

As a result of the District's many attempts to implement school reform, in 2007 the *Washington Post* and washingtonpost.com embarked upon the task of reviewing, researching, and analyzing the current state of the public school system. This year-long investigation provided detailed summaries illustrating the pitfalls, obstacles, missteps, and leadership turnovers that created an environment that was not conducive to implementing sustainable change that would make a difference in the lives of the students.[20]

The investigative research published over the course of the year won the Scripps Howard Foundation National Journalism Award for Web Reporting and two other awards. In cover stories, readers were provided unprecedented access to the inner workings of the public school system.[21] Unfortunately, the reporting painted a very bleak and dismal picture of the District's school system.

One of the first articles asked blatantly, "Can D.C. Schools Be Fixed?" This article was featured on the front page of the *Washington Post* on June 10, 2008.[22] By asking the question, the article leads one to think that there is no hope for the students who are products of the District's system. This question leads one to ponder the notion that failure is a realistic possibility for the students, teachers, and administrators. Some of the unfortunate, but noteworthy, statistics highlighted in this article include the following:

- In the areas of reading and math, students ranked at the bottom among eleven major city school systems. When this number was further aggregated to compare only poor children, it was found that 33 percent of poor fourth graders across the nation lacked basic skills in math, but in the District, the figure was 62 percent. It was 74 percent for eighth graders when compared with 49 percent nationally.

- In the area of finances, the District spends $12,979 per pupil each year, making it the third highest among one hundred of the largest districts in the nation. However, a majority of that money does not benefit the classroom. The District ranks first in its share of the budget spent on administration and last in its share of the budget spent on teachers and instruction.

- Another astounding notation mentioned in the article relates to what is described as a "hostile environment." Slightly over half of the teenage students attend schools that meet the District's definition of "persistently dangerous" due to the pervasive nature of crime throughout the system. On a typical day in DCPS, at least nine violent incidents are reported that include fights and attacks with weapons.[23]

The article went on to describe the physical conditions of many of the schools as a result of directional differences from the top. High personnel turnover rates have a direct correlation with shifts in priorities and how policies are implemented. Many of the administrators' attempts to alleviate some of the issues impacting the physical infrastructure of the schools were blocked in many instances, mishandled, or unfortunately made worse due to poor decision-making.

All stakeholders affiliated with DCPS are keenly aware of its problems. The news media have repeatedly reported on basic conditions that have gone without attention in the District. Unfortunately, students and their parents have grown accustomed to dealing with issues such as faulty heating and cooling systems, lead-tainted water, rodents, and the lack of transportation for students in special education. Many were able to list their agonizing concerns without any thought to the matter. Now a new mayor, chancellor, and administration are faced with not only repairing infrastructure issues, but also addressing deficits in student achievement. The new leadership team will also be responsible for meeting the challenge of restoring confidence in a city that has grown weary of broken promises and numb from unfulfilled reform initiatives. Restoring confidence and successfully implementing a reform initiative in the District is a huge responsibility for the mayor. It must, however, be attempted if students are to have any chance to live up to their fullest potential. Their destiny will depend upon how well the stakeholders can implement this reform plan.

Another poignant article published on New Year's Eve in 2007 chronicled the failed maintenance and upkeep of the District's schools. This article was titled *The Price of Neglect.* According to Fallis, Haynes, and Keating, during the 1990s the Army Corps of Engineers invested $80 million to replace heating systems with new boilers intended to last over twenty-five years. This initiative is another example that demonstrates poor decisions by those charged with caring for the students. Decision-makers failed to invest in the ongoing support needed to sustain the equipment. At the time of the reporting of this article, 40 of the 50 renovated heating systems were either broken down or in need of major repair. According to officials, it would have cost the District $100,000 a year to maintain more than four hundred boilers. As a result of not paying attention to the maintenance, the leaders were forced to expend more than $10 million for emergency repairs that caused students to be displaced due to cold classrooms.[24]

Because of the poor nature of the conditions of the schools, the City Council passed a measure that approved an additional $1 billion for school repairs totaling $2.3 billion to be spent over ten years. With approval of the Council, Mayor Fenty gave control of construction to Allen Y. Lew, a contractor with experience in managing major city projects. After accepting the appointment, Lew requested to expand his responsibilities and duties to include maintenance. This element is central for ensuring infrastructure, development, and maintenance. This directly impacted the learning environment for the students as it is very difficult for a student to excel in an environment that is not conducive for learning. Many parents mentioned during discussions their disappointment and discontentment with the leaders' inability to ensure a safe, adequate learning environment. It is an unfortunate commentary when elementary schools are not fully functional to serve their students during the winter months. How do you motivate and encourage students to compete when basic needs are not being met? The dynamics of the situation leads one to ponder the sincerity of the leadership and question whose best interest is being served throughout the decision-making process. All stakeholders with a vested interest in the community must galvanize their resources in opposition to deplorable conditions and poor decision-making by those charged with protecting and serving students. Each civic group must understand their connection to having school-age students equipped with the tools needed to succeed.

With mounting discontent by parents, civic groups, teachers, administrators, and Congress, Mayor Fenty, armed with the power and authority over DCPS, appointed Michelle Rhee as the new chancellor on June 12, 2007. Chancellor Rhee is considered a change agent because of her background of transforming other urban public school districts through her work with The New Teacher Project (TNTP). TNTP was organized to address teacher shortages and teacher quality concerns around the country. TNTP initiated three projects to create and implement high-quality alternative routes to staffing urban schools.[25]

Rhee's appointment was met with mixed reactions. Fenty was both criticized and praised for this appointment for several reasons, including her age and race. She was thirty-seven at the time of her appointment as chancellor (the youngest to be appointed to this position) and is Korean American, making her the first non-black to head the school district since home rule. More importantly, in a highly charged political environment, she is considered an outsider.

Upon arriving and accepting the appointment as chancellor, Rhee participated in an online question-and-answer period. During this session on June 21, 2007, Rhee answered questions that dealt with her qualifications, parents, student achievement, school violence, teacher support, the role of business leaders, philanthropists, and accountability. Rhee stated, "Everyone who has the privilege of working with our students must be willing to take personal responsibility for achieving outcomes that move student achievement forward in a significant way. Anything less is shortchanging our kids."[26]

This in-depth conversation provided insight into the new chancellor's thinking and priorities. When Rhee was asked what three important steps she would take in the next year to improve the academic performance of DCPS, she stated: "[First,] we need to set clear expectations for everyone in the system for what outcomes we want to see. Second, we need to give people the resources and tools necessary to be successful. Third, we need to hold people accountable for attaining their goals." This online discussion with the chancellor clearly provided her with a forum to demonstrate to those who questioned her passion to see how determined and focused she is in making a real change in the nation's capital.

After being on the job for several months, Rhee gave a presentation at the American Enterprise Institute on February 13, 2008, titled "The Future of Urban School Reform." Months after the online discussion, her passion, determination, and commitment to this city and reforming education were even more pronounced. Chancellor Rhee began her presentation by noting Mayor Fenty's unwavering support of her office. Rhee mentioned that she is in a unique position to have the support of a committed mayor who has realized that having a world-class city requires having a world-class educational system. Mayor Fenty has not only offered his support to Chancellor Rhee for implementing the changes necessary to move the city's school system forward, but also has offered the resources needed to make it happen.

During 2007, the city experienced a $100 million surplus. Like any urban city, the surplus could have been used in any of the departments that manage the city, but the mayor made an audacious decision to earmark $81 million to be allocated towards the public schools. This clearly demonstrated the mayor's commitment to improving the city's school. After completing her first year of appointment, Rhee has received mixed results. However, it is very obvious that the reform needed in DCPS will not happen overnight and will require some drastic changes in the areas of personnel and fiscal management. Hard decisions will have to be made that may not be popular and may create discontent among those stakeholders who feel that their voices are not being heard. Chancellor Rhee mentioned during her presentation that prior to accepting the role as chancellor, she warned Mayor Fenty that the type of changes needed in the District would mean a tremendous amount of opposition, noises would be made, and discontent would be a part of the process. According to Rhee, the mayor responded by stating, "Frankly, as long as you believe that what you're doing is in the best interests of children, then I have no problem with the noise."[27] This is an incredible show of support and commitment by a mayor who has a vested interest in the lives of the students within his city.

Almost one year after the *Washington Post* article "Can D.C. Schools Be Fixed?" graduation ceremonies were held around the city. Ballou Senior High School, one of the more problematic schools in the system, held its ceremony in a newly erected football stadium. It served as a gentle reminder that all stakeholders must play a participatory role in answering this question.[28] Parents, family members, friends, and other supporters came out to celebrate the achievements of the graduating class. The mayor noted that he wanted the responsibility of the school system to be placed on his shoulders, but the reform effort that is currently being implemented is a lot larger than the mayor and chancellor—the livelihood of an entire generation of students is at stake. Everyone must join in this process in order to ensure that a positive, productive answer to that question is the only solution for a city that is the backdrop for the White House and the Congress.

The students graduating from Ballou Senior High School, a school that has faced many challenges (including deaths), seemed to shine brighter than the sun that was beaming down that afternoon. The students were very optimistic and hopeful about the future and how they would play a role in shaping and competing in society. Stakeholders must continue to work to create an educational system that does not fail its students. As real estate values stabilize, buildings are torn down and rebuilt, and a new president comes in to serve the nation, society must be committed to creating an environment that will allow all students to fulfill their destiny.

President Obama ran on a platform that offered hope to all citizens with a particular emphasis on education. That same hope mirrored what was found during the afternoon of the Ballou graduation. According to President Obama, "in a global economy where the most valuable skill you can sell is your knowledge, a good education is no longer just a pathway to opportunity—it is a prerequisite. The countries that out-teach us today will out-compete us tomorrow."[29]

One way the president is offering much-needed support is with the American Recovery and Reinvestment Act of 2009 (ARRA).[30] The primary goals for this critical piece of legislation are to stimulate the economy in the short term and to invest in education and other essential public services to ensure the long-term economic health of our nation. DCPS will benefit from Title I, Part A Recovery Funds for Grants to Local Education Agencies. DCPS is expected to receive approximately $153,840,386. The new funding under this important legislation is designed to create an unprecedented opportunity for educators to implement innovative strategies in Title I schools that will improve education for at-risk students and close the achievement gaps while also stimulating the economy.[31]

The overall success of this mammoth piece of legislation will be judged by how school systems like DCPS are able to utilize those resources to transform the system for urban school students. Mayor Fenty will now share shouldering the responsibility of reforming this school system with President Obama, who has a vested interest in transforming urban and rural school districts around the country.

Citizens of the District of Columbia must hold political leaders accountable in order to ensure that competitive educational services are afforded to all students of DCPS. This country has a long history of misinterpreting and denying democracy to all of its citizens and has therefore created a divide among the citizenry in how various services impacting quality of life issues and other guaranteed rights under our laws are delivered. This disparity has existed in education, employment, voting rights, housing, and criminal justice matters. The quest for democracy has been an ongoing struggle for minorities, particularly in the area of education. Bridging the achievement divide requires an active, participatory approach to democracy.

Legislation has now been implemented and education has the support from the highest level, the office of the president of the United States. President Barack Obama and the secretary of education, Arne Duncan, have made educating the students of this country a national priority. Research conducted years from now will demonstrate if federal involvement in education has positively impacted conditions and overall achievement for students in DCPS.

The residents of the District of Columbia appear to be poised to make major gains at least in the area of education. Mayor Fenty and Chancellor Rhee must capitalize on this perceived support to ensure that progress is made to enhance and empower local students to compete globally.

NOTES

1. McKenzie, Floretta Dukes, "Education, Not Excuses," *The Journal of Negro Education* 53, no. 2, 1984.

2. District of Columbia Public Education Reform Amendment Act of 2007.

3. Press Release, Office of the Mayor, Washington, D.C., January 4, 2007.

4. Ibid.

5. Mayor Fenty's Education Proposal, Washington, D.C., 2007.

6. The Parthenon Group, *The Full Report*, 2006

7. Ibid.

8. *National Commission on Excellence in Education*, 1983.

9. Henig, Jeffrey R., Richard C. Hula, Marion Orr, and Desiree S. Pedescleaux, *The Color of School Reform: Race, Politics and the Challenges of Urban Education*, Princeton, N.J.: Princeton University Press, 1999.

10. Henig, Jeffrey, and Wilbur Rich, *Mayors in the Middle: Politics, Race, and Mayoral Control of Urban Schools*, Princeton, N.J.: Princeton University Press, 2004.

11. No Child Left Behind Act of 2002 (NCLB)

12. *National Assessment of Educational Progress*, National Center for Education Statistics, 2002.

13. schools.nyc.gov.

14. schools.nyc.gov.

15. de Tocqueville, Alexis, *Democracy in America*, written in 1848, ed. J. P. Mayer, New York: Harper Collins, 1969.

16. As quoted in Walter A. Rosenbaum's *Political Culture* (New York: Praeger, 1975).

17. Cohen, Sol, "The Urban School Reform," *History of Education Quarterly*, Fall 1969.

18. Harrigan, John J., Politics and Policies in State and Communities, New York: Harper Collins, 1991.

19. Rosenbaum, Walter A., *Political Culture*, New York: Praeger, 1975.

20. www.washingtonpost.com/wp-srv/metro/interactives/dcschools.

21. Ibid.

22. Keating, Dan, and V. Dion Haynes, "Can D.C. Schools Be Fixed?" *The Washington Post*, June 10, 2008.

23. Ibid.

24. Fallis, David S. V., Dion Haynes, and Dan Keating, "The Price of Neglect," *The Washington Post*, December 31, 2007.

25. www.tntp.com.

26. washingtonpost.com-DC Schools Chancellor.

27. Chancellor Michelle Rhee, February 13, 2008, American Enterprise Institute, "Future of Urban School Reform," February 13, 2008.

28. Keating, Dan, and V. Dion Haynes, "Can D.C. Schools Be Fixed?" *The Washington Post*, June 10, 2008.

29. President Barack Obama, White House, Office of the Press Secretary, March 10, 2009.

30. American Recovery and Reinvestment Act of 2009 (ARRA).
31. www.ed.gov/policy/gen/leg/recovery/fact-sheet/title-i.html.

BIBLIOGRAPHY

Article

Hess, Frederick M., and Michael Petrilli, "Wrong Turn on School Reform," *Policy Review*, Issue 14, February–March 2009, 55.

Books

Hill, Paul Thomas, Christine Campbell, and James Harvey, *It Takes a City: Getting Serious About Urban School Reform*, Washington, D.C., Brookings Institution Press, 2000.
Hill, Paul Thomas, and Mary Beth Celio, *Fixing Urban Schools*, Washington, D.C., Brookings Institution Press, 1998.
Hill, Paul Thomas, and James Harvey, *Making School Reform Work: New Partnerships for Real Change*, Washington, D.C., Brookings Institution Press, 2004.

Speech

President Barack Obama, February 24, 2009, Joint Session to Congress, "Saving and Creating Jobs and Reforming Education."

Legislation

Elementary and Secondary Education Act of 1965.

8

Can Washington, D.C., Youth Speak?
Youth, Education, and Race in the
Political Socialization Process

Darwin Fishman

But above all, nearly a century of congressional control had created a leaderless, passive city full of politically docile people.

Harry S. Jaffe and Tom Sherwood, *Dream City: Race, Power, and the Decline of Washington, D.C.*

WHAT IS POLITICAL SOCIALIZATION?

When we examine the percentage of eligible voters that have voted or when we try to ascertain the percentage of people who identify with a particular political party, all of this work is done with some core political principles in mind. In particular, we assume that the nature of our democracy not only gives us the freedom and the right to vote for whatever political party we like, but that we have a certain level of knowledge about these freedoms and rights. The way in which we learn about our political freedoms and rights has become an intrinsic part of our individual identity formation, as well as part of our broad understanding of what it means to be an American citizen. The study of the way that we learn about politics and how we form our political beliefs is called political socialization. There has been quite a lot of work done on the political socialization of people that live in the United States of America, and there has been a sharp divergence in opinions about the nature, scope, and significance of what this term might entail and how and when it can be used.

Nowhere does this debate about our political socialization process appear to be more pronounced and complicated than it has been for Washington,

D.C. Washington, D.C.'s unique status as the nation's capital has meant we have had limited voting rights here. The absence of the two U.S. senators and the limited voting rights for the one member of the House of Representatives' delegate, Eleanor Holmes Norton, means that District residents have limited political rights and privileges. These institutional barriers present a significant challenge for scholars attempting to study the political socialization process of Washington, D.C., residents. One could ask in general if Washington, D.C., residents are more inclined or less inclined to participate in the political process because of the limitations placed upon their political rights. The population in Washington, D.C., is 588,292 and out of this population there are 324,875 black people and 231,657 white people.[1] There are 377,007 registered voters and there were 124,199 people that voted in the 2008 presidential primary election.[2] These numbers are not extraordinary and these numbers can be shown to be similar to national and large-city voter patterns. Given the nature of the political landscape of Washington, D.C., the pertinent question is how is the political socialization process understood and acted upon by its residents? Are the factors that influence the political socialization process of black youth in other cities the same factors that influence youth in Washington, D.C.?

To begin to answer these questions and many others, this paper will focus on the political socialization process of youth in Washington, D.C., with special attention given to the role that educational institutions play in this process. There are 93,448 youth between the ages of fifteen and twenty-four in Washington, D.C.[3] Of the 53,945 students in the public school system, the vast majority are black (80.7 percent).[4] Given that Washington, D.C., has a majority of "minority" students in public schools, one could ask how this added element might influence the political socialization process of youth[5]: Does a marginal racial identity alter the political socialization process? Or is the political socialization process of youth in Washington, D.C., identical to the process other youth engage in and struggle with? Are Washington, D.C., youth not aware and/or interested in the unique political stature of their home?

To be able analyze the political socialization process of black youth in Washington, D.C., a broad overview of the historical and theoretical origins of political socialization will be used as a basis for this study. A more specific discussion of the political socialization process of the black youth in Washington, D.C., will be presented in a historical and a contemporary framework. This chapter will conclude with a current review of some of the scholarly work being done on political socialization and what the implications of this work might have for research that could be done on the political socialization process for black youth in Washington, D.C.

HISTORICAL AND THEORETICAL
ORIGINS OF POLITICAL SOCIALIZATION

The concept of "political socialization" originates with Herbert Hyman's seminal 1959 work. Richard Merelman's analysis of Hyman's work can be used to understand the significance of Hyman's contribution to the birth and development of the field of political socialization. In his article "The Adolescence of Political Socialization," Merelman describes the origins of the field of political socialization in the following way: "The appearance of political socialization as a distinct field of inquiry usually is dated from the publication, in 1959, of Herbert Hyman's *Political Socialization*." Even though there had already been a long, rich history of studying political attitudes and beliefs, Hyman's work helped to place this work within a distinct field. Hyman's most significant contribution to the field of political socialization is presented by Merelman:

> Hyman developed a new framework for them (development of political beliefs) to which he gave the name "political socialization." More importantly, Hyman helped stamp a particular cast of assumptions and research strategies upon the field he named.[6]

The field of political socialization was further refined by Merelman's theoretical assumptions:

> This (Hyman's) approach provided the foundation for two vital assumptions about socialization: 1) socialization should be conceived mainly as a process by which social institutions inculcated political values, rather than as a learning process by which innately different individuals develop their own brand of political orientations; 2) because social institutions and agencies change more slowly than the individual, political socialization inevitably acts as a brake upon political change. In short, the vulnerability of the child and the relative stability of social institutions destined political socialization to be an important conservation force in the polity.[7]

Political socialization began to be viewed by scholars as not just an easily identifiable process that all American citizens engage in and a process that is most noticeable and significant for adolescents, but also a process that supports a particular social, political, and economic status quo. The requirements of this socialization process were expected to mirror the goals and aspirations of our society, and one of the bedrocks of this ideology is the type of political cohesion and stability our society has enjoyed. Political acts and beliefs that have contributed and nurtured this stability, such as the right to vote and the way in which one acquires the knowledge about this right, have been the cornerstone of academic research done in the field of political socialization. These political actions and beliefs support some of our assumptions about what citizens should and can do in a healthy, well-functioning democracy. Hyman's work provided critical insight into the complex fashion in which people learn to be political agents in our society. He showed us how this process not only has an impact on our social, political, and economic institutions, but also how this process ultimately helps to bolster and solidify the ideals and institutions that were integral in the formation and development of the form of democracy that we live with now.

Hyman's work provided a great deal of insight into the necessity for, as well as the actual mechanics of the political socialization process in the United States. However his work also produced many complicated questions about this new field of political socialization. Questions about whether or not the political socialization process is primarily the domain of adolescence, or if this process is a part of a lifelong process that includes significant political shifts in attitudes and behaviors at every stage of development, are still being debated. Whether the appropriate subject of study for the field of political socialization should be an individual, a group, or an institution is another concern for scholars. There has also been a wide variety of opinions on whether a specific geographic region or a specific period of time should be viewed as the most influential components of a political socialization process, and which is thus more important to study. Even within the specific subject frame of psychological approaches, questions about which psychological-based approach should be utilized are also highly contested. For those scholars that have focused on institutions and/or larger societal units, questions about the influence of education, family, peer groups, media, and popular culture have attracted a great deal of scrutiny.

Arguably the most troubling theoretical question has been the implications and the meaning of who is included and who is excluded from research conducted on political socialization. In particular, questions about which people are left out of the previously described understanding of political socialization continue to plague the growth and development of this field of study. To shed light on these dilemmas, factors such as how youth, race, and education interact in the field of political socialization will be analyzed.

YOUTH, RACE, AND EDUCATION IN
THE FIELD OF POLITICAL SOCIALIZATION

Starting with Hyman's work, the scholarly definition and examination of our political socialization process began to logically flow from these modest beginnings. Considerable quantitative research was conducted on middle school and high school students in the 1950s and 1960s that supported the key components of Hyman's understanding of political socialization. Scholars were able to show that certain political beliefs and behaviors were developed by youth. Youth then provided the keys to unlocking the mysteries of our political socialization process. People did not just magically register to vote, align themselves with a political party, and vote in every single election at a certain age. The way in which students learned about themselves, as well as their surroundings, played a significant role in the development of their political beliefs and actions. In particular, a significant link emerged between childhood development and educational experiences in the political socialization process.

As this link between youth's social and political development and their educational experience was established as the foundation for a great deal of the political socialization research that was being conducted, it also became apparent that this academic work was rife with devastating flaws as well as inherent limitations. One of the most pronounced anomalies that appeared in the scholarly work done on the political socialization process was the omission of youth of color. The problem youth of color provided was not only a part of the larger theoretical problem of who is and who is not included in research done on the political socialization process, but it also provided for some very specific problems about how much contemporary research on political socialization can reveal about places, such as Washington, D.C.

Merelman's discussion of the significance of educational institutions in the political socialization process for youth provides an example of how prickly and complicated these subject areas can be for scholars to address properly. Merelman states that:

> There is evidence that the schools make a substantial contribution to the political socialization of both minority group and duller students through a process Langston has called "compensatory political socialization." Because few of these students bring parental support for democratic values or political participation with them to school, they find social studies offerings stimulating, not redundant. By contrast, their more fortunate peers apparently are bored by the social studies courses that recapitulate ideas already mastered elsewhere. Indeed, there is even some evidence that the school alienates bright twelfth graders from democratic values. Thus, the effects of the school appear to be both variable and selective.[8]

On one level, Merelman's assertion that educational institutions did not have the same positive or useful impact on the political socialization of all youth can be seen as providing support for the underlying assumption that there is a link between educational institutions and youth's political socialization process. On another level, one could ask about the implications of research that suggests that "minority group" and "duller students" are the chief beneficiaries of what educational institutions can offer by the way of a fully developed political socialization process. Merelman's inclusion of this research is unusual in its reference to "minority students" and his observation that a political socialization process might not be an even process. Whereas Hyman and many of the other trailblazing scholars from the 1950s and 1960s were more comfortable with a discussion of the political socialization process in a universal context and language, Merelman's work and that of more contemporary scholars of political socialization have attempted to draw attention to this notion of diverse audiences as recipients of this political socialization process.

"Minority youth" then, if captured at all, are typically used to confirm the resiliency and vitality of the previously discussed theoretical foundations. In Merelman's research on the role that educational institutions play in the political socialization process, he discovered that "minority groups" and "duller students" were the ones that were influenced the most by these "social studies" courses and that the "brighter twelfth graders" found these courses to be boring. In fact, one could infer from this research that these "brighter twelfth graders" developed their political ideas and beliefs in a healthy manner at home, and they did not need the educational support that social studies and other classes might have provided. It was presumed that the other students must not have been exposed to the important political ideals and practices that are needed in our society from other family members; therefore, educational institutions had more of an impact on their political socialization process.

The analysis of this research that Merelman provides begs the question of what this political socialization process looks like from a minority student perspective. Is it true that minority youth do not learn democratic values at home? Is it true that this lack of knowledge of democratic values imparted by family members would make minority students more interested in social studies classes? Does this then imply that educational institutions have more of an impact on the political socialization process for minority youth than their families do? These are some of the questions that can be asked after reading Merelman's analysis, and these questions begin to tug on and pull at the theoretical framework of the field of political socialization.

Many scholars have attempted to address these questions by providing a new theoretical lens throught which to view the field of political socialization. One of the more intriguing shifts in this research was the inclusion of race as an explanatory factor and as a meaningful variable. The work of Richard Niemi and Barbara Sobieszek illustrates this point:

Work in the early 1970s moved in several directions to fill in obvious gaps in earlier work and to expand its scope. First, investigators examined subgroups of the American population, especially groups likely to hold attitudes different from those of middle-class whites. Abramson cites 34 separate studies reporting on black-white differences in feelings of political efficacy or trust.[9]

As noted by Niemi and Sobieszek, the work that included race was primarily limited to work on "black-white differences." Paul Abramson is quite often credited with broadening the scope of research done on political socialization to include race.

Abramson's work provided a theoretical way to understand black youth's political socialization process as a way to distinguish this socialization pattern from the others that had been documented.[10] Unlike past scholarly work done on youth, Abramson's work acknowledged and identified black youth as a group that had a distinct political socialization process.[11] The distinction Abramson made between the political socialization of black and white youth became not just a discussion about a deviant and a normal group or even a brighter or duller group. It grew more into a well-rounded, sensitive discussion about the nature of the differences in the political socialization process for black and white youth and what these differences might mean for the overall field of political socialization.[12]

Abramson begins his work with the following insight:

> The six million black schoolchildren in the United States, like their white counterparts, have virtually no political power. Yet, socialization research suggests that black children feel less politically powerful than white children do.[13]

Abramson immediately establishes the premise that black school children not only have a marginal status in our society, but that the knowledge of this power difference must be the appropriate starting place for research done on the political socialization process of youth. Abramson suggests that social scientists have already documented that black school children "feel less politically powerful than white children do,"[14] and these insights provide the foundation on which the theoretical structure of his work is built. This provides a distinct break with the previous research that Merelman discussed. No longer would it be sufficient explanation of research results to simply lump "duller" and "minority" students together and, as Abramson argues,

> If we wish to begin to build theories about the differential political socialization of subcultural groups, we need to go beyond mere findings and progress toward the development of explanations.[15]

Henceforth, Abramson's research provides a marked departure from the neglect of racial differences in examining a political socialization process. He boldly suggests that racial differences can be observed in the political socialization process and these differences can also be explained. The oppressive social, political, and economic conditions of black life within our society are critical in developing explanations for the black political socialization process and why it is different from and similar to that of other racial groups. As a marked departure from the previous approaches that have been considered, it presents a new course for political socialization research.

THE NECESSITY OF QUALITATIVE RESEARCH

The field of political socialization has made great strides from its initial humble beginnings in the 1950s. The theoretical dilemmas that were previously mentioned have been largely addressed but not resolved in a satisfactory fashion. This is particularly true for political socialization research that has been done on youth, race, and education. There are still very few analyses that have been offered within the field of political socialization that adequately answer the myriad intriguing questions that youth, race, and education pose for the field. When Hyman's work was initially introduced as the most influential in the development of the field of political socialization there was no discussion of the quantitative research methods he utilized. These methods meant that it was not just a matter of whether subjects such as race were going to be addressed, but raised the equally intriguing question of how this subject matter would be addressed. It is from this vantage point that qualitative research methods could be utilized as a way to address some of the theoretical and methodological problems that have plagued the field of political socialization. A shift toward qualitative-based research could provide a more in-depth understanding of the field of political socialization. It could provide a different set of questions for some of the often neglected and discarded subject areas.

When a qualitative methodological approach is applied to the political socialization process of black youth in the Washington, D.C., metropolitan area, the potential value this approach has becomes easier to appreciate. As Merelman's analysis in the previous section suggested, this is especially true when methodological and theoretical debates are not just applied to abstract concepts, such as a healthy understanding of democratic political institutions, but also are placed in the specific context of a study of the political socialization of black youth. It becomes not just a simple methodological decision about the appropriate tool used to measure the phenomenon being studied, but also a decision that must include an analysis of the impact that the measuring device might have on the marginalized community being studied. When the discussion moves from an abstract discussion about the utility of a qualitative or a quantitative methodological approach to a discussion about what approach might provide the most insight into the political socialization process for black youth, it generates the potential for social change for black youth. At this point the lines between the various approaches become more murky and confusing.

LeCompte and Schensul's description of ethnography provides an excellent example of how a qualitative approach could be applied to the field of political socialization and, specifically, to black youth's political socialization.[16] Given the dilemmas and weaknesses that survey research has presented for the field of political socialization, an ethnographic approach that incorporates participant observation along with face-to-face interviews appears to be a well-deserved antidote for this quantitative research.[17] There are a variety of ways that ethnographic research techniques could be utilized in conducting research on black youth's political socialization. Participant observation is one of the key techniques that LeCompte and Schensul discuss. They identified this technique as being applicable for any group setting in which there were regular, noticeable patterns of social interactions.

It is at this point that a qualitative methodological approach could be proposed as a way to advance the research that has been done in the field of political socialization. In particular, an ethnographic approach that incorporates face-to-face interviews and participant observation could provide greater insight into the political socialization process for black youth. By starting with participant observation in a U.S. history or government classroom setting, the ability to observe the way in which the students interact with each other and with other school officials could be included in the analysis of the subject's political socialization process. This knowledge could be incorporated into a scholar's final analysis of the political socialization process of youth. Setting up follow-up interviews with some of the students allows for a scholar to probe more deeply into how some of the students construct their social and political worlds. This type of investigation can be more revealing as well as informative than a quantitative approach, especially in terms of such potentially delicate areas as an upsetting home life, overtly racist experiences, lack of interest in school, or personal feuds with other students, teachers, or staff. All of these areas would have a greater likelihood of being detected and documented by an ethnographic approach. Unlike standard survey questions that are used in quantitative research, these ethnographic methods can move well beyond written or oral answers to set questions. These qualitative techniques can open doors that quantitative research might not be able to access. Quantitative research documents the existence of a particular attitude or behavior, but the use of a qualitative approach can offer and provide greater insight into which attitudes or behaviors manifest themselves. Qualitative methods can also shed light on how these attitudes and behaviors are developed by youth. The potential for producing results that could move beyond the established literature and providing greater insight into the political socialization process of black youth is the most attractive prospect for qualitative methods.

BREAKING AWAY FROM THE FAMILIAR TERRAIN

Academic scholarship on political socialization has tended to lump this process into a larger framework dealing with youth development. As children grow up in our society it is expected that they also learn about their political rights and responsibilities. Scholars have attempted to illustrate the way in which institutions (school, parents, peer groups) as well as personal development (psychological models of youth development) have contributed to this process.

Some youth have been neglected or completely left out of this research. It is clear that youth of color have been left out of the standard models that have been developed for the political socialization process. The focus of research has not been based on these groups. Even when racial minority youth have been included in research, they have quite often been used to support previously established conclusions about the dominant (white) racial group. An analysis of the political socialization of black youth in Washington, D.C., can be used to evaluate the strengths and weaknesses of new theoretical and methodological approaches.

WHY WASHINGTON, D.C., MATTERS

Historical Significance and an Institutional Analysis

It is important to first return to some of the insights about Washington, D.C., that were presented at the beginning of this paper in order to place this information in a historical framework. It was mentioned earlier that Washington, D.C., has a population of 572,059 with 56 percent African Americans residents. Dramatic shifts in the demographics in Washington, D.C., were described in Harry Jaffe and Tom Sherwood's book, *Dream City: Race, Power, and the Decline of Washington, D.C.* In particular, they point out that "[o]f the city's eight hundred thousand residents in 1968, nearly 70 percent were of

African American descent, the highest proportion of any major city, but most were well off." One of the major thrusts of their book was that the decrease in the population was due in part to the riots that took place in Washington, D.C., in 1968: "In countless ways, the city of Washington never recovered from the uprising. People will always define the city's history as 'before the riots' and 'after the riots.'"[18]

The riots not only left hundreds of burned-out businesses in their wake but also started a white and black flight from the city into the Maryland and Virginia suburbs.[19] As part of this flight, a lot of financial resources left Washington, D.C. The problems that this loss of human and material capital has caused are still being grappled with by Washington, D.C.

Another key moment in Washington, D.C., history was the passage of a home rule charter by Congress that brought back local elections in the 1970s. Jaffe and Sherwood describe these developments in the following way:

> Nixon signed the historic legislation December 24, 1973. Four months later, on May 7, 1974 city voters gave overwhelming support to the new form of government. Even if their elected officials would still have to be supplicants before congressional committees, finally, after nearly one hundred years, the District would have a locally elected government again.[20]

The first mayoral and City Council elections held in 1974 ushered in an era in which the residents of Washington, D.C., could exercise one of their key democratic rights: voting. This is arguably the most significant component of the political socialization process for the people of Washington, D.C. Not only is their voting limited (the D.C. delegate in the House of Representatives can only vote in committee, but not on the House floor; no senators represent Washington, D.C.), but even these limited voting rights are relevantly new (about thirty years old).

Studying the political socialization process of any Washington, D.C., resident presents many challenges. Some of the institutional areas covered by scholars have to be accompanied by many caveats. For example, the role that families have on the political socialization process of future generations might be more meaningful for a family that can point to two, three, or four generations of a tradition of participating in politics. How does a scholar approach a family where there is only one generation that has had the opportunity to vote and the political offices available to vote for were limited? The expectation that voting will be valued and incorporated into the lifestyle of families in Washington, D.C., has to be carefully applied and has to be understood within this larger historical and institutional framework. This might mean that research done in Washington, D.C., on the role that family members play in the political socialization process of their children has to be specifically tailored to address the larger historical and institutional framework.

The same questions could be posed for an analysis of the impact of peer groups on the political socialization process of youth. The typical influence peer groups are supposed to have on the political socialization process of youth is also limited. Much of this research was built on the premise that some members of a peer group would be more likely to be engaged in and knowledgeable about political ideals and our democratic practices. Since everyone in Washington, D.C., had historically lacked voting rights there was no room for diverse experiences. It is true that D.C. youth today can vote for candidates running for most of the typical local political offices that other youth can vote for, but the value attached to this political practice has been permanently tarred by this legacy. In some respects, this historical inequity provides all Washington, D.C., youth, regardless of race, class, gender, or sexual orientation, with an identical political handicap to tackle. Whereas a combination of socio-economic status and peer group bonding might illuminate voting habits in certain places, it is less meaningful as an instrument in and of itself for Washington, D.C. Clearly the history of voting and the significant shift in demographics in Washington, D.C., should be included in any analysis of the political socialization process for youth in Washington, D.C.

These same questions could be posed for the role of educational institutions. It is a common practice for social studies and government classes to teach students about the freedom and rights that are part of our democratic form of government. Washington, D.C., students are currently exposed to the grim reality that they do not have the same political rights and freedoms as the fifty "normal" states. These students cannot simply consume the traditional knowledge that is provided in U.S. history and government classes. They have to learn that they have fewer political freedoms than other Americans, but they are expected to develop similar political beliefs and practices as all of the other Americans. Schools are one of the primary venues in which Washington, D.C., youth learn about political realities. The educational experience becomes a critical ingredient in their political socialization process.

There is one noteworthy exception to this rather gloomy political history for Washington, D.C. Washington D.C.'s second democratically elected mayor, Marion Barry, built up a significant youth following that was a critical component of his political power base. In fact, Jaffe and Sherwood suggest that "Barry needed the young blacks as much as (Labor Secretary) Wirtz did, but for different reasons: He wanted to organize them into a political force."[21] Even though his motives might be contested, it is generally agreed that "Barry's ability to connect with the black teenagers distinguished him once again from the city's other civil rights leaders," as well as from most of the political candidates he faced in elections.[22] Barry's work with youth paid off as he eventually won multiple citywide elections over four decades (and still holds office today as City Council representative for Ward 8.) This has helped to establish an historical precedent for the value and significance of the youth vote in Washington, D.C. From the very first school board election the city held in 1974 that started Barry's political career to the most recent election he won (Ward 8 councilmember) in 2004, the youth vote not only played a critical role in Barry's career but also a role in determining the winner in every election in Washington, D.C.[23]

Contemporary Youth Struggles

Any analysis of Washington, D.C., youth will uncover familiar and foreign terrain. As previously suggested there are ways in which the political socialization process of Washington, D.C., youth is indicative of national and other large urban area voting patterns. There are also ways in which this political socialization process is distinct. To evaluate these trends a few key areas of the study of the political socialization of youth will be covered. First, a comparison between Washington, D.C., and national trends will be reviewed. Second, how Washington, D.C., compares to two cities with similar demographics will be explored. Finally, how explanations of these trends should include an analysis of not only what makes Washington, D.C., unique, but also how the other dominant institutions in the study of the political socialization of youth should be included in any analysis will be presented.

Washington, D.C.'s youth voter participation records are similar to other large-city and national statistics. Two of the last elections in Washington, D.C., illustrate these points. In the 2006 general election there were 19,716 youth (age eighteen to twenty-four) registered to vote, and out of these registered voters only 2,043 actually voted.[24] In the 2008 presidential primary election there were 31,832 youth registered to vote of which only 4,660 actually voted.[25] The Center for Information and Research on Civic Learning and Engagement (CIRCLE) describe the national voting trends for youth in the following way:

> More than 6.5 million young people under the age of 30 participated in the 2008 primaries and caucuses. This marks a dramatic increase in youth voter turnout over the last comparable election cycle in 2000. In states where data is available for both the 2008 and 2000 primaries, the national youth turnout rate rose from nine percent in the 2000 primaries to 17 percent in the 2008 primaries.[26]

This slight increase in the percentage of voter participation (10 to 14 percent) in D.C. can be compared to the national shift from 9 to 17 percent that CIRCLE describes. Based on data provided by CIRCLE, Washington, D.C.'s youth 2006 midterm elections participation (29 percent) was lower than cities that had a similar percentage of black residents In particular, Detroit (38 percent) and Atlanta (36 percent) both had a higher percentage of voter turnout.[27] (It is also true that all of these cities had a higher percentage of voter turnout for the age category thirty and older [Washington, D.C., 58 percent; Detroit 60 percent; Atlanta 52 percent] and that the youth voter category tends to always have the lowest level of voter participation.[28]) Washington, D.C., youth face similar urban challenges as do youth in other cities. Within educational institutions these challenges can be observed through an examination of dropout rates, grade point average of students, and disciplinary actions utilized by school officials. Even the racial makeup of Washington, D.C., youth and educational institutions is not too different from other major cities.

Schley Lyons's work, "The Political Socialization of Ghetto Children: Efficacy and Cynicism," provides amazing insight into the political socialization process of black youth from over thirty years ago. Many of her insights can be used to understand the political socialization process for black youth today. Lyons's work provides a brilliant antidote for the previously cited pioneering political socialization studies. First, Lyons identifies race and the study of black youth as being of critical importance for the study of political socialization:

> Explanatory factors investigated in other socialization studies include the family unit, social class, sex, intelligence, school curriculum, peer groups, and the mass media. However, a potentially significant explanatory factor that has received relatively little attention is race. Does the fact that one's skin is black aid in predicting how a child will score on indices measuring a sense of efficacy and feelings of cynicism? After controls were introduced for race, it became evident that the association between milieu, the environment in which the children lived, and the dependent variables was primarily a result of attitude differences between white and black children.[29]

Lyons also finds it necessary to reach out beyond the previous political socialization research and to delve into social conditions of the participants in the research. Lyons's work is also emblematic of some of the new trends in political socialization research. The point then is not to simply study parents, peer groups, life cycles, generations, or other factors, or even to study multiple factors in a simultaneous fashion. Lyons advances the premise identified by Abramson and more contemporary scholars:

> It is obvious, however, that the slum child, particularly the Negro slum child, acquires his political values and beliefs within a milieu of poverty and racial discrimination that differs significantly from that of white, middle-class children. What is the effect of such early life experiences on the slum child's sense

of efficacy? Do children who grow up in the deprived milieu of the inner city develop more cynical feelings about government than children who grow up elsewhere?[30]

To address these questions, Lyons concludes that it is best to proceed with a discussion of real-world socio-political problems:

> Aside from adding to our knowledge of childhood political socialization, a second implication of these findings is that the prospects for the Negro fulfilling this aspiration through widespread use of the ballot are not encouraging. For adults a sense of political efficacy and low feelings of cynicism are positively related to political involvement. The weaker the sense of efficacy and the stronger the feelings of cynicism the less likely one is to participate in the political process.[31]

Finally, Lyons not only enmeshes her research results in real-life socio-political problems, but she also offers a very insightful prediction of why this problem might persist:

> In recent years legal barriers hindering the full participation of the Negro in the political process have been largely stripped away. The federal government is attempting to stimulate a kind of "grass roots" democracy among Negroes and the urban poor through the poverty and model cities programs. Various black spokesmen striving to arouse the Negro poor out of their apathy and self-hate have captured the headlines and news bulletins. Nevertheless, black youth continue to develop early in life fundamental political orientations that suggest that "nothing very basic is happening." When one projects into the future the kind of political behavior correlated with the low-efficacy and high-cynicism orientations of Negro youth, one is led to speculate that the next generation of Negro adults will still be operating far below its potential in the political arena.[32]

From a historical perspective, most of Lyons's comments can be borne out. It could be submitted that Lyons's work also provides some vital openings for future research on political socialization of black youth.

For these reasons the field of political socialization needs to continue to expand the scope and the depth of its research. The expansion of this research should be based on the study of how youth, race, and educational institutions interact with each other in the development of a political socialization process. The days in which quantitative research could be done on a limited sample of white males and then be utilized to explain larger political habits and beliefs, have passed. What can be gleaned from the political socialization process of youth of color is just as insightful and necessary for the development and growth of this field as research done on any other demographically distinct group.

CONCLUSION

Washington, D.C., represents a striking example of how race, youth, and education converge to form a unique political socialization pattern. More qualitative research conducted on youth of color in other localities, such as Philadelphia, Atlanta, and Los Angeles, could help to illustrate the potency of this new political socialization work, and it can also teach us a lot about American political identity formation and how this process has evolved. If the political socialization process of black youth in Washington, D.C., is going to be linked to or compared to other large metropolitan centers, then not only do the previously mentioned insights about race, youth, education, and urban trends need to be incorporated into the analysis, but the unique "undemocratic" status of Washington, D.C., must also be included. What is unique for Washington, D.C., youth are the limited voting rights that are available to them and the limited role they can play in the way that their government and government functions are operated and executed.

This does present specific challenges for any scholarly work done on the political socialization of black youth in Washington, D.C. Besides the previously mentioned dilemmas described for political socialization scholars, there is the added burden of being able to assess and evaluate the effect this unique political dynamic has on Washington, D.C., youth. A strong argument can made for the use of qualitative methods as well as the necessity of moving beyond some of the quantitative approaches that have been utilized before. Even expanding the methodological approaches will not ensure that all of the previously discussed shortcomings and deficiencies will be adequately addressed. The logic of political socialization does not necessarily pull in one direction, and some of the contradictory and confusing trends revealed by academic work on political socialization might be exacerbated by research based on Washington, D.C., youth. Washington, D.C., not only provides a window through which to view the political socialization process of black youth in large urban centers, but it can also offer insight into the city that has been referred to as "the last colony."

The particular dilemma that the political socialization process presents to scholars becomes more perplexing and difficult when Washington, D.C., is studied. Not only are the typical issues present (e.g., lower voter turnout and nontraditional participation) but the added burden of the nature and scope of the government (e.g., limited voting rights and limited control over legislative and financial matters) has to be included. As previously described, Washington, D.C., has a unique form of limited democracy and this limited democracy has been successfully challenged in some respects, but it has not been completely eliminated. In particular, even with the successful passage of a home rule charter by Congress and the reintroduction of local elections in the 1970s, it is also still a fact that Congresswoman Eleanor Holmes Norton does not have full voting rights and privileges as the elected congressional representative of Washington, D.C., and that the Washington, D.C., City Council and mayor have to receive approval for all financial and legislative matters from Congress.

This particular backdrop is unique to Washington, D.C., and this means that any analysis of the political socialization of Washington, D.C., residents has to include the more traditional large urban issues, such as education, housing, and budgetary concerns, but must also include the actual form and process of government, such as who has the power and authority to make decisions for Washington, D.C., residents. Washington, D.C., youth do not just learn about a lot of the same inner city problems that other youth experience, but they also encounter the limits and the weaknesses of the government that represents them and that is responsible for many of the most critical areas of their lives. This includes the funding and support of public schools and charter schools, the closing of hospitals, and crime bills. The success and failure of these local struggles are inextricably connected to the success or failure of the equally important struggles for expanded democratic rights, equal rights, and a more autonomous form of government for Washington, D.C. These added elements not only make the past work on the political socialization of black youth inadequate, but raise the possibility that even more recent attempts to conduct research on the political socialization of black youth will need to be reassessed when these approaches are applied to Washington, D.C., youth.

NOTES

1. Estimate for July 1, 2007, Office of Planning, Government of the District of Columbia, Washington, D.C.

2. Board of Elections and Ethics, Washington, District of Columbia (January 14, 2008).

3. Office of Planning, Washington, D.C., estimate for July 1, 2007.

4. Office of Data and Accountability, School Board, Washington, D.C. (2008–2009 School Year): white (6.5 percent), Latino (10.2 percent), Asian (1.8 percent), and Native American (.08 percent)

5. I use the term "minority" and "youth of color" throughout this chapter to refer to either a specific black racial population in the United States or to a broader category of any minority group in the United States that confronts systematic and institutional oppression on a regular basis.

6. Richard M. Merelman, "The Adolescence of Political Socialization," *Sociology of Education* 45 (1972): 135.

7. Ibid., 135–36.

8. Ibid., 150.

9. Richard G. Niemi and Barbara I. Sobieszek, "Political Socialization," *Annual Review of Sociology* 3 (1977): 215.

10. Paul R. Abramson, "Political Efficacy and Political Trust Among Black Schoolchildren: Two Explanations," *The Journal of Politics* 34 (1972): 1259–62.

11. Ibid., 1259–62.

12. "Previous studies of political sophistication and civic competence found gender but not race a significant variable"; Carol A. Cassel and Celia C. Lo, "Theories of Political Literacy," *Political Behavior* 19 (1997): 324.

13. Abramson, "Political Efficacy and Political Trust Among Black Schoolchildren: Two Explanations," 1243.

14. Ibid., 1244.

15. Ibid., 1244.

16. Besides the work of Margaret LeCompte and Jean Shensul in *Designing and Conducting Ethnographic Research*, specific ethnographic work done on black youth in educational settings can be found in Arnett Ferguson's *Bad Boys: Public Schools in the Making of Black Masculinity* (Ann Arbor: University of Michigan Press, 2001) and L. Janelle Dance's *Tough Fronts: The Impact of Street Culture on Schooling* (New York: Routledge Falmer, 2002).

17. Part of the problem with the research that Merelman described was the way in which quantitative research methods limited the possible knowledge that could be gained from the results. In particular, the questions I posed for the "minority students" are especially relevant in a discussion of qualitative methods. Their responses to this research could not have been limited to or forced into an analysis that simply suggested that social studies classes and educational institutions provided or did not provide assistance for their own political socialization process. Qualitative approaches can allow a researcher to produce a more nuanced and comprehensive analysis of students' responses to a wide range of topics directly or indirectly related to their political socialization process.

18. Harry S. Jaffe and Tom Sherwood, *Dream City: Race, Power, and the Decline of Washington, D.C.*, Simon and Schuster: New York, 1994, 81.

19. Ibid., 83.

20. Ibid., 104.

21. Ibid., 55.

22. Ibid., 56.

23. It should also be noted that the official voting age was lowered from twenty-one to eighteen in 1971. This was three years before Washington, D.C., held the historical elections of 1974, and this change in the voting age clearly contributes to Jaffe and Sherwood's analysis of Marion Barry and the youth vote in Washington, D.C.

24. Board of Elections and Ethics, Washington, D.C., 2008.

25. Ibid.

26. CIRCLE, "Quick Facts about Young Voters in Washington-Alexandria, DC-VA-MD WV1—The Midterm Election Year," Karlo Barrios Marcelo, research associate, 2 July 2007.

27. Ibid.
28. Ibid.
29. Schley R. Lyons, "The Political Socialization of Ghetto Children: Efficacy and Cynicism," *The Journal of Politics* 32 (1970): 290.
30. Ibid., 290.
31. Ibid., 303.
32. Ibid., 303–4.

BIBLIOGRAPHY

Abramson, Paul R. "Political Efficacy and Political Trust Among Black Schoolchildren: Two Explanations," *The Journal of Politics* 34 (1972): 1259–62.
Cassel, Carol A. and Celia C. Lo. "Theories of Political Literacy," *Political Behavior* 19 (1997): 324.
Center for Information and Research on Civic Learning and Engagement (CIRCLE). "Quick Facts about Young Voters in Washington-Alexandria, DC-VA-MD WV1 — The Midterm Election Year," Karlo Barrios Marcelo, research associate, 2 July 2007.
Dance, L Janelle. *Tough Fronts: The Impact of Street Culture on Schooling.* New York: Routledge Falmer, 2002.
Ferguson, Arnett. *Bad Boys: Public Schools in the Making of Black Masculinity.* Ann Arbor: The University of Michigan Press, 2001
Jaffe, Harry S. and Tom Sherwood. *Dream City: Race, Power, and the Decline of Washington, D.C.* Simon and Schuster: New York, 1994.
LeCompte, Margaret and Jean Shensul. *Designing and Conducting Ethnographic Research.* Walnut Creek, Calif.: AltaMira Press, 1999.
Lyons, Schley R. "The Political Socialization of Ghetto Children: Efficacy and Cynicism," *The Journal of Politics* 32 (1970): 290.
Merelman, Richard M. "The Adolescence of Political Socialization," *Sociology of Education* 45 (1972): 135.
Niemi, Richard G. and Barbara I. Sobieszek, "Political Socialization," *Annual Review of Sociology* 3 (1977): 215.

9

Banished: Housing Policy in the District of Columbia and the Struggle of Working Families

William G. Jones

INTRODUCTION

The housing conditions in the District of Columbia are influenced by national economic and housing policy and local housing policy. The particularly local housing markets, in regionally integrated areas, are subject to the influence of the national government's toolbox for the housing economy. Local housing markets in areas with diverse populations are sensitive in particular forms to the political economy of housing. The national government's housing policy toolbox includes potent tools such as affecting interest rates, mortgage regulations, and housing program funding. Congress is influential through its legislative, oversight, and budgetary roles in national housing policy. Full democratic participation in Congress is important to the District of Columbia because of its critical housing issues of affordability, gentrification, displacement, and housing resources. Full voting rights by representatives adds greater leverage to political participation. Local political leadership is limited in its responsiveness to housing conditions by the relative effectiveness of its interaction with national government. Working families in the District of Columbia have struggled with a severely stressed market for affordable housing. Local government and national housing policies have provided limited shelter from an overheated housing market and a variety of social problems that have exacerbated the banishment of low-income working families from the District of Columbia. The price of homeownership and rental housing has skyrocketed over the past decade, making living in the District a challenge. The District's mayors and City Councils have been challenged with the dual objectives of urban revitalization and providing affordable housing. National housing policy is also challenged in the same ways. These policy objectives have stood as either irreconcilable or complementary depending on the political orientation and economic interest of the local and national governments.

In the 1980s and early 1990s, the District of Columbia, like many Northeast and Rust Belt central cities, suffered from abandonment by upper- and middle-class families. Housing abandonment was epidemic with vacant and boarded housing characteristic of certain areas of cities. Urban economies suffered as industries, businesses, and, therefore, jobs left American cities and moved south and overseas. In contrast to cities of similar size, the District historically lacked a large scale industrial base. Corporations were attracted to suburbs, rural areas, and foreign countries out of sight and out of reach of many urban workers. Drugs flooded into cities as anesthesia for the pains of job loss, poor education, and community disinvestment. These conditions resulted in increased poverty rates and rising crime rates rooted in economic dislocation and drug importation, displaced aggression, and internal inferiorization.[1]

The District of Columbia government has found itself pursuing a multifaceted strategy of urban revitalization and housing policy aimed at ameliorating a housing crisis for low-income families. Its urban revitalization strategy has been focusing on facilitating an influx of new residents to address the housing abandonment and accompanying economic losses to the tax base, commerce, and jobs. Washington, D.C., unlike many other central cities, possesses tremendous assets that make it an attractive place to live. The city has a relatively stable economic base with the federal government as its core, and is surrounded by a deeply prosperous metropolitan area. Amenities abound with free, world-class museums, libraries, educational institutions, mass transportation, and recreation. The private market has accommodated the city's objective of attracting new residents in a robust fashion with vigorous gentrification, invoking the characterization of "phoenix" and "foul" from diverse observers. Despite the District's parallel policy efforts to protect long-term residents and encourage the growth of new residents, low-income residents are being pressed out of the jurisdiction by gargantuan social and private-market forces.

Two major housing policies have been the center piece of the city's effort to address working families' housing needs. The city has had "rent control" legislation for over a decade. The Housing Trust Fund is another key piece of legislation that has often been discussed as important to addressing housing needs.

The District's rent control legislation has been considered a model for local governments across the nation. It has been characterized as a reasonable means to address the needs of tenants and landlords. Under the legislation, tenants were provided rent stabilization, and landlords were provided up to 12 percent return on investment. Real estate interests viewed the District of

Columbia's rent control legislation as an impediment to a robust and healthy housing market that would attract both reinvestment and new investment in the city. James McGrath of the D.C. Tenants' Advocacy Coalition (TENAC) characterized the efforts by the real estate lobby to overturn rent control simply as "greed" wrapped in the promotion of "laissez-faire housing policy" and "market-driven pricing."[2]

FEDERAL AND LOCAL ASSISTED HOUSING POLICY

Aside from regulatory interventions in the private market, such as rent control and the Housing Trust Fund, the District of Columbia has an inventory of assisted housing in the form of public housing buildings and Housing Choice Voucher units. The District's public housing program, like many other programs in large central cities across the nation, has been vandalized by the constant hurling of negative reports by the mainstream media. A three-decade-long propaganda campaign managed to characterize public housing, along with other welfare programs, as impenetrable fortresses of the "culture of poverty" and "social ills." Certainly, housing policies that geographically concentrated unemployed and underemployed families contributed to concentrated social problems such as drug abuse and crime, but these are not social problems alien to middle- and upper-class suburbia. Social problems are viewed as pandemic in the "underclass" and viewed as treatable personal anomalies in the upper strata. While focusing on the plight of public housing and its residents, meager attention was given to the massive export of jobs and industry from urban areas during the same period. The era of deindustrialization, although coinciding with the accomplishments of the civil rights and black power movements, erased an opportunity ladder being counted on by many urban families. Instead, subsidized housing needs outweigh availabile affordable housing. In Washington, D.C., there were 10,599 public housing units and 7,352 housing vouchers in 2000.[3] The city had 8,643 public housing units and 11,385 housing vouchers in 2009. Between 1993 and 2007, the District received approximately $181 million in HOPE VI grants to revitalize existing public housing and develop new units.

Public housing policy in the District parallels the national policy. The thrust of the policy is to revitalize public housing by demolition of antiquated housing properties and the development of mixed-income, lower-density properties. The "Townhomes on Capital Hill" is characteristic of one approach to revitalizing public housing. Formerly, the site was developed as the Ellen Wilson Dwellings—low-rise apartments and townhouses. Unlike some large Northeastern cities, the District of Columbia never developed high-rise public housing properties or huge, sprawling public housing communities. The demolition of the Ellen Wilson Dwellings and construction of "Townhomes on Capital Hill" were partially financed with a $25 million grant from the Department of Housing and Urban Development (HUD). The project was designed to be a mixed-income cooperative providing ownership opportunities for residents with low incomes and incomes in the $90,000 bracket. This property was developed by the District of Columbia Housing Authority, Ellen Wilson Development Corporation, and Telsis Development.

At least some Capitol Hill residents had continuing concerns about whether the property would sooner or later devolve into a less-than-desirable state. James Didden, an executive of the National Capital Bank on Capitol Hill, was skeptical that the developers really met the objective of building a new concept in public housing. He considered the end product to be just another public housing project with the same occupancy qualifications as public housing rather than mixed income.[4] The architecture of the property blends with the historic character of the area, breaking the mold of public housing. The District's efforts to revitalize low-income housing have generally been met with optimism by low-income families and their supporters and skepticism by some existing and new property owners.

"Townhomes on Capitol Hill" is but one of seven efforts by the District to redevelop public housing and disperse low-income residents. Several HUD HOPE VI projects have been awarded to redevelop public housing complexes around the city. Other District of Columbia Housing Authority (DCHA) HOPE VI developments included the Arthur Capper/Carrollsburg development with a 2001 $34 million grant, East Capital Dwelling/Capital View Plaza development with a 2000 $30 million grant, and, more recently, Sheridan Terrace development with a 2007 $20 million grant. The city has also used city resources to build new housing. In Ward 8, homes at the Woodmount single-family development received a city-financed grant to build the $14 million homeownership project. This project used $1 million of city tax dollars. The project was developed primarily to attract middle-class homeowners, in part in response to neighborhood concerns over a proposal to develop apartments in an area already oversaturated with rental properties.[5] Houses in Woodmount would cost as much as $584,000.

DCHA has not been without internal problems, particularly those that surfaced during the 1990s and led to federal intervention in the form of HUD placing the agency under receivership. The housing agency was plagued with poor administrative practices that probably had their genesis in years of mismanagement prior to home rule. The authority had thirteen executive directors between 1979 and 1995, a 20 percent vacancy rate, and approximately thirty thousand unaddressed maintenance work orders.[6] As with other big urban housing agencies, political linkage with the city's patronage system and political machine played a role in the housing agency's flaws. The receivership would support adding some degrees of separation between city leadership and the housing authority.

One of the key thrusts of national housing policy and District of Columbia housing policy has been to revitalize low-income housing by physical modernization and mixed-income development. Some affordable housing organizations believe the approach has resulted in few government-funded, low-rent apartments. "By 2006, local authorities across the country have demolished at least 78,015 public housing apartments under the HOPE VI program, according to HUD data," according to Linda Couch, deputy director of the National Low-Income Housing Coalition. She also added, "In 1998, Congress did away with the one-to-one replacement rule which required rebuilding one unit for each unit torn down."[7] The revitalization of public housing arose out of "general public concern cultivated by a media campaign to malevolently portray endemic social problems as inherent in the welfare state instead of continuing racial discrimination and the structure of the political economy."[8] The prevailing political climate has shown considerable resistance to any programs designed to significantly improve the life chances of the "truly disadvantaged."[9] Given the conservative political climate and federal-local institutional relationship present for the past few decades, the liberal-led District government exercised a blend of political leadership styles highly sensitive to its special structural relationships with federalism. The District political leadership in the form of the mayors and City Councils tended toward a style that emphasized a leadership image of power politics and concern for the population, and emphasized a policy work orientation that supported the status quo while acknowledging the needs of low-income African American constituents. This political leadership style was embodied in the housing programs in the District. National housing programs come to local governments generally already structured to meet nationally determined policy objectives with some parameters for local policy discretion and flexibility. In many respects, leadership style and effectiveness are contingent and situational based on the institutional context.[10] When local governments such as the District leadership act in an institutional context where national policy is more conservative, there is a greater tendency toward bargaining and maintaining relationships, rather than concentrating on purely local-orientated goals that emerge from democratic processes in close proximity. Because of the District of Columbia's limited geography and limited national political leverage, its political leadership style and effectiveness are more susceptible to federalism's institutional context as a factor than states'.

HOUSING IN THE WASHINGTON METROPOLITAN AREA

In the 1990s, the Washington area led the nation in home building permits and by 2000 experienced record highs in homeownership.[11] At the same time, low-income working families experienced exceptional difficulty finding affordable homeownership opportunities or in renting a two-bedroom apartment. Nicolas Retinas, director of Harvard University's Center for Housing Studies, announced, "It used to be that if you played by the rules, worked hard, you could afford a place to live, but even in the midst of all this prosperity, it just isn't so anymore." In terms of homeownership, "we barely made a dent in disparities between whites and minorities. . . . If we can't change the disparities in the good times, what does this mean for the bad times?"[12] Working families in the District were squeezed between escalating prices for apartments and homeownership in both the District and its suburban areas. Even in Arlington, Virginia, a solidly middle-class suburban county, low-income and middle-class residents found housing too expensive. Arlington voters failed to approve creation of a local housing authority twice, yet adopted a housing policy that put providing for housing needs in the hands of nonprofit and for-profit developers.[13] A number of northern Virginia counties adopted housing policies similar to Arlington County. These policies forestall the easy entrance into the suburbs for families with housing vouchers from other jurisdictions such as the District. Federal requirements allowed assisted families the opportunity to "port-in" (transfer housing choice vouchers) to any jurisdiction where a housing authority exists. Washington's surrounding suburbs provided few rental or homeownership options for low-income working families. For housing voucher families, a submarket exists of properties that accept housing vouchers. This market provides limited access to the private housing where landlords can make a profit and are willing to risk the negative perceptions that might impact property values, and put forth management effort associated with some low-income housing units. Given the amount of subsidy in a hot rental market, many property owners opt for lucrative unsubsidized renters from middle-income individuals and families.

Prince George's County was one of the few suburban areas where rare affordable housing opportunities were available. Prince George's County is a mostly middle-class, predominately African American county immediately east of Washington, D.C. The county's leadership and some residents were concerned about the influx of low-income families from the District and concerned about existing, privately owned low-income housing properties in the county. Former Prince George's County executive Wayne Curry complained that the District's public housing demolitions were resulting in an increased number of low-income families moving to the county, thus creating a greater demand for certain public services associated with the poor. In a meeting, Curry encouraged the District's former mayor Anthony Williams to consider the impact of demolitions on neighboring Prince George's County and beckoned other surrounding "communities to do their fair share" to accommodate alternative housing jurisdictional choices sought by the District's low-income families.[14] While the county could easily track housing-voucher assisted families moving from the District, the number of residents moving because of public housing demolitions was probably dwarfed by those who moved into the county because of private-market housing economic dislocation resulting from rising costs. Both Washington's mayor and Prince George's County executive had made commitments to strengthen their local economies. Mayor Williams's strategy, in part, included revitalizing low-income neighborhoods considered burdened by a dysfunctional opportunity structure and sometimes obsolete public housing projects. Likewise, Executive Curry was concerned about the county's image related to business development prospects and residential development.

The political leadership in the District's surrounding jurisdictions exercised a democratic leadership style seeking to conciliate two different objectives: that of optimal attainment of group goals and that of limited external controls on the actions of individuals. This conciliation is possible only if conditions for close collaboration between the leaders and the members exist or can be created. Conditions for close collaboration are enhanced when the distance between leadership and groups is narrowed by a common history, empathy, and active participation in goal setting and decision-making.[15] The expression of differing goals and housing policy orientations tailored by leaders to represent perceived needs of their jurisdiction demonstrates that the democratic leadership style was present. District of Columbia political leadership expressed interest in greater regional integration and burden-sharing consistent with a less politically potent and less wealthy area. Other surrounding jurisdictions expressed a tendency toward avoidance of regionalism in burden-sharing and exercising political leverage where available on a national and regional level to advance the collective goals consistent with the collegial leadership style in their jurisdictions.

HOMEOWNER INCENTIVES AND HOUSING PRESERVATION, REHABILITATION, AND PRODUCTION OMNIBUS AMENDMENT

Mayor Anthony Williams appointed Milton Bailey as director of the Housing and Community Development department in an effort to provide new leadership at the agency charged with developing important public-private partnerships for affordable housing. Bailey was the former director of the city's housing finance agency. During Bailey's stay at the District of Columbia Housing Finance Agency, the agency moved from $14 million in debt to $16 million in net worth. Also, Bailey's leadership was credited with expanding the agency's target areas for single- and multifamily loans to 82 percent of the District.

In his 2001 testimony before the City Council Committee on Economic Development, Bailey remarked, "Over the past two decades, the City lost many of its working class families."[16] The city had four thousand vacant housing units, and the real possibility of losing ten thousand affordable rental units due to having federal subsidies expire in five years. A goal of attracting 130,000 new residents was mentioned.

Bailey's testimony introduced the mayor's proposed "Housing Preservation, Rehabilitation, and Production Omnibus Amendment Act of 2001." The mayor's proposed bill countered two housing legislative proposals from the City Council related to homesteading and non-targeted tax incentives for employer-based homebuyer assistance to employees. The Omnibus Housing Act was a comprehensive package of incentives and assistance aimed at low- and middle-income renters and homebuyers. As housing policy legislation, the bill was considered the most significant of the past two decades. Its goals included preserving some 2,700 units of affordable housing, and building or rebuilding 4,300 units of housing for extremely low-, low-, and moderate-income families.[17] Councilperson Linda Cropp introduced legislation number B14-0167 on March 30, 2001, also called the Housing Preservation, Rehabilitation, and Production Omnibus Amendment Act of 2001, and Council passed it into law on January 8, 2002. In an editorial published by the National Association for Restoration of Pride in America's Capital, a writer described the bill as noteworthy as an effort to provide for affordable housing for low-income families but argued that the bill would further burden the District with a class of people who cost more in services than the taxes they pay and could attract more low-income residents stressed with the increasing housing costs in neighboring jurisdictions. Surrounding jurisdictions had consistently shown themselves uninterested in providing anything more than well-crafted housing policies designed to limit, where possible, infiltration of low-income residents from nearby jurisdictions, in particular the District of Columbia.

INSPECTING HOUSING

The *Washington Post*'s editorials acknowledged that "in the Washington area's white-hot housing market, the poor are getting squeezed. Tenants cling even to dilapidated units, fearing they won't be able to afford anything else."[18] A point highlighted in one of the editorials involved another housing policy being implemented in both the District and Montgomery County. Aggressive enforcement of housing code violations emerged as both a blessing and a difficulty. In some cases, it was suspected that landlords used deferred maintenance as a tool to encourage low-income tenants to move in order to reposition the real estate for higher-income tenants or condominium conversion. The District has conducted waves of major inspection pushes to address complaints from tenants and citizens concerned for better maintenance service. In 2008, the District's mayor, Adrian M. Fenty, announced the city plans to inspect all eleven thousand rental properties in an effort to launch a more comprehensive approach to improving the city's rental housing stock.[19] The results of the inspections were mixed; they sometimes resulted in encouraging landlords to make needed repairs. In other cases, the inspections resulted in new opportunities for ownership by tenants or dislocation of tenants. Efforts to raise the quality of housing have reached all the city's eight wards, including the Southeast Ward, which contains the city highest concentration of low-income families.

Another *Washington Post* editorial addressed the issue that many low-income residents were worried that District "officials intent on rebuilding the District's economic base are more concerned with attracting business and wealthy residents" than with preserving affordable housing.[20] The editorial compliments the District of Columbia City Council for targeting half the funding in the "housing production trust fund" included in the Omnibus Housing Act to residents earning less than half the area's median income. The trust fund was originally authorized in 1988, but not initially capitalized with significant funding until 2002 when $25 million was obtained from the sale of city property.

COMPREHENSIVE HOUSING STRATEGY TASK FORCE

The Comprehensive Housing Strategy Task Force created by the mayor and City Council in 2003 examined the trust fund, and concluded it was inadequate to address the scope of housing needs in their 2006 report. The Task Force estimated that the implementation of its major recommendations would require average expenditures of $399 million per year over the next fifteen years. This amount was almost twice the $202 million annual flow available from the 15 percent of the recordation tax designated in the Housing Act of 2002.[21] The Task Force recommended increasing the amount of the recordation tax dedicated to the Trust as one way to support its housing recommendations. The main focus of the strategy was to address steep housing prices by increasing private housing production while using subsidies, incentives, and regulatory controls to support production and preservation of affordable housing. Between 2005 and 2020, the strategy will be aimed at producing fifty-five thousand affordable housing units distributed throughout the city. City efforts were to result in both creating new production of nineteen thousand affordable housing units and preserving approximately thirty thousand affordable housing units.[22] The Task Force membership, nominated by Mayor Anthony Williams in 2004, was composed of a broad base, including the banking and financial community, developers, affordable housing advocates, low-income residents, and the District government.[23] The twenty-two people who served on the Task Force included co-chair Alice Rivlin, senior fellow and director, Greater Washington Research Program under the Brookings Institution, and co-chair Adrian Washington, president, Anacostia Waterfront Development Corporation (former president and CEO, Neighborhood Development Corporation).[24] The District's effort to establish a local trust fund was paralleled by a regional effort to provide a regional approach to the problem of soaring housing prices which were infecting the area.

REGIONAL HOUSING TRUST FUND

In 2002, before the city's Task Force was established, Washington, D.C., metropolitan area leadership attempted to set up a trust fund to address affordable housing as an inter-jurisdictional concern. The leaders of three core jurisdictions—the District's Mayor Williams, Montgomery County's Executive Douglas Duncan, and Alexandria's Mayor Kerry Donley—called on the federal government to appropriate $5 million in seed money for the Washington Area Housing Trust Fund.[25] The regional fund is run by the Washington Area Housing Partnership, a group focused on regional affordable solutions by soliciting funds from local governments in the region and from major employers such as the federal government, Lockheed Martin, Marriot, and others. From 2003 to 2005, the federal government provided approximately $1 million including earmarks sponsored by the Washington-area congressional delegation. The Washington Area Housing Trust Fund functions as a regional trust fund that provides funds for predevelopment, new construction, rehabilitation, bridge financing, and down-payment and closing-cost assistance for individual homebuyers. The fund's goals are to 1) increase affordable homes by providing loans, grants, and equity investments; 2) engage new corporate partnerships; 3) advocate for affordable housing needs and opportunities; and 4) encourage affordable housing as a means of connecting housing, jobs, and transportation.[26] This regional housing partnership was a rare project, given the propensity of jurisdictions to cling to localism out of prejudice and fear that such efforts might lead to proposals to increase inter-jurisdiction mobility of the District's concentration of African American low-income residents. In surrounding areas, local leadership faced resource constraints. Local housing advocates focused on lobbying City Council and the mayor to prioritize affordable housing challenges for a demographic group that would be considered solidly middle-class families in the District. In the surrounding jurisdictions professionals such as teachers, police officers, and retail managers cannot find housing in Alexandria, Virginia, or Rockville, Maryland.

ATTRACTING NEW RESIDENTS VITAL TO ECONOMIC STABILITY

Washington D.C., had its only unique challenge as articulated by the former mayor Anthony Williams in 2003 at the beginning of his second term. Mayor Williams set a goal to attract one hundred thousand new residents. The administration promised to make a concerted effort to target recruitment of residents from among the black middle-class residents that left the city for the suburbs. However, by 2003 an escalating trend of gentrification was already established. The majority of residents moving into the District were white middle-class individuals and families.[27] Many could identify with the somewhat antiquated term of the 1970s and 1980s as yuppies (young urban professionals). However, this new wave of yuppies was socially and economically different from the old group. They identified more readily with the new "hip-hop" urban culture. This new wave was more likely to have inherited substantial assets from firmly established middle-class parents and grandparents. In some cases, they may have been beneficiaries of the technology boom of the 1990s, also referred to as the "dot-com" bubble.

The period covering Mayor Williams's administration is the high watermark for the city's accelerated economic turnaround. Washington has always held a special attraction for commercial real estate interests over the past two decades. However, under the Williams administration, both commercial development and particularly housing development saw an unprecedented boom. Housing values in many communities—even some dominated by barred or boarded-up windows—soared to the point where political debate dwelled not on urban blight but on the perils of gentrification. A number of factors contributed to the boom. Low-mortgage interest rates and creative mortgage-financing instruments were factors. Another contributing factor was growth in personal wealth among a new generation of young adults intrigued by urban living along with growing transportation costs. The Williams administration provided a facelift to the city's image, bringing it closer to a comfort zone of some middle-class traditionalists less likely to see former Mayor Barry as a welcoming face of good governance and stability. The Barry administration suffered from a storm of media-manufactured perils, the associated dilemmas of internal neocolonialism, and real personal controversies. The Barry administration found itself caught in the dilemma of trying to meet years of pent-up demand for justice and equality for the District's working-class and poor residents while the local economy was limited and controlled by an external political structure that included Congress. The Williams administration grew the city investment climate and used the congressionally mandated Financial Control Board as a basis to subordinate popular demands to a neoconservative path to financial stability. Both mayors could count real estate interests as partners and substantial contributors.

PROPERTY TAXES

As property values sharply increased in the region, local government valuation and taxes increased as well. By 2005, property assessments in some Maryland counties increased as much as 40 percent or more. Thomas Branham, the District's chief assessor, said that the assessment increases in the city was comparable to those in the surrounding areas. Robert Reid of the Center for Housing Policy said that people at the lower end of the income range were experiencing an extreme challenge with choices limited to either commuting three hours or living in undesirable neighborhoods.[28] District policymakers aimed tax legislation at reducing the stress on low- and middle-income property owners. A year earlier in 2004, the City Council introduced two proposals for alleviating the tax burden on homeowners. One proposal would cap property tax bill increases to 10 percent per year. Another proposal would cap increases at 20 percent and change the homestead deduction from $30,000 to $50,000. The homestead deduction is the amount automatically excluded from the assessment. Analysis of the proposals indicated that the first tax relief proposal would provide a greater portion of relief to higher-value properties and homeowners living in the city's wealthier wards. Washington's wards 1, 2, and 3 can be counted as the higher-income wards. The second proposal provided for broader and deeper tax relief for low-income homeowners with lower-valued properties. Although lower-income families had properties with lower assessments, nonetheless, the relative increase in values and assessments resulting from the real estate boom was putting intense pressure on the financial viability of low-income seniors and families. In the District, approximately 55 percent of homes were valued under

$250,000. The financial impact extended to renters as well. Landlords passed the increases in property tax on to tenants, further stressing affordable housing. A salient issue for policymakers was that the District could not afford to fully fund the proposed tax relief. This was unfortunate in that it offered the greatest relief to low-income families and low-value properties that offered refuge for the renter pressed by increased rent related to property taxes. Tax relief for District property owners came with a price tag. Available estimates indicated that the District could afford to provide approximately $24 million in tax relief. The District's chief financial officer reported that in 2005 his projection was that $100 million might be available. This amount would be needed to support tax relief as well as a number of other competing prospective commitments. For the District policymakers, their alternatives regarding tax relief would be artificially restrained by the relationship with the national government, particularly the Congress, and its oversight, rather than the locally controlled electoral process as is the case in other state and local governments where large nonprofit or governmental institutions impact the tax base. Congress limited the District's effort to adopt measures such as commuter taxes or payments in lieu of taxes (PILOT) that might have provided adequate resources for more robust tax relief supporting affordable rental properties and homeownership. Tax relief is another brake on gentrification and banishment of low-income families.

RENT CONTROL POLICY

Rent control policy was another key component in the effort to maintain affordable housing in Washington, D.C. The District has one of the nation's most progressive rent control policies. Rent control legislation in Washington initially took effect in 1985 in what is considered the second generation of these programs. This second generation included Washington D.C., Boston, San Francisco, and Los Angeles. Then the major push for rent control was bolstered by a spiraling inflation rate and protection of those on fixed income, particularly the elderly.[29] Programs in some of these cities have been substantially modified or dismantled. Rent control was threatened in Washington in 1995 when the law was up for renewal. The city had lost a pro-tenant mayor in Sharon Pratt Kelly, but then presiding Mayor Marion Barry and the Council supported renewal. However, at that time the city was under a federally mandated financial control board overseeing the fiscal impact of any legislation under consideration.[30] In 2005, the City Council and mayor began consideration of an amendment and extension of the rent control legislation. After passage, the Rent Control Reform Amendment Act of 2006 went into effect in August of that year.[31] This legislation was generally considered a needed update to the policy that closed loopholes to exploitation by real estate interests and furthered rent control's original legislative intent. Two of the leading sponsors on the City Council were Jim Graham of Ward 1 and Phil Mendelson, an at-large member. Some affordable housing advocates still concluded that the amended rent control legislation was a step in the right direction, yet inadequate to address the many tenants and units affected by soaring rental costs that were outside of the legislative umbrella. Real estate interests such as the apartment owners and managers association believed the renewed policy was detrimental to the housing market. Shaun Pharr of the Apartment and Office Building Association of Metropolitan Washington remarked that rent control was a failed policy, but an enduring fact of life in D.C. Linda Couch of the National Low-Income Housing Coalition offered that in an environment of "neighborhoods gentrifying beyond the range of anyone's income," maintaining rent control and tenants rights is a way to assist.[32]

The program in the District provided two measures in response to growing increases in housing costs and gentrification. First, rent control legislation provided for stable, rational rent increases. This feature provided a hedge against rapid rent increases by limiting the increase to once a year. Then, rent increases were limited to an inflation index plus two percent. The feature discouraged real estate speculation in the city's affordable rental housing stock. Rent control primarily applies to housing units built before 1975.[33] Secondly, a unique feature of District rent control policy is "Right of First Refusal." This feature required landlords of buildings with four or more units to offer first to tenants the opportunity to purchase property being sold. Subsidized housing units are exempt from rental control. The District has housing units that are both federally subsidized and District-subsidized with both types being exempt from rent control. Federally subsidized units have been the most stable refuge for low-income workers and families in an unprecedented upward spiral of rent increases and development of high-rent units in the District.

HOUSING WITH PREDATORY AND SUBPRIME LENDING

In late 2007 and 2008, the nation began enduring a broad and deepening financial crisis spurred by predatory and subprime lending in the housing market. While the financial crisis affected citizens involved with an array of industries from financial services to the auto industry, those most impacted were and are typical renters and homeowners. Renters and homeowners living in properties financed by nontraditional mortgages were acutely impacted by the crisis. Lending practices experienced by many citizens became tantamount to usury and fraud after deregulation of the financial services industry. The deregulation of the financial services industry was orchestrated by the industry, its congressional supporters, and the Clinton and Bush administrations. The economic philosophy of "free market" capitalism reigned supreme as creative financing and esoteric financial instruments permeated segments of the market. Unsophisticated and more seasoned borrowers alike became victims of financing featuring adjustable rate mortgages, no documentation ("no-doc") loans, no down-payment, back-end loaded loans, balloon loans, and their variations.

Organizations that studied predatory lending practices found that predominantly African American communities appeared to be targeted by efforts to market these usury-based products. Washington, D.C., was hard hit by the crisis because of its demographic profile. New homeowners were lured into risky mortgages by the prospect of getting easy-in mortgages and a sparkling new condominium or townhome. Many existing low-income homeowners in Washington found these innovative financial products irresistible. For many years people have held dreams of homeownership as a means of establishing a base for wealth building. Those homeowners found using money from the home equity loans convenient and sometimes a necessity for the purpose of addressing repairs, education loans, medical necessities, car loans, or sometimes nonessential amenities. The loans were based on real and sometimes fictitious equity. A segment of appraisers aided predatory lenders by providing appraisals that were either overly optimistic or did not reflect a conservative approach prudent in a boom-to-bust real estate market. In certain cases, tradition underwriting criteria would have shown the borrowers could not sustain anticipated payments. Elderly low-income homeowners and homeowners living on low wage and fixed incomes were impacted. Low-income homeowners who inherited longtime family homes would have been among the victims of predatory lending practices.

Renters were not spared. Landlords and real estate investors were also subject to the foreclosure crisis infecting the housing market. In turn, tenants faced evictions and dislocation as a result of financing arrangements made by property owners and managers. A number of regions experienced an intense upswing in housing values. The housing market bubble and the escalation of property values had federal policy influences as well as local-market influences. Federal policy had its impact most significantly from Federal Reserve interest rate policy and Treasury Department mortgage banking regulation. The Federal Reserve Board of Governors, under Chairman Alan Greenspan's leadership, systematically established lower interest rates and maintained lower interest rates between 1987 and 2006.[34] The housing bubble and unsustainable value escalation were caused by a complex combination of historically low interest rates, predatory lending practices, immigration related demand, and a greedy exuberance in real estate speculation. The general direction of federal housing policy was a laissez-faire approach toward the housing market including lenders, brokers, investors, home seekers, and renters. The policy favored lax regulation and greatly favored finance companies and real estate interests. Finance businesses were among the top campaign contributors to presidential candidates in the 2000, 2004, and 2006 election campaigns.[35]

SUMMARY AND CONCLUSION

The District of Columbia's mayors and City Councils have predominately practiced a democratic leadership style in the area of housing policy. It can be argued that legislation and policy have not been robust enough to address the needs of the low-income and moderate-income families most of whom are African American. Real estate business interests are also seen by representatives as an important constituency contributing to the economic well-being of the jurisdiction. Some low- and moderate-income homeowners received significant financial benefits as a result of rising property values. Questions abound whether housing legislation and programmatic compromises have been sufficient to alleviate the banishing effect of gentrification and the real estate market boom.

The ability of the District's elected and appointed officials to address critical issues voiced by residents and affordable housing advocates is greatly affected by financial resource restraints and supportive federal policies and programs. District elected officials have often decried how the federal presence in the District affects its tax base, and therefore its ability to address local needs expressed through the democratic processes available to residents. In addition to the financial challenge of having a restrained tax base, the District uniquely faces political restraints to expanding revenues for affordable housing solutions. The District has long sought to implement a commuter tax like similarly situated jurisdictions where large proportions of the real estate inventory has a non-taxable institutional status. The District's attempts to implement a commuter tax have been consistently met with opposition from the congressional subcommittee in charge of oversight for the District of Columbia. The complexity of these structural and artificial constraints also constrains the exercise of democratic practice to the extent that the complexity of the federal and local relationship is less than transparent to the general public. District residents and citizen advocates often find it difficult to make the connection between national and local policy, particularly in areas assumed to be within the realm of local governance. Housing policy adds an additional layer of complexity because even fewer members of the general public are fully aware of the hidden federal hand in the housing market. This hidden federal hand influences mortgage interest rates, lender practices, and the availability of federal funding for affordable housing. The extent of the federal influence is not fully understood by many District residents. Compared to the District government, the breath of the federal government's ability to affect the real estate market is enormous. The federal influence on national, and therefore, local housing policy makes it critical that, for effective democratic participation, the District of Columbia have full representation in Congress. The District of Columbia's congressional representation would certainly impact the national policy leverage toward more progressive urban policies and programs aimed to increase affordable housing, interjurisdictional mobility, and the city's economic development.

Low- and moderate-income families have been experiencing tremendous economic pressure in the District of Columbia that has put in peril their right to shelter and freedom to enjoy a stable sanctuary. Over the past decade and a half, low- to moderate-income residents have been required to consider the limits of local democracy in the context of the power of the market and national government. The booming private housing market and other social and political factors have been influential in this effect. District of Columbia government policy has made efforts to ameliorate the impact on low- and moderate-income working families. The local government has at its command many of the tools available to both state and local governments elsewhere. However, without national government assistance, the District has a limited scale of economy compared to most states. The City Council members and mayors have put forth and implemented legislation and programs aimed at addressing the plight of many families forced to consider leaving the District to find affordable shelter. Some housing advocates argue that the efforts have been at best half-measures considering the depth of the housing crisis for low-income residents. The record indicates a level of programmatic responsiveness from the District government commensurate with measures undertaken by other large jurisdictions. The structure of the relationship with the national government is influential in limiting the scope of political options and financial resources available to address the housing situation. Even more influential and less accessible to local democratic authority are private market forces unleashed from national regulatory control and aided by a lack of national urban economic and housing policy.

The District's mayors have promulgated policies that have supported a local goal of lifting the city out of declining economic fortunes in part resulting from restraints on District revenue and national urban policy. Some policy emphases have been both complementary and counteractive to the goal of retaining low-income residents. Federally assisted housing in the form of public housing has afforded some District low-income residents the opportunity to weather the storm of a real estate boom. The District of Columbia Housing Authority, like many other large, urban, public housing agencies, worked with HUD to revitalize public housing through private-public partnerships to develop new housing featuring mixed-income tenancy and using a combination of public and private financing. Demolition of old public housing projects in Washington raised concerns from officials in neighboring Prince George's County that the District's housing policy encouraged assisted housing tenants to relocate, thereby burdening the County with their presence. The demolitions concerned housing advocates interested in abating displacement and gentrification. At the same time, the effort to revitalize public housing based on a new model improved the quality of public housing in the District. It also complemented economic and community development goals.

The structure of metropolitan governance, which can be inter-jurisdiction and inter-state, is set by Congress. It is administrated through the Council of Governments (COG) and Metropolitan Planning Organizations (MPOs) that direct regional planning, transportation funding, and coordination of public safety programs and, at the council's discretion, regional housing planning and programs. Washington's metropolitan area provides limited housing choices for low-income residents seeking affordable housing. The three Washington, D.C., area jurisdictions that have housing authorities are Prince George's County, Montgomery County, and the City of Alexandria. The majority of the members of the Washington Metropolitan Council of Governments do not have housing authorities thereby limiting inter-jurisdictional mobility for District residents and other jurisdictions with housing authorities. Residents in public housing are generally afforded the opportunity to transfer to other jurisdictions particularly with the housing choice voucher program. Jurisdictions surrounding the District have sought to narrowly tailor affordable housing programs to meet the needs of their own stressed middle- and working-class residents. In 2002, the region's leaders such as Mayor Williams, Montgomery County's Executive Douglas Duncan, and Alexandria's Mayor Kerry Donley set up a regional Washington Area Housing Trust which raised several million dollars for affordable housing projects. In the end, the trust fund never found the substantial financial support it sought from private employers or the national government. Lack of a coordinated regional effort further exaggerated the difficulty of low-income residents in the District. A Washington Area Housing Partnership was set up by the COG. The partnership focused mostly on educational programs and technical assistance on housing policy issues. While the Washington Metropolitan COG, like other regional metropolitan COGs, was set up to the address region's problems in a highly integrated area, the format, whether democratic or consensus decision-making, in many cases, fails to address issues that may be critical to central cities like the District. Some low-income families found themselves banished from the District and banned from some suburban communities by the high price of housing and unsupportive housing policies. Many central cities are not well served by the congressionally mandated structure of metropolitan governance. The District's full representation in Congress would likely provide an experienced voice to the consideration of more justifiable structures of democratic governance for regional bodies, related to the burden carried by central cities.

In the period between 2002 and 2008, the District government took a number of major steps toward addressing the housing crisis for low- and moderate-income families. Mayor Williams and the City Council passed the Housing Preservation, Rehabilitation, and Production Omnibus Amendment Act in 2002. The bill updated and expanded the city efforts toward preserving and creating affordable rental and homeownership units through incentives and assistance to residents and developers. A housing trust fund was established. In 2003, the mayor and City Council created a Comprehensive Housing Strategy Task Force to formulate a clearer view of the housing situation and develop a more coherent housing effort. The task force established benchmarks and resource objectives to address affordable housing. The group recommended that a $399 million annual expenditure was needed from the housing trust fund over fifteen years. Mayor Anthony Williams and the City Council were not able to fully fund the financial commitment needed to support the plan's recommendations. Mayor Adrian Fenty, who won election in 2007, has been criticized by housing advocates for not providing more support for housing as promised during the campaign. Mayor Fenty formerly served on the City Council and was a key member of the Housing Task Force. Mayor Fenty appointed Leslie Steen in 2007 as housing chief. A task force strategy recommendation was that a position such as housing chief was needed to perform high-level coordination. Ms. Steen resigned February 29, 2008, saying she was "not satisfied with the relevance and powers of the new position."[36] She indicated in her resignation letter that the position was not structured to allow her to play the role the task force had envisioned.

Other major measures the District of Columbia government implemented included property tax relief and rent control. Property tax relief was structured to help homeowners stay in their homes against the tide of escalating assessments due to gentrification, new condominium construction, and national housing and economic policy. Alternative property tax proposals were considered by the District. One approach was more beneficial for higher-value properties and their high-income owners. The other approach was for a deeper tax relief policy targeted for low-value properties and low-income residents. The District eventually adopted a moderated tax relief policy, given that the proposed approaches scored in 2005 by the city's chief financial officer were estimated to cost as much as $24 million. By 2008 the District had adopted tax relief capping increases at 10 percent per year, reducing the overall property tax rate, and increasing the homestead deduction. The measures lacked targeted relief for low- and moderate-income homeowners and low-income renters who are equally affected by soaring property values.

Rent control legislation was updated to limit rent increases. The policy applies to rental units built before 1975 and provides tenants with a first right of refusal when landlords with four or more units sell rental properties. The Rent Control Reform Amendment Act of 2006 was passed on May 2 of that year. The legislation eliminated rent ceilings but did not address newer units that have been developed. The Apartment and Office Owners Association spokesman Shaun Pharr vowed that expanding rent control to newer units would mean "World War III."[37] Rent control legislation in the District covers approximately one hundred thousand rental units.

The rental housing inspection program was one of the District policies that had dubious public appeal. The inspection program featured large-scale sweeps of low-income rental properties. Policymakers considered it a means to increase housing quality and enforce needed repairs to substandard rental properties. Some housing advocates expressed concern that the policy forced tenants out of units and provided landlords with a sound reason to remove low- and moderate-income tenants. Mayor Williams made part of his strategy to revitalize the District the objective to bring one hundred thousand new residents into the city. The objective seemed appropriate given that the District, like other many older central cities, suffered from an extensive housing vacancy and abandonment problem. The inspection policy along with the effort to attract new residents helped create a feeling of mistrust among some of the government's low-income constituents.

Adding to the numerous housing problems faced by low- and moderate-income families was the national housing crisis that came to prominence in 2008. The crisis was the culmination of federal deregulation of policies in the financial and mortgage industries. The lending system adopted practices that would be considered one of the greatest redistributions of wealth in American history. A major feature of the lending practices was predatory lending that preyed on low-, moderate-, and middle-income families by using usurious-loan terms that would result in foreclosure and property disenfranchisement.

The national housing foreclosure problem provides insight into the nature and limits of democracy for citizens in the District of Columbia as well as other local jurisdictions. The District of Columbia is a special case because it is the seat of the national government and, therefore, is a supernumerary factor influencing output of the democratic process. Congress's policy restraining the District's efforts to use certain revenue tools such as a commuter tax, which is otherwise available to similarly situated local governments, affects resources to support housing policy. National policies governing the housing market are far beyond the District's control and reach of Washington's citizens. At best the District of Columbia mayor and City Council can act to mitigate the effects, while its local democratic institutions are simultaneously limited by national policy and national market forces. Many low- and moderate-income families are being banished from the District of Columbia while the structure of opportunity for democratic participation toward effective policy is limited.

NOTES

1. Robert C. Smith, *Racism in the Post-Civil Rights Era, Now You See It, Now You Don't* (Albany: State University of New York Press, 1995), 29–30.

2. James McGrath, "Gentrification and Rent Control," OP-ED, *Washington Post*, October 3, 1998, A18.

3. Picture of Public and Assisted Housing, database published by U.S. Department of Housing and Urban Development, 1998

4. Daniela Deane, staff writer, "A New Face for Public Housing," Real Estate Section, *Washington Post*, May 8, 1999, Final Edition, G01.

5. Lyndsey Layton, staff writer, "High Hopes, and Higher Home Prices, in Anacostia; Development Is Part of Plan to Diversify, Mend Worn D.C. Area," *Washington Post*, October 19, 2006, A1.

6. Linda Fosburg, Susan J. Popkin, and Gretchen P. Locke, *An Historical and Baseline Assessment of HOPEVI, Volume I, Cross-site Report*, Prepared by Abt Associates for HUD, July 1996.

7. Matthew Cardinale, "Public Housing on the Chopping Block in the US," *Atlanta Progressive News* from Inter Press Service, August 30, 2007, www.atlantaprogressivenews.com/news/0218.html (accessed January 21, 2009).

8. Eric Alterman, *What Liberal Media? The Truth About Bias and The News* (New York: Perseus Book Group, 2003), 81–97.

9. William J. Wilson, *When Work Disappears: The World of the New Urban Poor* (New York: Random House, 1996), 201.

10. Joseph Cooper and David W. Brady, "Institutional Context and Leadership Style: The House from Cannon to Rayburn," *The American Political Science Review*, Vol. 75, No. 2 (June 1981), 411–25.

11. "State of the Nation's Housing, 1999," Joint Center for Housing Studies, Harvard University, Boston, 1999, 6; "State of the Nation's Housing, 2001," Joint Center for Housing Studies, Harvard University, Boston, 13–14.

12. Daniela Deane, staff writer, "D.C. Region Leads U.S. In New Home Permits: Industry Set Records in '98, Study Shows," *Washington Post*, Final Edition, June 21, 1999, A10.

13. Henrietta Warfield, Arlington Co. Republican Party chairperson, and Michael D. Lane, former Republican candidate, Arlington Co. Board of Supervisors, OP-ED, "Close to Home," *Washington Post*, Final Edition, Sunday, April 26, 1998, C08.

14. Carol D. Leoning and Paul Schwartzman, "Housing Crisis; Anger Over D.C. Demolitions; Curry Says Pr. George's Is Suffering," Metro Section, *Washington Post*, Final Edition, March 29, 2000, B01.

15. Léon Dion, "The Concept of Political Leadership: An Analysis," *Canadian Journal of Political Science*, Vol. 1, No. 1, Canadian Political Science Association (March 1968), 14, www.jstor.org/stable/3231692, accessed July 27, 2009.

16. Milton J. Bailey, "Testimony of Milton J. Bailey, Director, Department Of Housing and Community Development, before the Committee on Economic Development," June 11, 2001.

17. National Association to Restore Pride in the American Capital (NARPAC), Editorials, July, 25, 2005, www.narpac.org/EDIT02.HTM, accessed August 17, 2007.

18. "Decent Place to Call Home," *Washington Post*, editorial, A22, Final Edition, July 14, 2000.

19. Debbie Cenziper, "D.C. Plans to Inspect All Rent Housing, Proactive Tack Part of Crackdown on Negligent Landlords," Metro/District Section, *Washington Post*, Final Edition, B01, June 25, 2008.

20. *Washington Post*, Final Edition, editorial, B06, January 6, 2002

21. Thomas G. Kingsley and Barika X. Williams, "Policies for Affordable Housing in the District of Columbia: Lessons from Other Cities," The Urban Institute, January 2007 (submitted to Fannie Mae Foundation), 3.

22. Comprehensive Housing Strategy Task Force, "Homes for an Inclusive City: A Comprehensive Strategy for Washington, D.C.," April 2006, 38–39.

23. Mayor Anthony A. Williams to Linda W. Cropp, chairperson, District of Columbia City Council, letter dated March 14, 2004.

24. Ibid.

25. Roger K. Lewis, "Affordable Housing Fund Is a Start, but It Needs a Helping Hand," under Real Estate, "Shaping the City," *Washington Post*, Final Edition, H03, September 21, 2002.

26. Karen Sibert, Metropolitan Washington Council of Governments, Press Release, "Washington Area Housing Trust Fund Grants First Loan," November 5, 2003, www.mwcog.org/news/press/detail.asp?NEWS_ID=71.

27. Craig Timberg, "Williams Aims To Be Mayor of a Bigger D.C.: Attracting Residents Is Goal As 2nd Term Begins Today," *Washington Post*, Final Edition, January 2, 2003, A1.

28. Tim Craig, "Md. Home Valuations Increase Sharply; D.C., Va. Expecting Double-Digit Jump," *Washington Post*, January 6, 2005, A01.

29. Richard Arnott, "Rent Control" in *The New Palgrave Dictionary of Economics and the Law*, ed. Paul Newman (Basingstoke, Hampshire: Macmillan, September 1997), 3.

30. Karen Cerasco, "Spotted Owl, Snail Darter and . . . Rent Control, Is Rent Control Heading for Extinction?" Shelterforce Online, National Housing Institute, March/April 1995, www.nhi.org/online/issues/80/spotowl.html, accessed October 10, 2008.

31. Sara Gebhardt, "Getting a Handle on the District's Rent Control Changes," *Washington Post*, August 19, 2006, T09.

32. Eric M. Weiss, "Rent Control Extension Finds Backing; Council Members Propose Measures to Regulate District Landlords," Metro Section, *Washington Post*, Final Edition, January 19, 2005, B01.

33. "What You Should Know About Recent Control in the District of Columbia," pamphlet, District of Columbia, Department of Consumer and Regulatory Affairs (n.d.).

34. Board of Governors, Federal Reserve System, www.federalreserve.gov/bios/boardmembership.htm, accessed November 2, 2008.

35. Center for Responsive Politics, Campaign Contributions Database at Open Secrets.org.

36. Jonanthan O'Connell, staff reporter, "D.C. Mayor Fenty's Housing Chief Quits, Says She Was 'Marginalized,'" *Washington Business Journal*, March 6, 2008. washington.bizjournals.com/washington/stories/2008/03/03/daily43.html, accessed March 18, 2009.

37. Eric M. Weiss, staff writer, "D.C. Rent Ceilings Set to Come Down," *Washington Post*, May 3, 2006, A1.

BIBLIOGRAPHY

Books

Alterman, Eric. *What Liberal Media? The Truth About Bias and The News*. New York: Perseus Book Group, 2003

Arnott, Richard. "Rent Control." *The New Palgrave Dictionary of Economics and the Law*, ed. Peter Newman. Basingstoke, Hampshire: Macmillan, 1997.

Smith, Robert C. *Racism in the Post-Civil Rights Era, Now You See It, Now You Don't*. Albany: State University of New York Press, 1995.

Wilson, William J., *When Work Disappears: The World of the New Urban Poor*. New York: Random House, 1996.

Journals

Cooper, Joseph, and David W. Brady, "Institutional Context and Leadership Style: The House from Cannon to Rayburn," *The American Political Science Review*, Vol. 75, No. 2 (June 1981), 411–25.

Dion, Léon, "The Concept of Political Leadership: An Analysis," *Canadian Journal of Political Science*, Vol. 1, No. 1, Canadian Political Science Association (March 1968).

Newspapers and News Online

Atlanta Progressive News, www.atlantaprogressivenews.com/news
National Association to Restore Pride in the America Capital (NARPAC)
Washington Business Journal
Washington Post

Public Documents

Bailey, Milton J. "Testimony of Milton J. Bailey, Director, Department Of Housing and Community Development, before the Committee on Economic Development" June 11, 2001.
Cerasco, Karen. "Spotted Owl, Snail Darter and . . . Rent Control, Is Rent Control Heading for Extinction?" Shelterforce Online, National Housing Institute, March/April 1995.
Comprehensive Housing Strategy Task Force, "Homes for an Inclusive City: A Comprehensive Strategy for Washington, D.C.," April 2006.
Fosburg, Linda, Susan J. Popkin, and Gretchen P. Locke. *An Historical and Baseline Assessment of HOPEVI, Volume I, Cross-site Report*. Prepared by Abt Associates for HUD, July 1996.
District of Columbia, Department of Consumer and Regulatory Affairs, "What You Should Know About Recent Control in the District of Columbia," pamphlet.
Federal Reserve System, Board of Governors, Membership List from webpage.
Kingsley, Thomas G., and Barika X. Williams, "Policies for Affordable Housing in the District of Columbia: Lessons from Other Cities," The Urban Institute, January 2007 (submitted to Fannie Mae Foundation).
National Association to Restore Pride in the America Capital, (NARPAC), Editorials, July 25, 2005, www.narpac.org/EDIT02.HTM, accessed 4:10 p.m., August 17, 2007.
Sibert, Karen, Metropolitan Washington Council of Government, Press Release, "Washington Area Housing Trust Fund Grants First Loan," November 5, 2003.
"State of the Nation's Housing, 1999," Joint Center for Housing Studies, Harvard University, Boston, 1999.
Williams, Anthony A. to Linda W. Cropp, chairperson, District of Columbia City Council, letter dated March 14, 2004.

Databases

Center for Responsive Politics, Campaign Contributions Database at OpenSecrets.org
U.S. Department of Housing and Urban Development, Picture of Public and Assisted Housing Database

10

Democracy and Its Impact on Rehabilitative Resources in the District of Columbia

Kevin L. Glasper

INTRODUCTION

Crime in the District of Columbia continues to be a significant public policy issue. It always seems to be one of the top policy issues along with improving education, affordable housing, and unemployment. One of the first mayoral actions that newly elected D.C. mayor Adrian Fenty performed on January 2, 2007, was the appointment of a new D.C. police chief, Cathy Lanier. Washington, D.C., has a majority African American population with some of the most highly successful and educated blacks in the country. There is also the criminal element that confronts the nation's capital resulting in high rates of criminal activity and the need to adequately prepare ex-offenders and D.C. residents alike for prisoners' release.

Washington, D.C., is a city that has a unique political alignment unlike any other urban location when it comes to federalism. It is a city that includes both local and federal political dynamics because it is home to the U.S. capital. However, federal power does not always translate into local resources for deprived D.C. citizens. For example, many ex-offenders from the District of Columbia return from prison to the area each year without adequate preparation to function sufficiently in society. This study addresses the administrative services of the Court Services and Offender Supervision Agency (CSOSA), a federal program, and how it works with some other D.C. local government agencies to provide access for the distribution of rehabilitative resources to African American male ex-offenders reentering D.C. communities. CSOSA is a federal executive branch agency responsible for parole and probation services in the District of Columbia.[1] I argue that the inadequate or restricted distribution of rehabilitative resources for African American males

181

can be attributed to three key components: 1) institutional racism in the D.C. prison system, 2) a tightly controlled federal judicial system, and 3) the lack of strong family support among African American families which leads to limited understanding and restricted access to rehabilitative resources.

Ex-offender reentry is the process through which an individual goes to prison and returns, trying to establish a crime-free life, reconnect with family, and contribute to his or her community.[2] The objective here is to determine what local and federal resources have been used to prevent individuals from returning to prison. This chapter examines the following critical areas: (1) the D.C. rehabilitative process and its resources, i.e., housing, employment, education, health benefits, and so on; (2) the type of crimes committed by individuals that receive the most resources for rehabilitation; and (3) the most effective rehabilitative resources used to curtail reentry back to jail. The methodology used for this study consisted of a comparative data analysis of secondary statistics and a critical analysis of the literature and other studies and reports provided on the subject matter.

DEMOCRACY AT THE LOCAL LEVEL

In an urban area that is predominantly African American, citizens are heavily impacted by regressive policies or the lack of effective programs that can assist them. In addition to the political layout of the city, Washington, D.C., is similar to other large metropolitan areas in that it has multiple classes of African American citizens, including the upper echelon, the working class, and the lower class, that coexist in one city within blocks of one another. However, the working class and the poor are more heavily impacted by the inept capability of both local and federal government officials to work together to solve common problems like properly preparing the release of ex-offenders back into the city. Some of the most highly problematic and publicized national policy issues are even more perplexing to resolve in Washington, D.C. This is partly due to the breech in the democratic process with limitations to home rule. A prime example of this inadequacy in the democratic process is demonstrated in the D.C. criminal justice process.

Washington, D.C., embodies the utmost in democratic authority and power in terms of its governmental structure and geographical location. D.C. local government often has the most inadequate political and structural means of obtaining adequate resources to combat the most common urban problems. In this regard, there seems to be no advantage to being a resident of the District of Columbia in close proximity to the federal government as compared to any other U.S. city. Symbolically, citizens can easily make the argument that they reside in the most powerful city in the United States and the world. Neverthe-less, attempting to look for practical policy solutions to resolve the most com-mon urban problems resulting in a distribution of resources provided by the federal government transferred down to the local government causes one to take a closer look into how effective the democratic transfer of power works in the District of Columbia.

Like most cities, Washington, D.C., has to contend with urban decay and gentrification that adds to the skyrocketing housing costs, alarming rates of crime, a biased criminal justice system, high unemployment rates, and an ed-ucational system where students often do not meet national standards. Many of the problems are certainly interrelated. For example, usually if there are pockets of high unemployment in a community then you will probably find high crime rates in that same community as well. If the educational system has major challenges then you can also discover that unemployment rates will be impacted in the area. Most people who live in Washington, D.C., as well as outside the beltway area can hardly understand how a national capital city seems to always lack adequate resources in the above areas particularly for communities of color. Although any one of the above areas would make for an interesting study of how democracy has impacted policy implications or a lack thereof in the District, this study only focuses on the District of Columbia's efforts to rehabilitate its African American male ex-offender population.

An ideal democracy should provide adequate, effective and equitable distribution of rehabilitation programs for its citizens, in this case African American males and particularly for those who have committed crimes that are nonthreatening to our society. African American men between the ages of eighteen and thirty seem to be easy targets for the criminal justice system in most urban areas across the United States. There are still a host of criminal justice discrepancies that potentially frame or trap young black men in the judicial system such as racial profiling, police brutality, and excessive drug sentencing laws.

Young African American males are more apt to come in contact with the police on a daily basis and can potentially become a victim of one of these discrepancies. Frequently, a young black male is pulled over by police for just driving down the street or for being in the wrong neighborhood. He is more likely to be subjected to a police search after the stop than any other group of people with the exception of Hispanic males. He is also more likely to experi-ence police brutality if the situation escalates. According to Kenneth Meeks, "the practice of racial profiling became institutionalized through a 1986 Drug Enforcement Agency Program called Operation Pipeline, which trained over 27,000 police officers in forty-eight participating states."[3] The worst part was that over the next ten years a series of Supreme Court decisions fueled the practice by allowing the police to use traffic stops as a pretext to fish for evidence of wrongdoing.[4]

Issues of racial profiling and police brutality are more severe in areas where a high concentration of black males and white officers come in contact, as in cities like Washington, D.C., New York, and Los Angeles. Furthermore, a 2002 Justice Department report on racial disparities in policing showed that African American males, as compared to white and Hispanic males, have a greater chance of being harassed after a stop. Harassed means that African American males may be threatened force or put in handcuffs by police. The study showed that African American males have a 5.8 percent chance of being arrested as compared to a 5.2 percent chance for Hispanics and a 2 percent chance for whites.[5] This same report also showed that blacks were exposed to threats or force by the police 2.7 percent of the time as compared to 2.4 percent for Hispanics and 0.8 percent for whites.[6] Also, handcuffs were used on African Americans 6.4 percent of the time, 5.6 percent of the time on Hispanics, and 2 percent of the time on whites.[7]

Cities that have a majority black population cannot be taken for granted in terms of having good policing by establishing better relationships between the black community and law enforcement and also by trying to find better ways to reduce crime without creating suspicious and hostile relations. Some black citizens have committed violent crimes and should be incarcerated. Majority black cities like Washington, D.C., should not become so marginalized that lawmakers conclude that the criminal discrepancies are unwarranted because one cannot possibly claim racial profiling or police brutality in a city that has a majority population of African Americans. American cities have been experiencing a high volume of crime because of the growing number of gangs, the expansion of drug abuse, and the lack of quality social programs that assist ex-offenders returning home to their communities. In most urban cities, correlations exist among those who have a limited education, and high rates of unemployment and crime. One should not assume that every person that has a limited or poor education is unemployed or commits a crime, but studies have shown that in some cases the three main components that are usually interrelated with high rates of incarceration include lack of education or inadequate job skills, unemployment, and a criminal element.

D.C. had problems managing and overseeing its overcrowded prison population and local officials decided to allow the federal government to preside over its prison system back in 1997. Prior to this federal intervention, the city was burdened with some of the costs for housing its prisoners at the Lorton Prison in northern Virginia. Limited space also became a problem at the Lorton Prison. After federal involvement a decade ago, the Federal Bureau of Prisons was given authority to find locations for D.C. offenders wherever space was available. A federally run program does not automatically guarantee efficiency or improvements, but it usually does mean tighter governmental controls. The federal takeover of D.C. prisoners resulted in decisions on the confinement, drug treatment, rehabilitation, sentence duration, and conditions of parole for D.C. felons resting solely with the federal government.[8] District residents have no voice regarding the treatment of their friends and loved ones in this prison system or in how the offenders will be prepared to return to society after serving their sentences.[9]

CHALLENGES OF THE D.C. CRIMINAL JUSTICE SYSTEM

The D.C. criminal justice system has several organizations that are involved in its criminal justice process that include both D.C. local agencies and federal agencies. The D.C. agencies that receive local funds that are involved in the process are the Metropolitan Police Department, the Office of Corporation Counsel, the Department of Corrections (DOC), and the Office of the Medical Examiner. On the federal side the agencies involved include the Office of U.S. Attorney for D.C., Bureau of Prisons (BOP), the U.S. Marshals Service, U.S. Parole Commission, the Court Services and Offender Supervision Agency for D.C. (CSOSA), and the D.C. Pretrial Services Agency. There are some D.C. agencies that are federally funded which include the D.C. Superior Court, the Public Defender Service, and the Office of the Corrections Trustee. According to a General Accounting Office report, the D.C. criminal justice system needs better coordination among the various agencies that are involved the process.[10]

The D.C. Department of Corrections (DOC) is the local organization that oversees the safety, security, and human confinement of pretrial detainees and sentenced misdemeanant prisoners. The Department of Corrections received data between October 1, 2007, and March 31, 2008, that was published in a report in April 2008 about their inmate population. The report provides statistical data on the D.C. prison population that include various components of the D.C. prison administrative and correctional process. However, emphasis is placed on only the specific components that are relevant to this study, including the following percentages of the intake and release of inmates, age distribution of inmates, inmate population by race, offenses by most serious active charge of inmates, and the length of stay for inmates in custody. According to the D.C. Department of Corrections statistical study, 90.4 percent of the male inmate population is African American, 4.7 percent is Hispanic, 2.6 percent is white,

1.1 percent is considered other, and 1.1 percent is not declared.[11] The DOC study further acknowledges:

> The category "other" includes Asians and those who have declared their race as other. Those who have not declared a race are reported as not declared. Blacks are overrepresented compared to the DC population which is 60 percent Black. Whites and Asians are under-represented compared to the DC population which is 30 percent White and more than 2 percent Asian.[12]

The percentages show an overwhelming number of African American males that are incarcerated in the D.C. jail system as compared to males of other races in the Washington, D.C., area.

Another main component of this study is its scrutiny of the age distribution of the male inmates. For example, only 9 percent of males under the age of twenty-one are incarcerated. In the twenty-one to thirty age range, 36 percent of males are incarcerated; the thirty-one to forty age range reported only 22 percent of males; forty-one to fifty only 23 percent; fifty-one to sixty only 9 percent; and over the age of sixty-one only reported 1 percent.[13] The median age of male inmates is 33.13 years.[14] These numbers indicate that as the African American male gets older, the percentages of inmates incarcerated are lower with the exception of those under twenty-one. It is not clear from reviewing the report, but the under twenty-one age group at 9 percent could mean that the data only reflect the adult population numbers and not the juvenile figures which could be much higher than 9 percent if one includes the seventeen to twenty-one age population. The percentage rate among those under twenty-one and the fifty-one to sixty age group is the same at 9 percent. The over sixty-one group has a 1 percent incarceration rate, indicating that as the inmates get older the number significantly decreases, which could also indicate that 9 percent is a more reliable number for the fifty-one to sixty group than for the under twenty-one group because of the unknown juvenile numbers that are not provided in the report.

DISTRICT OF COLUMBIA INCARCERATION PROBLEMS
AND PLANS FOR A COLLECTIVE APPROACH

According to the U.S. Department of Justice, more than eight thousand previously incarcerated persons from federal prisons have returned to the District in the last four years seeking a new start.[15] This situation happens annually in the District and most of the ex-offenders are not adequately prepared to reenter society. Some of these ex-offenders are released to an organization called the Court Services and Offender Supervision Agency

(CSOSA). This agency was created to work with D.C. governmental officials and the criminal justice system. CSOSA also has responsibility for increasing public safety and crime prevention programs while reducing recidivism. CSOSA also works to reduce rearrests, improve education levels, increase employment rates, and reduce drug use among the population it serves.[16] It does this in a partnership effort with a host of other local governmental agencies such as the D.C. Department of Health, Department of Employment Services, and so on. CSOSA also works with the church and nonprofit community in the D.C. area.

CSOSA has an instrumental role in providing D.C. rehabilitative services to ex-offenders through multiple functions and services. The Community Supervision Services (CSS) division of the Court Services and Offender Supervision Agency is responsible for the delivery of parole and probation services in the District of Columbia for offenders sentenced by the D.C. Superior Court.[17] The Community Supervision Services division has a total staff of 581, including four hundred community supervision officers (CSOs, also called parole/probation agents or parole/probation officers in other jurisdictions).[18] There is an administrative overload when one considers the ratio between CSOs and ex-offender cases. For instance, the total caseload at CSS is 15,284 offenders and the average offender-CSO ratio is fifty cases to one in the general supervision units, including those concerned with domestic violence, substance abuse, mental illness, and sexual offenses.[19]

The federal government control hinders progress for the ex-offenders receiving rehabilitative resources in some areas. For example, ex-offenders are restricted from getting Pell grants to go to school, cannot live in public housing, and are limited from applying for certain jobs.[20] Most are restricted from having the right to vote and obtaining certain jobs. These restrictions prevent the progress that ex-offenders often need to make in order to become more productive citizens in society. Employment restrictions were lifted. In 2004, D.C. councilwoman Kathy Patterson (D-Ward 3) sponsored the Omnibus Public Safety Ex-Offender Self-Sufficiency Reform Act that lifted restrictions that otherwise prevented ex-offenders from obtaining licenses to work as asbestos workers, barbers, cosmetologists, commercial bicycle operators, electricians, funeral directors, operating engineers, plumbers/gasfitters, refrigeration and air-conditioning mechanics, and steam engineers.[21]

In addition to the restrictions, the social stigma that ex-offenders have to contend with does not help with their confidence and sometimes allows them to return to the same type of lifestyle which causes them to easily become repeat offenders. Some ex-offenders have even developed the mindset that it is almost better remaining in or returning to prison, where they at least have a bed and regular meals that they can rely on. Once they are out of prison, the minimum of food and a place to sleep become uncertainties if they do not have access to adequate resources and a strong family support system.

While there is federal assistance, the majority of rehabilitative services are provided by the District of Columbia's local government. Some of these services include drug treatment, job placement, health and mental health initiatives, and so forth.[22] The D.C. government has also partnered with nonprofit organizations to help with the provision of specific services to ex-offenders. The majority of D.C.'s offender population has a history of substance abuse estimated at 75 percent.[23] Approximately 30 percent of D.C. offenders have temporary housing arrangements. Many have complex issues, like mental illness or medical problems.[24] The correlation between substance abuse and criminal behavior is usually an important marker for someone who needs substance abuse treatment. Despite the fact that incarceration is a unique opportunity to treat offenders with substance abuse problems, most correctional facilities are unable to meet the need for substance abuse treatment.[25] Resources are limited and often costly, but many groups have joined forces to offset some of the costs and because they are more effective when working together.

Former mayor Anthony Williams, local public officials, and other local organizations joined forces to address the problem of prison recidivism by establishing a comprehensive plan to combat this issue. In October of 2002, Williams created the Ex-Offender Reentry Steering Committee. The main objective was to determine the appropriate method between the Reentry Strategy and the Memorandum of Understanding guiding the use of funds granted to the city under the Serious and Violent Offender Reentry Initiative.[26] Five working groups in the District of Columbia were organized to develop a comprehensive action plan with a community-based perspective. The workgroup action plan provides a road map to address important safety concerns by improving the planning and continuity of services that are necessary for offenders to return from prison and establish successful, productive lives in the community.[27] This comprehensive action plan is illustrative of a unique intergovernmental relationship that involves both local and federal involvement.

A point of contention regarding the D.C. prison system is that although most of the services are provided by the local government, the federal government assumes control of its prisoners. This means that the federal government can provide more funding to D.C. for rehabilitating ex-offenders, but it can also influence how federal dollars are spent which can have an impact on the outcome of rehab programs. Federal intervention also means tighter controls over the prison system.

TREATMENT OF D.C. INMATES AT
RIVERS CORRECTIONAL INSTITUTION

Findings have shown disparities in the treatment of D.C. inmates as compared to other inmates at prisons where D.C. inmates are housed. There are discrepancies in the treatment as well as the accessibility of resources depending on the location of the prison. Some prisons have better resources and are more organized than others. In other words, the more organized prisons usually have scheduled activities for the inmates that provide more structure and discipline for their lives. The lack of structure or organization at a prison impacts how effective the rehabilitative programs will be for the offender. Some D.C. inmates are incarcerated in various prisons in North Carolina, Ohio, Florida, West Virginia, and Texas.[28] According to the U.S. Bureau of Prisons, there are approximately one thousand D.C. inmates housed in the Rivers Correctional Institution, a private North Carolina prison.[29] The inadequacies of the Rivers Correctional Institution were discovered by the bureau's director, Harley G. Lappin, and Delegate Eleanor Holmes Norton (D-D.C.) after receiving complaints for several years from inmates, their families, and prisoner advocates.[30] The complaints centered on the need for the institutional standards to be improved and to have resources comparable to other prison institutions. Washington, D.C., inmates are sometimes transferred to this prison location because of limited space in D.C. and other areas.

According to Delegate Norton, the problem does not stop in North Carolina. She contended that the seven thousand D.C. inmates in seventy-five institutions nationwide get second-class treatment compared with the rest of the two hundred thousand inmates under federal control.[31] Norton evaluated several prisons and their organizational effectiveness in terms of treatment and the rehabilitation of D.C. prisoners. She compared the River's Institution with a federally funded prison in Cumberland, Maryland. Regarding Rivers, she stated that "inmates had too much unproductive free time. At Cumberland, programming was more organized, with inmates shuttling from one event to the next."[32] Another major distinction between D.C. inmates and other inmates is that at Rivers, the D.C. inmates were held alongside immigrants who were serving their time before being deported to their home countries. Those inmates often are not offered the same programs in prisons as U.S. citizens.[33]

Another finding of Lappin and Norton was the physical location of D.C. offenders located near the immigrants who do not receive the same type of programs slated for U.S. citizens. What is not clear is whether this was a temporary location for D.C. prisoners or was part of marginalization and institutional racism that exist in the judicial system for D.C. prisoners. The problem becomes even more burdensome if offenders do not have family members who possess the resources to fight against the criminal justice discrepancies. Those offenders who lack the necessary resources to fight against the system and family members who will follow up to hold law enforcement officials accountable usually become victims of judicial and legal neglect. This also translates into prisoners receiving poor or inadequate rehabilitative resources.

Lappin and Norton also discovered that nonviolent federal offenders get a year off their sentence if they complete a five-hundred-hour drug treatment program.[34] However, prisoners serving time for D.C. offenses get no such consideration, even though the D.C. government passed a law two years ago that said they deserved the time off.[35] The D.C. law sought to grant this one-year reduction for nonviolent offenders who had demonstrated good behavior and also if they were able to complete the five-hundred-hour drug treatment program by remaining free of drug use. The premise is that for good behavior and the completion of the drug treatment program the incentive for the nonviolent offender is a sentence reduced by one year.

The complaints by the inmates and their families coupled with the findings by Delegate Norton about the conditions of the D.C. inmates speak to a couple of issues worth noting here. First, it appears that D.C. inmates are not afforded the same type of treatment as their counterparts from other parts of the country. Does this mean that inmates from D.C. are considered more dangerous or is it because they come from a majority African American city that lacks the political controls to demand improvements to the system? It also speaks to the distant physical location of D.C. inmates. In other words, if you are a D.C. inmate who is transferred to a prison outside of Washington lacking timely, efficient inspections and reviews of the prison system, there is a greater likelihood for mistreatment of inmates.

NATIONAL IMPLICATIONS OF PRISON POPULATIONS

The issues of strict sentencing laws, overcrowding of jails and prisons, the increase in funding to build more prisons, and the privatization of prisons in the United States have had an impact on rates of incarceration. These conditions will inevitably continue to impact how efficient and expeditiously individuals are rehabilitated to return to society. A great deal of planning went into the incarceration of violators of the law, but it appears that very little planning went into developing an exit strategy to adequately rehabilitate those individuals who would be returning home. According to the Pew Center on the States, for the first time in U.S. history, more than one of every one hundred adults is in jail or prison.[36] The report stated that while one in thirty men between the ages of twenty and thirty-four is behind bars, for black males it is one in nine.[37] This implies that African American men have a greater likelihood of being incarcerated even for crimes that are low risk and nonviolent than men of other races. This idea alone has other negative consequences that adversely impact the black community such as the burden on the black family of removing the head male figure and reducing the number of eligible voters in the black community even after they have served their time. The burden on the black family is twofold; first, it takes away another potential income earner for the family, and second, it removes the black father from the wife and children for other protection and child-rearing needs. One exception is Hispanic men, whose incarceration rate is comparabale to that of African American men.

The study conducted by the Pew Center also has international ramifications because it found that the United States incarcerates more people than any other nation, far more than the more populous China where 1.5 million people are behind bars. It said that the U.S. also is the leader in inmates per capita (750 per 100,000 people), ahead of Russia (628 per 100,000) and other former Soviet bloc nations which round out the top ten.[38] In *Criminalizing a Race*, Charshee C. L. McIntyre discusses the historical perspective on crime as it relates to African Americans. She argues the following:

> The portrait that the African repository and like minded publications reinforced in the national mentality imprinted the idea that African Americans represent an inherently criminal race. So, it is not surprising that many of the prominent white leaders turned from the colonization project to developing the modern penitentiary system, which they predictably began with a disproportionate number of African-American inmates.[39]

McIntyre is referring to the dominant American cultural perspective of the African American community, with black males in particular being perceived as violent criminals. This persistent perception has plagued black communities and has created a very unstable and hostile relationship between blacks and law enforcement communities. For example, in most urban areas blacks also have to contend with issues of police brutality, racial profiling, or driving while black. This is largely because the perception held by the dominant culture is that blacks are more prone to commit crimes than other groups. Such a presumption is especially harmful to persons who have a history of marginalization and unjust discrimination.[40] This is harmful because such a group of people seem to always become the poster group for criminal behavior based on perceptions held by the dominant culture even when some incidents are discovered to be isolated cases. Howard

McGary argues that these negative police perceptions regarding certain groups can be attributed in part to the way in which police view their role in the community.[41] For instance, if police believe that the perception held by the community is positive, then this can encourage them to respond to the community in a nonthreatening or nonsuspicious manner. Their role in these communities appears to be one of a helper or to restore order in the community. On the other hand, if they think that their perception is one of contempt or untrustworthiness, then instead of attempting to change this community perception the police will sometimes respond in a negative way to the community. McGary's argument further supports the historical claim that the police community and the African American community have not maintained a healthy respect for one another.

There are several ways prisoner reentry affects the public safety of society. In some cases, the community fears the release of ex-offenders because most prefer not to have halfway houses built in their neighborhoods. Second, there are concerns by citizens regarding the health of the community, as ex-offenders include those inflicted with sexually transmitted diseases, mental illness, and drug and alcohol dependency. Other community concerns highlight issues surrounding reincarceration.

Over the past two decades, there have been several public instances of police brutality and racial profiling that have caught the attention of the national media. For example, in 1992, D.C. public defender Robert Wilkins, an African American male, was stopped by a Maryland state police officer while with three other African American males on the way to his grandfather's funeral in Chicago.[42] It was only later that Wilkins learned he'd been stopped because of a written profile (prepared by the Maryland State Police) that described him perfectly—a black male in a rental car.[43] These recurring problems of police misconduct continue to create conditions for young black men to get caught up in a very biased and unjust penal system particularly if the individual has unpaid traffic tickets, for example.

The American penal system perpetuated the judicial perspective of making it easy to get into prison, but providing a very difficult means of exiting prison and providing very limited rehabilitative resources that prepare individuals for a vastly changing world. This prescription for prison entry also provides a means for returning to prison by virtue of happenstance and the lack of adequate training and preparation. The type of training that ex-offenders need when they enter prison is often different by the time they are released. The skills that ex-offenders often receive are sometimes already obsolete by the time they are released because of the rapid technological advances in society. Some of these technological advances include having computer skills for the most basic and entry level positions.

Paula Ditton, Caroline Harlow, and Christopher Mumola found that 61 percent of state prisoners receive mental health treatment, which is a 20 percent increase over Distric jail inmates.[44] Jennifer Karberg and Doris James found that 69 percent of jail inmates are regular drug users, and 29 percent of convicted jail inmates report drug use at the time of their offense.[45] James further argues that more than half of all jail inmates have a current criminal justice status at the time of arrest.[46]

The allotment of federal funds for reentry programs for ex-offenders may be a challenge for D.C. ex-offenders. In most cases the federal government will just transfer the money for the programs to the states and allow them to distribute it locally as needed. However, in Washington, D.C., the federal government presides over the prison system that provides a more restricted scrutiny over federal dollars for programs in D.C.

THE SECOND CHANCE ACT OF 2007

Legislation known as the Second Chance Act (H.R. 1593/S.1060) was introduced in the U.S. Congress by Representative Danny Davis (D-Ill.) in March 2007. President Bush signed H.R. 1593 into law on April 9, 2008. The purpose of the act is to provide federal grants to states and local governments to promote the safe and successful reintegration into the community of individuals who have been incarcerated. It specifically authorized $362 million in grants to state and local government programs, new reentry courts, and nonprofit agencies to expand mentoring, drug treatment, education, job training, and other reentry services for ex-inmates.[47] The act also supports early release for elderly inmates convicted of nonviolent offenses and calls for the development of alternatives to incarceration, such as family-based drug treatment for nonviolent drug offenders with children.[48] Money and other resources are needed for these individuals to be trained for work, prepared and supported in the areas of employment, education, housing, and health care, among many other needs. According to the National Treatment Accountability for Safer Communities (TASC), the Second Chance Act is critically important legislation that can address such issues as the lack of jobs, parenting issues, lower educational attainment, housing, mental problems, and medications for HIV and other communicable diseases.[49]

The key component of any legislation after it passes is its proper implementation and oversight of the dollars to be used for its targeted population. It is imperative for states to make sure that the funds are used according to their created purpose. However, the District of Columbia must make sure that its money is applied across the board to support ex-offender programs that have the greatest need in terms of drug, alcohol, and mental health issues as well as across racial lines. Furthermore, the democratic lines of checks and balances are not as sufficient in D.C. as they are in other geographic locations. Unlike other locations that will supposedly benefit from this type of act, D.C. has direct federal involvement that could prove to be even more of a bureaucratic nightmare with obtaining the necessary funding to provide the services needed. Since D.C. has approximately thirteen combined agencies with federal and local levels of responsibilities, the more the roles and responsibilities seem to cross over into another agency's jurisdiction. In order for the act to benefit the D.C. criminal justice system there must be a clear and direct link to all agencies in the process and multiple monitors to track the monetary trail will have to be implemented. All of the agencies may have to divide up the money for the D.C. criminal justice system, and when each organization has its own administrative and bureaucratic processes, it is imperative to monitor funding sources and expenditures to make sure that the money is being used as intended. In other words, for the D.C. criminal justice system to work well, it may require a streamlining of the process.

The Urban Institute also identified some general obstacles that most ex-offenders face nationwide. They include obstacles in the areas of housing, employment, health care, mental and substance abuse, and economic and social disadvantages in their home communities. The grant money will be allocated as a result of the Second Chance Act to provide assistance in these areas.

CULTURAL NOTIONS ABOUT THE
PERCEPTION OF U.S. PRISONS AND PRISONERS

The United States has basically produced a cultural mindset for some prisoners such that they would rather return to prison, so that they can receive shelter, clothing and food rather than take the risk of having to try to survive in a very competitive society that has very little place or sympathy for them. Some talents of ex-offenders have yet to be discovered and they are either dormant or oftentimes misguided. Misplaced values and limited opportunities have been the dominant mindset of some of the ex-offenders and with the proper guidance and mentoring sometimes they can discover interests and talents that they never thought were possible to use that will benefit them. However, prisons, public officials, and probation officers must provide a means for them to have these opportunities to explore their talents. The lack of access to or the continuation of unequal distribution of rehabilitative resources perpetuates an inadequate rehabilitative system across the United States as well as in Washington, D.C.

Some former prisoners are very capable of making valid contributions to our society provided they are granted access to adequate resources.

RISK FACTORS OF RE-OFFENDERS

Studies have shown that there are some known risk factors for repeat offenders. Recent research on prisoner reentry indicates that those who re-offend are more likely to be unemployed, to use drugs or abuse alcohol, and to have extensive criminal histories.[50] The evidence produced by such studies continues to acknowledge that if ex-offenders are provided adequate rehabilitative resources, they stand a better opportunity of staying out of jail. On the contrary, if rehab services are limited, ineffective, or not available, then the ex-offender stands a greater chance of returning to prison. Those who re-offend also tend to be younger and have more negative attitudes toward police and the legal system than ex-offenders who do not return to prison.[51]

Timing also plays a role in identifying risks of re-offending: according to a 1989 study by Allen J. Beck and Bernard E. Shipley, released prisoners are at greatest risk of re-offending during the early months of their release, with nearly one-third (29.6 percent) of them rearrested during their first six months of freedom.[52] This study shows that the first six months after the release of an ex-offender are crucial to ensuring that he or she receives the most adequate rehabilitative resources available. Otherwise, the individual could easily resort to a life of crime. According to this study, an increase in educational and employment opportunities combined with more efficient drug and alcohol prevention programs all implemented within the first six months could decrease the recidivism rate of ex-offenders returning to prison.

There are many other conditions that play a significant role in determining whether or not an individual returns to prison. National demographics show that 88 percent of returning prisoners are male.[53] Fifty-five percent of returning prisoners are white, 44 percent are African American, and 21 percent are Hispanic, and the median age at the time of release is thirty-four.[54] The statistics indicate that a vast majority of returning prisoners are white and black males, while the recidivism rate for Hispanic males is on the rise. The statistics further show that white males are released at a higher rate than black and Hispanic males. The statistics do not imply that more white males are incarcerated as compared to their black and Hispanic male counterparts, but that they are released into their communities at higher rates. Statistics have shown for years that black and Hispanic males are arrested at more alarming rates than white males and are given longer sentences for the same crime in many cases, particularly with drug charges such as crack versus white powdered cocaine.

The release of the prison population back into the community has other health-related concerns. For example, compared to the general population, prisoners have higher rates of chronic medical problems and infectious diseases, including asthma, hypertension, HIV/AIDS, Hepatitis C, and tuberculosis.[55] Infectious diseases such as HIV/AIDS, Hepatitis C, and tuberculosis pose the most dangerous threat to the general population. It is imperative that the proper health care resources be administered to the offenders before they are released, and mandatory check health checkups should be monitored after they are released beyond the first six months.

In addition to drug and alcohol dependencies and infectious diseases, some of the ex-offenders in the District of Columbia, and across the nation, are in need of mental health treatment. Typically, mental health disorders are more prevalent among the prison population as compared to the general population.[56] Although most inmates have access to health care while incarcerated, upon release their access to treatment services and medication is often limited.[57] In the District of Columbia, the Department of Health, along with other local organizations and nonprofits, provides health care services to ex-offenders. For instance, in the Department of Health, there is the Addiction Prevention and Recovery Administration. Another important transitional component for the ex-offender is to have the support of family members. Family relationships are key among the sources of tangible and emotional support for returning prisoners.[58] Family support is extremely important for a number of reasons. First, it keeps the offender's morale and confidence up while in prison. Second, it gives the offender hope that once released, family members will be waiting and willing to help the person get back on his or her feet. Third, it sends a message to jail officials and probation officers that the individual has a strong, loving, and supportive family that will more than likely provide the necessary support once the person is released. Fourth, if the family is active in the institutional and administrative procedures of the prison process, then it shows prison officials that they should legally and properly administer good judicial prudence for their family member.

In some cases when family support is lacking or in families that do not have the legal resources to support an individual, there is often a breakdown in judicial or institutional prudence of the process for the offender. In cases where family resources are restrained or limited, the offender can be subjected to injustices in the administrative process of the judicial system such as inaccurate reports on behavior and denial of appropriate probation and release. When families are able to use their resources to understand the system, monitor the progress of the individual, and fight against the injustices of the criminal justice system, then the process sometimes works better for the offender and everyone involved.

One of the most immediate needs of any ex-offender is the need for housing. Twelve percent of state prisoners reported that they did not have housing at the time of their arrest, and the likelihood of homelessness increases for those with mental health and substance abuse problems.[59] There are some cases when, even with the best of family support, it is in the best interests of both the family members and the ex-offenders that they do not immediately return to their original family setting. In cases where the person has substance abuse dependencies then a more controlled setting with the proper treatment and monitoring is much better than a family setting that is unstructured, less rigid, and uncontrolled.

Employment prospects for ex-offenders are limited. While more than two-thirds of prisoners were employed prior to their incarceration,[60] unemployment rates are high among released prisoners.[61] African American men are having a difficult time finding employment anywhere in the United States even if they are college educated, according to Princeton University professor and sociologist Devah Pager.[62] Furthermore, her findings suggest that "being Black in America today is basically equivalent to having a felony conviction."[63] Findings discussed in the report acknowledge that a white male ex-offender with no college degree has a better chance of getting a job than an African American male with a college degree who has never been to jail.[64] In fact, this issue becomes even more alarming for African American male ex-offenders. When one considers the lack of educational and job training skills coupled with a criminal record, the situation becomes even more challenging. Because the prison industry is big business in America, more interest and financial support is placed on the front end of this problem that feeds into the criminalization of black men in particular and people of color in general.

SOLUTIONS TO THE PROBLEMS

Some of the federal and local agencies involved in the process should refine their roles and responsibilities and let each organization do what it is designed to do. The federal government should only provide the funding resources and federal guidelines to the local organizations. Another solution should be to consolidate services within some organizations. This would make it less costly for certain agencies as well as streamline the rehabilitative process.

Some criminal justice scholars and organizations have also argued that community policing and other types of police involvement strategies can help provide an effective transition for ex-offenders back into society. In fact, arrest frequencies for returning prisoners are thirty to forty-five times higher than for the general population.[65] Police agencies stand to benefit from their involvement in reentry because successful efforts to reduce recidivism among released prisoners can, by definition, prevent future crimes and help improve community relations with police.[66] This research by Tom Tyler suggests that better policing and more police involvement would improve perceptions of police. However, this notion goes against the "don't snitch" mindset that is operating in communities of color as well as the long history of poor perceptions or interactions between the black community and police. On the contrary, having police more involved on the back end of when the ex-offender returns home could create even more animosity in the black community; the ex-offender and the police provide old stereotypes and perceptions that are not changed. The problem is really a three-tier challenge. There is the poor perception that the black community has of the police, the negative perception that the police has of the black community, and, lastly, the issue of providing effective public safety for law-abiding African Americans without the fear of retaliation from ex-offenders or the police. Providing effective public safety often has to be done within the constraints that exist between the African American community and the police. Community forums and healthy exchanges should be provided in an attempt to erode some of the negative perceptions that exist. This process should take place before or at least in conjunction with the implementation of community policing as a strategy to assist the ex-offenders back into the community.

CONCLUSION

In conclusion, the data have shown that both in Washington, D.C., and nationally, African American communities, policymakers, and the criminal justice community in attempting to provide a place for ex-offenders as well as prepare them to become productive citizens, continue to face an uphill battle. The passing of the Second Chance Act seems to be a start in the right direction, but much more has to be done. There are just as many black males going into prison as there are being released due to overcrowding or completion of their sentences. If these young men are not provided the adequate resources to transition back into society then they will easily fall prey to the revolving door of prison life. The African American female incarcerated population is also on the rise and will require just as much attention from policymakers, scholars, criminal justice professionals, and the legal community.

The D.C. criminal justice system has some unique institutional and systemic problems as well as some common problems that can be identified across the country. For instance, some of its unique problems involve the federal administering of the D.C. criminal system. CSOSA is one of many agencies that should refine and review what is working versus what is not working. The perpetual continuation of such issues as 1) institutional racism in the D.C. prison system, 2) a tightly controlled federal judicial system, and 3) the lack of strong family support, which leads to a limited understanding and restricted access to rehabilitative resources, provide a challenge to CSOSA and others. For example, the institutional racism demonstrates that African American offenders and ex-offenders are not always provided equal and adequate services within the prison system as was noted in the findings about the North Carolina prison by Delegate Eleanor Holmes Norton. D.C. prisoners are sent all over the country without having the proper supervision, oversight, and guidelines of D.C. officials. If a D.C. prisoner is sent to Connecticut or Ohio, then he more than likely will fall under the jurisdiction of those states' guidelines. How can D.C. officials effectively keep up with D.C. prisoners who are sent all over the country?

What seems to be working are the coalitions that have been created at the local and nonprofit levels. These coalitions are partnerships between churches and local government but even their involvement needs to be improved. Washington, D.C., probably has more nonprofit organizations that can assist with the transition of ex-offenders back into society than any other city. However, if the federal government is involved, then it may hinder local nonprofit organizations from involvement because of federal regulations and the concern of more federal scrutiny for D.C. nonprofit organizations. Federal oversight of the D.C. criminal justice process is overdue. However, what appears to be more efficient in terms of receiving more federal dollars to invest in rehabilitating the ex-offenders also has led to the creation of more federal intervention in agencies at the local level. This means funding has to be divided up according the need and function of the multiple agencies involved. The D.C. criminal justice process now has more agencies than before involved in the process with some overlapping responsibilities and objectives. The long, convoluted D.C. criminal justice process only complicates the process for everyone involved such as the offender, criminal justice professionals, court system, attorneys, and the many families.

Federal oversight is key in making sure that the criminal justice system is functioning properly, but if too many restrictions exist or if the process becomes too bureaucratically large to accomplish the main rehabilitation objectives for the ex-offender then the process needs revision. Democracy at its best is a system that allows the unavoidable ebb and flow of government to work at each level at a high and effective level. It becomes fragmented and convoluted when too many rules are put into place, while too loose a system will cause decay and corruption in the criminal justice system. In addressing the critical and controversial issue of rehabilitating ex-offenders, it becomes crucial to get it right and to make sure the appropriate values and priorities are established, not only in the District of Columbia, but also all over the country. In a highly political town like D.C., it becomes even more important because if the criminal justice system works well then the tone can be set for the nation to replicate. On the contrary, if the system continues to work poorly, then the ex-offenders and the entire criminal justice system continue to be used in a political game, and that is not fair for those who have paid the debt for their crimes, especially for nonviolent criminals.

NOTES

1. Leonard A. Sipes Jr., "We Save Neighborhoods: Parole and Probation Patrols in Washington, D.C." National Crime Prevention Council, www.ncpc.org/publications/catalyst-news, 2004 (last accessed July 2008).

2. Court Services and Offender Supervision Agency: Offender Reentry in Washington, D.C. Fact Sheet, 1.

3. Kenneth Meeks, *Driving While Black: Highways, Shopping Malls, Taxicabs, Sidewalks, How to Fight Back if You Are a Victim of Racial Profiling* (New York: Broadway Books, 2000), 172.

4. Ibid.

5. Monica Lewis, "Critic of Justice Department Effort to Suppress Data on Racial Profiling Demoted," www.blackamericaweb.com, August 24, 2005 (last accessed July 2008).

6. Ibid.

7. Ibid.

8. *The Washington Post.* Author unknown, October 3, 2000, 1.

9. Ibid.

10. Richard M. Stana, "D.C. Criminal Justice System: Better Coordination Needed Among Participating Agencies," United States General Accounting Office (GAO-01-708T), May 11, 2001, 3.

11. D.C. Department of Corrections: Facts and Figures, April 2008, 14.

12. Ibid.

13. Ibid.

14. Ibid.

15. Valencia Mohammed, "Over 2,000 Inmates Released Each Year: Coming Home not Easy," *The Afro American Newspaper*, August 4, 2006, 1.

16. Ibid.; CSOSA Fact Sheet.

17. Thomas H. Williams, "What Works? Evidence-Based Practices in Parole and Probation," *Journal of Community Corrections*, Summer 2007, 5.

18. Ibid.

19. Ibid.

20. Ibid.; Mohammed, *The Afro American Newspaper.*

21. Ibid.

22. Ibid.; Sipes, 2.

23. Ibid.; Sipes, 3.

24. Ibid.

25. Ibid.; Thomas Williams, 5.

26. Comprehensive Reentry Strategy for Adults in the District of Columbia: Action Plan, October 15, 2003, 3.

27. Ibid., 2.

28. *The Washington Post*, January 7, 1998.

29. Robert E. Pierre, "Church Pledged at N.C. Prison," *The Washington Post*, October 17, 2007, B1.

30. Ibid.

31. Ibid.

32. Ibid.

33. Ibid.

34. Ibid.

35. Ibid.

36. David Crary, "More Than One in 100 Adults is Behind Bars, Making the U.S. the World's Top Incarcerator," BlackAmerica.com: www.blackamericaweb.com, February 29, 2008, 3.

37. Ibid., 3.

38. Ibid.

39. Charshee C. L. McIntyre, *Criminalizing a Race: Free Blacks During Slavery* (New York: Kayode Publications, Ltd., 1993), 150–51.

40. Howard McGary, *Race and Social Justice* (Oxford: Blackwell Publishers, Inc., 1999), 177.

41. Ibid., 179.

42. David A. Harris, *Profiles in Injustice: Why Racial Profiling Cannot Work* (New York: The New Press, 2002), 8.

43. Ibid., 10.

44. Paula A. Ditton, "A Mental Health and Treatment of Inmates and Probationers," Washington, D.C., Bureau of Justice Statistics, U.S. Department of Justice, 1999; Caroline Harlow, "Profile of Jail Inmates," 1996, Washington, D.C., found in Bureau of Justice Statistics, U.S. Department of Justice, 6.

45. Jennifer Karberg and Doris J. James, "Substance, Dependence, Abuse, and Treatment of Jail Inmates, 2002," Washington, D.C., found in Bureau of Justice Statistics, U.S. Department of Justice, 2005, 11.

46. Ibid.

47. Elaine Shannon, "Congress Passes Second Chance Act to Ease Ex-Inmate Reentry," The Public Welfare Foundation, 2007, 1.

48. Ibid.

49. "An Examination of Drug Treatment Programs Needed to Ensure Successful Reentry," testimony of Scott A. Sylak, House Committee on the Judiciary: Subcommittee on Crime, Terrorism and Homeland Security, February 8, 2006.

50. Nancy G. LaVigne, "Why Map Prisoner Reentry?" *Crime Mapping News* 6 (4): Washington, D.C., The Police Foundation, 2004, 1–3.

51. Christy Visher, Nancy G. LaVigne, and Jerome Travis, "Returning Home: Understanding the Challenges of Prisoner Reentry," Maryland Pilot Study, Washington, D.C.: The Urban Institute, 2004.

52. Allen J. Beck and Bernard E. Shipley, "Recidivism of Released Prisoners in 1983," Washington, D.C., Bureau of Justice Statistics, U.S. Department of Justice, www.ojp.usdoj.gov/bjs/pub/pdfrpr83.pdf (1989).

53. Paige M. Harrison and Allen J. Beck, "Prisons in 2003," Washington, D.C., Bureau of Justice Statistics, U.S. Department of Justice, 2004.

54. Ibid.

55. Nancy G. LaVigne, Amy Solomon, et al. "Prisoner Reentry and Community Policing: Strategies for Enhancing Public Safety," Office of Community Oriented Policing Services, U.S. Department of Justice, prepared in partnership with Urban Institute Policy Center, March 2006, 13.

56. Ibid.

57. Theodore M. Hammett, Cheryl Roberts, and Sofia Kennedy, "Health-Related Issues in Prisoner Reentry," *Crime and Delinquency* 47 (2001) (3): 390–409.

58. Ibid.; LaVigne and Solomon, 2006, 13.

59. Ibid.; Ditton.

60. Ibid.; Harlow.

61. Ibid.; LaVigne and Solomon.

62. Soledad O'Brian, "Black in America," CNN Report, July 24, 2008.

63. Ibid.

64. Ibid.

65. Richard Rosenfeld, Joel Wallman, and Robert Fornango, "The Contribution of Ex-Prisoners to Crime Rates," in *Prisoner Reentry and Crime in America*, eds. Jeremy Travis and Christy Visher (London: Cambridge University Press, 2005), 80–104.

66. Jason Sunshine and Tom R. Tyler, "The Role of Procedural Justice and Legitimacy in Shaping Public Support for the Police," *Law and Society Review* 37 (2003): 513–48.

BIBLIOGRAPHY

Books

Meeks, Kenneth. *Driving While Black: Highways, Shopping Malls, Taxicabs, Sidewalks, How To Fight Back If You Are a Victim of Racial Profiling.* New York: Broadway Books, 2000.

McGary, Howard. *Race and Social Justice.* Oxford: Blackwell Publishers, Inc., 1999.

McIntyre, Charshee C. L. *Criminalizing a Race: Free Blacks During Slavery.* New York: Kayode Publications, Ltd. 1993.

Rosenfeld, Richard, Joel Wallman, and Robert Fornango. "The Contribution of Ex-Prisoners to Crime Rates" in *Prisoner Reentry and Crime in America,* edited by Jeremy Travis and Christy Visher (80–104). London: Cambridge University Press, 2005.

Supplementary Reports

"An Examination of Drug Treatment Programs Needed to Ensure Successful Reentry." Testimony of Scott A. Sylak, House Committee on the Judiciary: Subcommittee on Crime, Terrorism and Homeland Security, February 8, 2006.

Beck, Allen J., and Bernard E. Shipley. "Recidivism of Released Prisoners in 1983." Washington, D.C.: Bureau of Justice Statistics, U.S. Department of Justice, www.ojp.usdoj.gov/bjs/pub/pdfrpr83.pdf (1989).

Comprehensive Reentry Strategy for Adults in the District of Columbia: Action Plan, October 15, 2003.

Court Services and Offender Supervision Agency: Offender Reentry in Washington, D.C. Fact Sheet.

D.C. Department of Corrections: Facts and Figures, April 2008.

Ditton, Paula A. "Mental Health and Treatment of Inmates and Probationers," Washington, D.C.: Bureau of Justice Statistics, U.S. Department of Justice, 1999.

Harlow, Caroline Wold. "Profile of Jail Inmates," 1996. Washington, D.C.: Bureau of Justice Statistics, U.S. Department of Justice, 1998.

Harrison, Paige M., and Allen J. Beck. *Prisons in 2003.* Washington, D.C.: Bureau of Justice Statistics, U.S. Department of Justice, 2004.

James, Doris J. "Profile of Jailed Inmates," 2002. Washington, D.C.: Bureau of Justice Statistics, U.S. Department of Justice, 2005.

Karberg, Jennifer, and Doris J. James. "Substance, Dependence, Abuse, and Treatment of Jail Inmates, 2002." Washington, D.C.: Bureau of Justice Statistics, U.S. Department of Justice, 2005.

LaVigne, Nancy G., Amy Solomon, Karen A. Beckman, and Kelly Dedel. "Prisoner Reentry and Community Policing: Strategies for Enhancing Public Safety." Office of Community Oriented Policing Services, U.S. Department of Justice, prepared in partnership with Urban Institute Justice Policy Center, March 2006.

Shannon, Elaine. "Congress Passes Second Chance Act to Ease Ex-Inmate Reentry." The Public Welfare Foundation, 2007.

Stana, Richard M. "D.C. Criminal Justice System: Better Coordination Needed Among Participating Agencies." United States General Accounting Office, May 11, 2001.

Visher, Christy, Nancy G. LaVigne, and Jeremy Travis. "Returning Home: Understanding the Challenges of Prisoner Reentry." Maryland Pilot Study: Findings from Baltimore. Washington, D.C.: The Urban Institute, 2004. www.urban.org/url.cfm?ID=410974.

Journals

Hammett, Theodore M., Cheryl Roberts, and Sofia Kennedy. "Health-Related Issues in Prisoner Reentry." *Crime and Delinquency* 47 (2001) (3): 390–409.
LaVigne, Nancy G. "Why Map Prisoner Reentry?" *Crime Mapping News* 6 (4): 1–3. Washington, D.C.: The Police Foundation, 2004. www.policefoundation.org.
Sunshine, Jason, and Tom R. Tyler. "The Role of Procedural Justice and Legitimacy in Shaping Public Support for the Policing." *Law and Society Review* 37 (2003): 513–48.
"Supervising Criminal Offenders in Washington, D.C." *Corrections Today,* February 2006.
Williams, Thomas H. "What Works? Evidence-Based Practices in Parole and Probation," *Journal of Community Corrections,* Summer 2007.

Newspapers

Mohammed, Valencia. "Over 2,000 Inmates Released Each Year: Coming Home not Easy." *The Afro American Newspaper,* August 4, 2006.
Pierre, Robert E. "Changes Pledged at N.C. Prison." *The Washington Post,* October 17, 2007, B1.
Wilson, Timothy. "Church Helps Ex-Cons To Live on the Outside." *The Washington Post,* October 26, 2006, DZ3.
The Washington Post. Title and author unknown, October 3, 2000.

Internet Sources

Crary, David. "More Than One in 100 Adults is Behind Bars, Making U.S. the World's Top Incarcerator." Black America.com. www.blackamericaweb.com. February 29, 2008.
Lewis, Monica. "Critic of Justice Department Effort to Suppress Data on Racial Profiling Demoted." Black America Web.com, www.blackamericaweb.com. August 24, 2005.
Sipes, Leonard A., Jr. "We Save Neighborhoods: Parole and Probation Patrols in Washington, D.C." National Crime Prevention Council, www.ncpc.org/publications/catalyst-news, 2004.

Television Report

O'Brien, Soledad. "Black in America." CNN Report, July 24, 2008.

11

The Dynamics of Poverty in the District of Columbia

Angelyn Flowers

INTRODUCTION

The District of Columbia will never be able to make significant inroads in reducing poverty as long as federal prohibitions exclude two-thirds of the income generated and substantial portions of the real property within the District of Columbia from taxation. The U.S. Government Accountability Office

> has documented that the District has a structural imbalance of $500 million to $1 billion per year. The structural imbalance results from two primary factors. First, the District has a higher service delivery cost than any other state—due to the high rates of poverty and crime associated with an urban area. Second, the District's revenue capacity is restricted by the federal presence—the District cannot tax non-residents and 41 percent of the land value is tax exempt. Due to these factors, the District imposes relatively higher tax burdens in order to meet basic service delivery requirements.[1]

This nonresident income exclusion is imposed only in the District of Columbia and its imposition deprives the District of Columbia of a right held by states and localities throughout the country. The property tax exclusion, while on its face has uniform applicability, nonetheless has what can only be considered a disparate impact on the city. The overall result is to leave the District of Columbia grappling with the dynamics of poverty.

Poverty in the District of Columbia is visual. For those who look closely, it can be seen in the homeless sleeping on heat grates outside federal office buildings or panhandling outside the Metro subway stations. It can be seen in those waiting in line for the dwindling number of available beds in shelters provided by the city or nonprofit organizations. More tragically, poverty can be seen when families are sleeping in shelters and cars. It can be seen in the children showing up at schools or recreation centers for free breakfast and lunch even in the summer months when school is not in session. Poverty can be seen in the increasing numbers of brown and black faces standing outside the Home Depot hoping for day labor. Poverty is endemic, and as a result of the global economic downturn its reach is expanding.

The one common legacy of the myriad approaches to eliminate poverty over time has been the continuation of poverty and the rise in income of those who are hired in the vast array of nonprofits and for-profit organizations funded by federal anti-poverty dollars. The nineteenth century and the "workhouse" movement represented the notion of keeping the poor out of sight. From charitable approaches that provided food to the "deserving" poor, to the social uplift approaches of the twentieth century and the 1960s "War on Poverty," to the Reaganomics–Bush I and II economic doctrine that "a rising tide lifts all boats," we have gone full circle back to the notion that the poor are to blame for their plight. Whether it is attributable to character flaws such as laziness, irresponsibility, and so on, or religious reasons—i.e., sufficient lack of devotion to God, lack of virtue, poor behavior in a previous life— the reality is that blaming the poor for their plight absolves the larger society of any responsibility to address this issue. Most importantly, it fails to focus on the underlying economic issues and structural arrangements in society.

Another common element is that while these approaches may vary, they are generally single-focused in nature and do not challenge the structural arrangement of the economy or related institutional arrangements like schools, entrance requirements, and so on. For example, the goal of charitable models is to provide food, clothing, or shelter to address an immediate individual or family need. The goal of social-service type models is to improve the condition of individuals/families through providing job training, jobs, education, and so on. The goal of the economic-development or business model is premised on the notion that supporting businesses will lead to job creation, therefore decreasing unemployment. However, while single-focus initiatives address specific problems of poverty, they do not look at poverty comprehensively to address the complex array of social, political, and economic problems affecting those that live in poverty.[2] That type of comprehensive strategy above all else requires the ability to generate the resources required for its implementation. But it also requires the elimination of bureaucratic silos.

It is difficult to fully discuss poverty without also discussing the symptoms of arrest and incarceration rates, educational failure, availability of affordable housing, family stability, the lingering effect of discrimination, teenage pregnancies, and above all else—jobs. In an unending cycle of poverty, any of these factors can be both cause and effect of other social ills. Overriding all discussion is the question of what government can and will do to address poverty. There are diametrically opposed viewpoints on what the role and reach of government should be. In its short history since the reestablishment of home rule, the District of Columbia has generally had elected officials who believe that the role of government is to serve the people by helping those it represents. These officials have been confronted by the fact that in governmental affairs in this city there is often a disconnect between the "will" to do something and the "means" to accomplish it.

The legislative and financial difficulties faced by the District of Columbia government in addressing poverty can be traced to three federally imposed constraints on the city's revenue-generating ability. Two of these prohibitions are specifically directed toward the District of Columbia and represent a deliberate undermining of home rule: the District of Columbia may not tax income earned in the District by nonresidents; nor can the District of Columbia require that employees of the District of Columbia government live in the city. The third limitation, while not applicable exclusively to the District of Columbia, impacts the city as no other jurisdiction in the country is impacted. This is the tax-exempt status of the federal government and nonprofit organizations which has the result of rendering the majority of the city's property exempt from taxation. The combination of these three factors places an economic stranglehold on the District significantly restricting the revenue-generating ability necessary to effectively address poverty. These structural impediments have compounded a poverty dynamic characterized by race, ethnicity, and class.

A city of contrasts, the District of Columbia is the capital city of the leading world proponent of democratic forms of government for other nations. Yet it is a city whose citizens are denied the right to completely control their own destiny with full representation and voting rights despite the fact that its residents pay more per capita in federal income taxes than the residents of several states. The District of Columbia has one of the most highly educated and affluent populations in the nation, with at least thirty years of African American mayoral leadership, and a legislative body that has seen the size of its majority African American membership decline, but still persist. Yet this city contains intractable pockets of poverty, located in geographically specific areas that over thirty-five years of home rule with local governance have been unable to eradicate or significantly reduce. After examining the dynamics of poverty in the District of Columbia, this chapter will describe the federally imposed structural constraints that contribute to the continuation of this dynamic.

THE FACE OF POVERTY

Within the District of Columbia, two geographic barriers are synonyms both for the socio-economic stratification of the city, as well as its racial stratification. The area of the city "west of Rock Creek Park" or "Upper Northwest" is predominantly white and affluent. The area "east of the (Anacostia) River" is predominantly African American with its residents perceived as more likely to live at or below the poverty level. Overly simplistic, this perception varies somewhat from reality, as the area east of the Anacostia River also includes affluent African American enclaves as does the affluent northwest quadrant east of Rock Creek Park. The perception often relegates to invisibility the city's growing Latino population which lives primarily in the northwest quadrant of the city, with the major concentration along 16th Street, north of K Street.

The "face of poverty" in the District of Columbia is a face of color. More disconcerting, however, is that the face of poverty in the District is more likely to be employed than not. Thirty-four percent of employed Asian residents, 37 percent of employed Latino residents, and 57 percent of employed black residents of the District of Columbia live in poverty.[3] Twelve percent of white residents of the District of Columbia are employed and also live in poverty.[4] However, the figure for white residents is actually inflated in that it includes college students living off campus and interns who may have lower salaries but are single with no dependents and living in group homes. This "color of poverty" is mirrored in the geographic distribution of poverty across the city.

With a few isolated examples, in the overwhelming number of communities in the "upper northwest" section of the city fewer than one out of ten people lives in poverty. Moving eastward across the city, the percentage of poverty in communities increases.[5] The racial and ethnic composition of the city changes as well. The upper northwest section is predominantly white. The mid-section of the city has a mixture of gentrified neighborhoods where white newcomers are settling into communities of black and Latino residents as they purchase or rent newly renovated and highly priced condos, apartments, and houses that are increasingly no longer afforable for the working poor households that once lived in those communities. Pockets of affluence in the southern part of the city, east of the Anacostia River, are also visible. Excluding Bolling Air Force Base in the southwestern section of the city, these pockets of affluence in "east of the river" communities are primarily inhabited by African Americans.

The "face of poverty" in the District is not only a face of color, but it overwhelmingly tends to be a young face The southern section of the city (Wards 7 and 8), which contains the largest concentration of neighborhoods

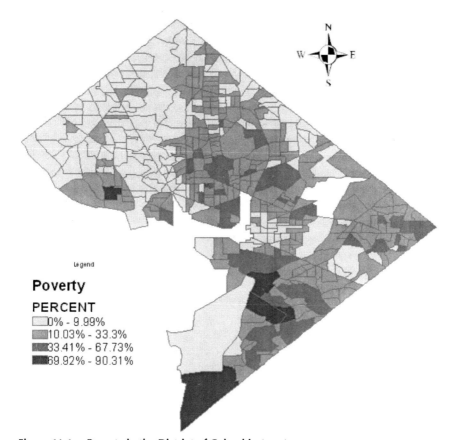

Figure 11.1. Poverty in the District of Columbia (map)

with people in poverty, also contains the largest percentage of children. In a city of almost six hundred thousand people, twenty out of every one hundred District residents are under the age of eighteen. However, in the typical east-of-the-river community, that figure is thirty to fifty out of every one hundred residents.[6] This is particularly significant when one considers that the leading indicator of juvenile offending is poverty and conversely that poverty tends to be pervasive in communities with high levels of juvenile offending.

The large number of juveniles living in poverty in the District of Columbia continues to have long-term consequences both for the youth and the city. These children primarily live in households with at least one working adult. However, they are less likely to start school "ready to learn," with consequences that can extend throughout their schooling. Their parents or caregivers are less likely to have the resources to provide the type of quality leisure time activities that build self-efficacy and coincidently serve as delinquency prevention strategies, and they are less likely to have had successful schooling experiences themselves. This means that parents and caregivers have less knowledge about pathways for success and the support systems that they can access for their children. Because of their economic status, these children will gain access to computers at a later age than their more affluent counterparts, again delaying their ability to acquire an essential set of skills. More than likely, if they have recreation activities, the options will be more limited than those of their white counterparts. Thus, economic disadvantages translate into a set of systemic disadvantages within every institutional resource that are cumulative over time in the harm produced. These cumulative disadvantages inhibit efforts designed to bridge the gap beween advantaged youngsters and those growing up in disadvantaged circumstances.

The District of Columbia leads the nation with a median personal income of $62,484.[7] This represents a 22 percent increase over a two-year period.[8] The District's median household income of $54,312 exceeds that of thirty-five states.[9] Approximately 18 percent of the households in the District of Columbia have a household income under $15,000, with approximately 70 percent of those households (under $15,000) having an annual income under $10,000.[10] The median monthly owner cost for households with a mortgage is $2,094 as compared to the median gross monthly rent (including averaged monthly utility costs) in the District of Columbia of $934.[11] Even using the median monthly rental cost, this represents $11,208 annually. Those households with a household income under $10,000 are already operating at a deficit before the inclusion of additional costs such as food, transportation, clothing, day care, and so on in their budgets.

These figures are particularly striking when it is considered that in the District of Columbia, 67.2 percent of children under the age of six have all

Table 11.1. Household Income in the District of Columbia

Income and Benefits in Adjusted 2006 Dollars	Number of Households	Percentage
Less than $10,000	33,380	13%
$10,000–$14,999	13,313	5%
$15,000–$24,999	23,719	10%
$25,000–$34,999	25,975	10%
$35,000–$49,999	33,274	13%
$50,000–$74,999	40,429	16%
$75,000–$99,999	24,654	10%
$100,000–$149,999	24,293	10%
$150,000–$199,999	12,439	5%
$200,000 or more	16,787	7%

Total Households = 248,263

parents working either full- or part-time. This is the sixth highest percentage in the nation. It suggests that significant numbers of households are operating near or below poverty levels despite having at least one working adult.

An examination of selected poverty indicators is illustrative of the plight of many residents in the nation's capital. When compared to other states, the District of Columbia has the highest infant mortality rate.[12] Its poverty rate is tied with the state of Mississippi and ranked second only to a pre-Katrina Louisiana.[13] The District of Columbia also has the highest unemployment rate at 8.2 percent.[14] By June 2009 that rate has risen to 10.9 percent and was the highest, not only in the region, but also in the nation.[15] This despite news reports that because of the federal government and associated businesses, the Washington metropolitan region had been relatively immune from the economic and job constriction pervading the rest of the country. That regional immunity however, does not extend to the city of Washington itself.

The District of Columbia's extremely low home-ownership rate increases the vulnerability of individuals already "living on the edge." Fifty-five percent of the housing units in the District of Columbia are occupied by renters.[16] Aside from the fact that home ownership is an asset-generating activity, not owning your home means that you are dependent on a variety of circumstances over which you have no control. Poverty restricts housing choices, relegating individuals to old, run-down, overcrowded, and deteriorating housing. The substandard nature of the housing units in turn makes them vulnerable to being torn down in "urban renewal" and "economic development" projects which then dislocate the residents making them even more vulnerable. A sizeable population in the District of Columbia lives precariously on the edge. A slight increase in rent or transportation costs will push them over that edge into greater poverty.

Table 11.2. Selected Poverty Indicators

| | Percentage | | State |
| | District of | | Comparison |
Indicator	Columbia	National	Ranking
People below the poverty level	19.9%	13.1%	4th
Persons under the age of 18 living below the poverty level	33.9%	18.4%	1st
Persons 65 and over living below the poverty level	14.4%	9.4%	3rd
Unemployment Rate	8.2%	5.5%	1st
Infant Mortality Rate	11.3		1st
	(per 1,000 live births)		

Many reasons have been presented for this phenomenon. Among those cited in a report on state and local approaches to poverty in Washington, D.C., by the Woodrow Wilson International Center for Scholars were lack of education, lack of low-skilled jobs paying adequate wages, lack of affordable transportation to jobs outside the District, lack of experience, lack of job-matching experience, insecure jobs, criminal record, poor service delivery, and inefficient city management.[17] However, these explanations do not begin to address what it means to be poor in the District of Columbia.

The poverty indicators in this city are related to the educational levels of its residents. Despite having one of the largest percentages of college-educated adults in the nation, the District of Columbia also has one of the lowest high school completion rates. Almost 46 percent of the residents of the District of Columbia age twenty-five and over have a bachelor's degree or higher.[18] However, 15 percent of the city's residents over the age of twenty-five have neither finished high school nor earned a GED, and one-third of those residents have less than a ninth-grade education.[19] In some sections of the city the percentage of residents over twenty-five who have not finished high school exceeds 30 percent.[20] It is not a coincidence that those are the areas of the city with the largest percentage of people living below the poverty level.[21] It is also not a coincidence that these are the areas with the highest levels of unemployment or underemployment.

Globalization and an increasingly technological society mean that the opportunities that once existed in the United States for underskilled and undereducated people no longer exist. A 2007 discussion paper prepared by the Brookings Institution noted that less than 10 percent of the jobs that are the most accessible to those that are the least skilled have a salary level that will lift a single mother with two children out of poverty.[22] This is despite working full-time. Inadequate education will increasingly condemn individuals to the bottom rungs of a society, which has no jobs they can perform, except to fill prison cells and thereby provide employment opportunities for others.

The impact of education on the ability to emerge from poverty is irrefutable. The relationship between education and poverty is best illustrated by a rephrasing of Lao Tzu, the ancient Chinese philosopher and founder of Taoism, within the language of the twenty-first century: "give someone a fish, feed them for a day; teach someone how to fish, feed them for a lifetime." Average annual earnings for individuals with a four-year bachelor's degree working full-time year-round is $52,200, as compared to $30,400 for a high school graduate, and $23,000 for those who have not finished high school.[23] Advanced and professional degrees boost that difference even more.

Over the course of a lifetime, bachelor's degree recipients can expect to earn approximately $2.1 million as compared to $1.2 million for a high

Table 11.3.   Earnings Comparison by Educational Level Attained

Highest Education Level Attained	Average Annual Earnings	Annual Lifetime Earnings
Four-Year Bachelor's Degree	$52,200	$2.1 million
High School Graduate	$30,400	$1.2 million
Non–High School Graduate	$23,000	$1 million

school graduate and $1 million for someone who did not finish high school.[24] It should be expected that the difference in lifetime earnings will also widen. So important was the connection between educational level and income considered that among the first pieces of legislation passed following the restoration of home rule was D.C. Law 1-36 establishing the University of the District of Columbia.[25] The University was legislatively mandated "to offer a comprehensive program of public postsecondary education" and intended to provide a range of higher education opportunities and upward mobility for the working-class population of the District of Columbia.[26]

Despite a promising start, the university has subsequently been plagued by mission confusion, an imbalance in the use of its financial resources, and most importantly, what some consider an unspoken determination by powerful interests that the university not actually succeed in educating the previously uneducated. William Spaulding, former councilmember and chairperson of the Committee on Higher Education that established the University, noted in a recent interview that

> given the nature of the regional economy, without a comprehensive University, the Mayor and City Council have no way to create a strategy to lift people out of poverty in the 21st century. . . . When you look at things like the dropout rates in K-12, and teen pregnancies it is clear that the city must have a two-prong strategy: first, to combat those problems, but also we must provide pathways for upward mobility.
>
> Ultimately we are confronted not simply with a political question, but also a moral question: Do we want to consign the poor in DC to prison, homelessness, and permanent underclass status?[27]

Excluding the 8,837 students who have received an associate's degree, and the 53,901 who have taken some college classes, there are still another 73,873 residents of the District of Columbia over the age of twenty-five who have a high school diploma or a GED, but have not been to college.[28] That represents a cumulative annual salary difference of $1,610,431,400. Even if only ten percent of that potential target population received a bachelor's degree, it still represents an annual cumulative salary difference of $1.6 million.

In addition to employability, there are significant financial advantages to increased educational attainment, both at the micro and the macro level. The financial benefits accruing to the individual and his or her family represent a micro-level impact. A macro impact is represented by the increased purchasing power generated from that higher income feeding into the larger economy. Rather than being primarily consumers of city services, through government-financed or subsidized health care, housing subsidies, and other types of public assistance, these individuals have theoretically become providers of city services as taxpayers.

Unfortunately, oftentimes for the District of Columbia, the question becomes: "Taxpayers where?" The trend of middle- and working-class abandonment of the city enriches surrounding jurisdictions, while further eroding the tax base of the District of Columbia. In one effort to reverse the tide, the District's nonvoting delegate, Congresswoman Eleanor Holmes Norton, was successful in obtaining federal funding to establish the D.C. Tuition Assistance Program (DC-TAG). DC-TAG pays the difference between in-state and out-of-state tuition costs for D.C. residents at any state university in the country, up to $10,000.[29] This program has had some success both in retaining and attracting middle- and upper-class residents with college-age children.

It would be remiss to not also mention small businesses as well as the construction industry which are frequently cited as two sectors that are alternatives to success for those without a college education. However, racism and other barriers limit these options. Timothy Jenkins, Esq., president of Unlimited Visions, Inc., and former interim university president and former vice-chairperson of the Board of Trustees for the University of the District of Columbia, noted that

> the trades are the step ladders out of poverty. There is a lot of wisdom in offering ranges of training for economic survival . . . the trades will have to be there as long as things have to be maintained and built. The problem is that the D.C. population of tradesmen is not renewing itself. . . . [We] need a systematic way to get around the racism in the trade unions and the performance failures of the school system.[30]

It is assumed that vocational training is the panacea for poor academic preparation in K–12. It is assumed that those who "missed out" can simply go into vocational training. It is overlooked that the most highly compensated of these professions require that the individual possess a minimum level of skill and knowledge prior to training. For example, the building trades require math and science skills beyond the ability of the typical high school dropout.

Similar to black and Latino residents who have been driven out of their neighborhoods by gentrification, small business are also under siege in the "new" Washington. The local beauty and barber shops, or nail salons, are often the first to go when neighborhood commercial development goes "upscale." The smallest of these businesses, but also the most accessible for those with limited resources, is street vending. However, Jenkins, in his capacity as the legal representative for a local vendor's organization in their challenge to proposed legal and regulatory changes, also noted that

> Street vendors have been an object of attack by downtown developers who consider that street vending . . . has a negative impact on the cityscape . . . toward that end they propose to gentrify street vending by the introduction of newly improved design specifications for vending facilities that can cost up to $75,000 for new carts which existing vendors can't afford. . . . They [downtown developers] want to move street vendors from being "mom and pop" entrepreneurs to being indentured servants in vans provided by the big businesses.[31]

It is no small irony that the various means which would enable individuals to lift themselves out of poverty are in different ways under attack from one direction or another.

FEDERAL CONSTRAINTS ON DISTRICT REVENUE GENERATION

In the Home Rule Act, the federal government retained the right to veto legislation passed by the elected council of the District of Columbia, or simply to pass federal legislation to control any aspect of life in the city that they choose.[32] The most far-reaching aspect of this federal control are the constraints on the District's ability to generate revenue. The most egregious was the prohibition against taxing nonresident income earned in the District of Columbia, also known as a "commuter tax." This prohibition applies even when the income in question is paid by District tax dollars. Also affecting the city's generation of revenue is the sizeable amount of property in the District of Columbia that is exempt from property taxes due to federal income tax regulations.

The unique relationship between the federal government and the District of Columbia exacerbates the poverty dynamic. The District of Columbia is unique within the United States. It operates simultaneously as a city, county, and state, as well as the seat of the national government. This presents agencies in the District of Columbia with a variety of roles to fill. Its population of 591,833 residents is a larger population than sixty countries.[33] With a landmass of sixty-one square miles and a resulting population density in excess of nine thousand persons per square mile, the District of Columbia's population density far exceeds that of every state in the nation. Seven months into 2009,

District of Columbia residents have already paid $1,986,922,724.78 in federal taxes but have no voting representation in the House and no Senate representative.[34] To place this in the proper perspective, the residents of United States territories such as Puerto Rico, Guam, the Virgin Islands, and so on, like the residents of the District of Columbia, are United States citizens and also like the residents of the District have a nonvoting delegate in the House of Representatives. However, unlike the District of Columbia, the residents of Puerto Rico, Guam, the Virgin Islands, and so on do not pay federal income taxes.

The District of Columbia confronts the twin demons of lack of adequate revenue funding and the lack of power to increase its revenue base through taxation.[35] Two-thirds of the revenue earned in the District of Columbia is earned by nonresidents.[36] However, the District of Columbia is precluded from taxing this income. Section 602 of the Home Rule Act specifically prohibits the City Council of the District of Columbia from imposing "any tax on the whole or any portion of the personal income, either directly or at the source thereof, of any individual not a resident of the District."[37] Taxing income at its source, or where it is earned, is a right enjoyed by other jurisdictions at both the state and local level.

Unlike other jurisdictions in the country, the District of Columbia is unable to benefit from the wealth generated within its own borders. Examples abound. The City of Philadelphia imposes a tax on all wages earned in the city at a rate of 3.9296 percent for residents and 3.4997 percent for nonresidents.[38] New Jersey and Connecticut residents, working in New York City, pay New York state income tax on all wages earned.[39] It should be noted that these out-of-state residents no longer also pay New York City taxes on those same wages. In 1999, in an effort to appease the suburban New York state counties whose residents were working in New York City, the state legislature eliminated New York City's thirty-year tax on nonresident wages while keeping in place the New York state tax on nonresidents.[40] The significant difference is that, unlike the residents of the District of Columbia, the residents of the city of New York had a vote in the legislative body that made decisions on their local tax policy.

It is acknowledged that in the tri-state region encompassing the District of Columbia, Maryland, and Virginia, most jurisdictions choose to send the tax on wages earned within their borders to the jurisdiction where the wage earner resides. This largess does not cost Maryland and Virginia significant revenue since in most instances this operates primarily in one direction: the revenue flows from the District to the surrounding jurisdictions. It is also important to keep in mind that every jurisdiction in the region, with the exception of the District of Columbia, has the power to make a change and to impose its own tax on those wages earned within its jurisdiction. The federal prohibition against the imposition of a commuter tax in the District of Columbia has served to increase the tax coffers of many of the surrounding jurisdictions substantially beyond the revenue generated within their own borders. This is most likely the reason why the federal legislators most opposed to the District being able to tax this revenue have been the congressional delegations from the states of Maryland and Virginia; if the District of Columbia were able to tax all revenue earned within its borders, the taxpayer's jurisdiction of residence would have to forego those taxes.

Not only can the District of Columbia not tax the millions of dollars earned in the city by nonresidents annually, it also is precluded from even taxing the wages earned by nonresident employees of the District of Columbia government—wages paid with taxes collected from District of Columbia residents. Approximately 70 percent of the individuals who work for the District of Columbia government live outside the city. In an effort to mitigate the hemorrhaging of District tax dollars from the city as well as to facilitate employment of its own residents, the District of Columbia's Comprehensive Merit Personnel Act of 1978 included a requirement that all new city employees had to either be residents of the District of Columbia or move into the city within a prescribed time period after hire. In a pattern that was to remain to this day, Congress quickly vetoed that provision. In the past thirty years, Congress has continued to veto any provision of District law requiring residency in the city as a condition for obtaining employment paid for with city tax dollars. The one exception has been a "residency preference" and a limited ability to impose a residency requirement for senior-level, executive-type appointments.

In an effort to provide employment for its residents, the District has frequently imposed conditions on those receiving District government contracts that a certain percentage of the employees paid with those city funds have to be District residents. This approach has been permitted, but has generated varying levels of success. These economic development approaches have increasingly been "project oriented" with the prospect of "job creation" as an added enticement. Too often, however, the jobs "created" tend to be temporary or seasonal, offering at best short-term solutions. Those longer-lasting jobs that are created and produce a level of economic stability also often result in the recipient moving their residence outside of the District while continuing to work in the District.

Nor is the District of Columbia able to rely on that other mainstay of revenue generation for local jurisdictions, property taxes. Approximately 41 percent of the land in the District of Columbia is tax-exempt.[41] Approximately two-thirds of this exemption is attributable to either a federal government or diplomatic presence; the remaining one-third exists for other reasons including religious organizations, or the plethora of nonprofit organizations desiring a national office location or access to the federal government.[42] This is federal property tax policy, applicable to all jurisdictions, and is not uniquely applied in the District of Columbia. What is unique to the District of Columbia is the amount of property exempted from taxation by the operation of these rules.

In an effort to partially offset the lost revenue from the inability to impose a commuter tax, as well as the large amount of tax-exempt land located in the District, the federal government until 1997 made a "federal payment" to the District of Columbia. However, the federal payment was eliminated in the District of Columbia Revitalization Act of 1997.

CONCLUSION

The combined effect of these restrictions is that, in a variety of ways, they restrict the ability of the District of Columbia government to address poverty in a sustained manner. While the District of Columbia has been very successful in its efforts to provide a "safety net" for those at the bottom, in terms of housing subsidies, health insurance, and so on, it has faced challenges in its ability to move individuals and families from dependency to sustained self-sufficiency. This has become even more challenging in a sustained global economic downturn. In the District of Columbia, individual income tax collections from October 2008 to May 2009 were down 18.6 percent from the previous year.[43] When one considers that in difficult economic times the demand for government-provided services increases while the financial ability of the government to continue to provide basic services decreases, the implications of declining revenue are even more acute in the District of Columbia.

Economists often speak of the "multiplier" effect, which refers to the fact that expenditures of money are often respent, thus increasing their original value. An individual is paid a salary. They go to the store and buy food, clothing, and so forth. The store takes that money, pays the salary of its employees, and pays their suppliers for the merchandise received. The employees then go spend their money. The suppliers pay their employees and the cycle continues. Theoretically, everyone pays taxes on the money that passes through their hands. Traditional applications of the multiplier effect do not necessarily work for the District of Columbia because the overwhelming amount of wages earned in the District of Columbia are paid to nonresidents who the District government is congressionally prohibited from taxing.

The District government has been resourceful in its efforts to compensate for the impact of these structural limitations on its ability to generate revenue. For example, the efforts of the District government to use business generation as a mechanism for encouraging money to be spent in the city have been successful.

Downtown has been revitalized with restaurants, movie theatres, and so on. U Street has once again become a vibrant corridor. But, in economic downturns, the first category of discretionary spending reduced or eliminated is entertainment. Relying on an entertainment sector for revenue can be unreliable.

The federally imposed prohibitions restricting the District of Columbia's revenue-generation ability, whether intended to do so or not, also restrict its ability to have the resources necessary to address the poverty causation cycle. Unlike other jurisdictions across the country, the District of Columbia is congressionally prohibited from taxing income earned within its boundaries, as well as from taxing the income of nonresidents working for the city. Combined with the exclusion of almost 40 percent of the city's real property from the property tax rolls, these prohibitions have the effect of placing a stranglehold on the city's ability to generate revenue.

NOTES

1. Wyatt, E. August, 2008. "Tax Rates and Tax Burdens in the District of Columbia—A Nationwide Comparison 2007." Washington, D.C.: Office of Revenue Analysis, Office of the Chief Financial Officer, 32.

2. Malombe, J. 1999. *State and Local Approaches to Poverty in Washington, D.C.* Washington, D.C.: Woodrow Wilson International Center for Scholars.

3. U.S. Census. *District of Columbia: State & County Quick Facts 2008.* www .census.gov.

4. Ibid.

5. The map was created using ArcGIS 9.2; the data was obtained from the U.S. Census 2000 block group datasets; see also Lane, C. Winter, 2009. "Juvenile Offending in the District of Columbia." Washington, D.C.: University of the District of Columbia, Institute for Public Safety and Justice.

6. Ibid.

7. U.S. Bureau of Economic Analysis. 2008. www.bea.gov/bea/regional/data.htm

8. The median personal income in the District of Columbia in 2005 was $48,484. Ibid.

9. U.S. Census Bureau. State Rankings: Median Houshold Income 2007. *Statistical Abstract of the United States.* www.census.gov

10. U.S. Census Bureau. District of Columbia General Selected Economic Characteristics. *2005 American Community Survey.*

11. U.S. Census Bureau. District of Columbia General Selected Housing Characteristics. *2005 American Community Survey.*

12. U.S. National Center for Health Statistics. 2006. www.cdc.gov/nchs/default. htm; see also U.S. Census Bureau. Table 105. *Statistical Abstract of the United States.*

13. U.S. Census Bureau.

14. Ibid.

15. Haynes, V. Dion. July 18, 2009. Unemployment inches up across the D.C. region. *The Washington Post.* www.washingtonpost.com/wp-dyn/content/article/2009/07/17/AR2009071702215.html

16. U.S. Census Bureau. District of Columbia General Selected Housing Characteristics. *2005 American Community Survey.*

17. Malombe, J. 1999. *State and Local Approaches to Poverty in Washington, D.C.* Washington, D.C.: Woodrow Wilson International Center for Scholars.

18. U.S. Census Bureau. District of Columbia General Social Profile. *2004 American Community Survey.*

19. Ibid.

20. District of Columbia Office of Planning: State Data Center. *2000 Educational Level by Ward.*

21. District of Columbia Office of Planning: State Data Center. *1999 Percent of Population below Poverty Level by Ward.*

22. Ross, M., and DeRenzis, B. March 2007. *Reducing Poverty in Washington, D.C. and Rebuilding the Middle Class from Within.* Washington, D.C.: The Brookings Institution Greater Washington Research Program.

23. Day, J. C., and Newburger, E. C. July 2002. "The Big Payoff: Educational Attainment and Synthetic Estimates of Work-Life Earnings." *Special Studies.*

24. Ibid.

25. The Committee on Higher Education, chaired by Councilmember William R. Spaulding, had but one purpose, which was to establish a comprehensive system of higher education for the District of Columbia. Passed by the council on first and second readings on July 15, 1975, and July 29, 1975, the bill was signed by Mayor Walter Washington on August 25, 1975, designated as Act No. 1-50, and transmitted to the Congress of the United States for review.

26. D.C. Code 38-1202.05. An activist Board of Trustees oversaw the consolidation of three separate institutions and provided the important preliminary policy framework which would enable the university to comprehensively address the educational, vocational, and training needs of a previously underserved population. The chairperson of that first board, Ronald Brown, Esq., was later elected chairperson of the Democratic National Committee in 1989, and was appointed by President Clinton as U.S. secretary of commerce in 1993.

27. Spaulding, W. July 6, 2009. Former councilmember, City Council of the District of Columbia. A. Flowers, interviewer.

28. U.S. Census Bureau. District of Columbia General Social Profile. *2004 American Community Survey.*

29. The University of the District of Columbia was not included in this program because D.C. residents already pay in-state tuition to attend. Subsequently, DC-TAG was expanded to include payment of $2,500 for private HBCUs.

30. Jenkins, T. July 27, 2009. Former interim president, University of the District of Columbia. A. Flowers, interviewer.

31. Ibid.

32. The earliest residents of the District of Columbia settled in the Brookland neighborhood in 1688. Following passage of the Organic Act of June 1878, Congress stripped District of Columbia residents of all local self-government. Passage of the District of Columbia Self-Government and Reorganization Act of 1973, also known as the home rule charter, restored some measure of local self-government. However, Congress retained the power to review all legislation passed by the Council of the District of Columbia. Congress also retained a line item veto over each item in the city's budget even though approximately 90 percent of those items are funded by District of Columbia taxes paid by city residents.

33. U.S. Census. *District of Columbia: State & County Quick Facts 2008.* www .census.gov; U.S. Census. *International Data Base 2009: Countries Ranked by Population.* www.census.gov.

34. This was as of July 22, 2009.

35. Malombe, J. 1999. *State and Local Approaches to Poverty in Washington, D.C.* Washington, D.C.: Woodrow Wilson International Center for Scholars.

36. Wyatt, E. August 2008. *Tax Rates and Tax Burdens in the District of Columbia—A Nationwide Comparison 2007.* Washington, D.C.: Office of Revenue Analysis, Office of the Chief Financial Officer.

37. District of Columbia Home Rule Act Sec. 602(a)(5)(2009), as amended. D.C. Official Code § 1-1-206.02(a)(5). December 24, 1973, 87 Stat. 813, Pub. L. 93-198, title VI, § 602.

38. Philadelphia Revenue Department. 2009. *Tax Rate Effective Date: July 1, 2009.* Retrieved July 18, 2009, from Philadelphia Revenue Department, Tax Revenue and Water Revenue Bureau: www.phila.gov/revenue/pdfs/Wage_Tax_Notice__Jun_1.pdf

39. Byrd, D. 2006. "Political Conflict and Intergovernmental Fiscal Relations." In R. F. Pecorella and J. Stonecash. *Governing New York State, fifth ed.* Albany: State University of New York, 42.

40. Ibid.

41. Wyatt, E. August 2008. *Tax Rates and Tax Burdens in the District of Columbia—A Nationwide Comparison 2007.* Washington, D.C.: Office of Revenue Analysis, Office of the Chief Financial Officer.

42. Ibid.

43. Alleyn, B. 2009. *D.C. Economic Indicators July 2009.* Retrieved July 24, 2009, from cfo.dc.gov/cfo.

BIBLIOGRAPHY

Alleyn, B. (2009). *D.C. Economic Indicators July 2009.* Retrieved July 24, 2009, from cfo.dc.gov/cfo.

Byrd, D. (2006). Political Conflict and Intergovernmental Fiscal Relations. In R. F. Pecorella and J. Stonecash. *Governing New York State, fifth ed.* Albany: State University of New York.

Centers for Disease Control and Prevention. (2006). Table 105. *Statistical Abstract of the United States.*

District of Columbia Home Rule Act Sec. 602(a)(5) (2009), as amended. D.C. Official Code § 1-1-206.02(a)(5). Dec. 24, 1973, 87 Stat. 813, Pub. L. 93-198, title VI, § 602.

D.C. Code 38-1202.05.

D.C. Office of Planning: State Data Center. *2000 Educational Level by Ward.*

D.C. Office of Planning: State Data Center. *1999 Percent of Population below Poverty Level by Ward.*

Day, J. C., and Newburger, E. C. (July 2002). "The Big Payoff: Educational Attainment and Synthetic Estimates of Work-Life Earnings." *Special Studies.*

Haynes, V. Dion. July 18, 2009. "Unemployment inches up across the D.C. region." *The Washington Post.* www.washingtonpost.com/wp-dyn/content/article/2009/07/17/AR2009071702215.html.

Jenkins, T. (July 27, 2009). Former interim president, University of the District of Columbia (A. Flowers, interviewer).

Lane, C. (Winter 2009). *Juvenile Offending in the District of Columbia.* Washington, D.C.: University of the District of Columbia, Institute for Public Safety and Justice.

Malombe, J. (1999). *State and Local Approaches to Poverty in Washington, D.C.* Washington, D.C.: Woodrow Wilson International Center for Scholars.

Philadelphia Revenue Department. (2009). *Tax Rate Effective Date: July 1, 2009.* Retrieved July 18, 2009, from Philadelphia Revenue Department: Tax Revenue and Water Revenue Bureau: www.phila.gov/revenue/pdfs/Wage_Tax_Notice__Jun_1.pdf.

Population Division, U.S. Census Bureau. (Release Date: December 22, 2005). Table 1: Annual Estimates of the Population for the United States and for Puerto Rico: April 1, 2000 to July 1, 2005 (NST-EST 2005-01).

Ross, M., and DeRenzis, B. (March 2007). *Reducing Poverty in Washington, D.C. and Rebuilding the Middle Class from Within.* Washington, D.C.: The Brookings Institution Greater Washington Research Program.

Spaulding, W. (July 6, 2009). Former councilmember, City Council of the District of Columbia. (A. Flowers, interviewer)

U.S. Bureau of Economic Analysis. (2008). www.bea.gov/bea/regional/data.htm.

U.S. Census Bureau. www.census.gov.

- Census 2000 Demographic Profile Highlights. Retrieved July 15, 2009
- District of Columbia General Selected Economic Characteristics. 2005 American Community Survey.
- District of Columbia General Selected Housing Characteristics. 2005 American Community Survey.
- District of Columbia General Selected Housing Characteristics. 2004 American Community Survey.
- District of Columbia General Social Profile 2004. 2004 American Community Survey
- District of Columbia: State & County Quick Facts 2008.
- International Data Base. (2009). Countries Ranked by Population.

- State Rankings: Median Houshold Income 2007. Statistical Abstract of the United States
- Table 689: Statistical Abstract of the United States, 2006.
- Table 699. Statistical Abstract of the United States 2006.

U.S. National Center for Health Statistics. (2006). www.cdc.gov/nchs/default.htm

Wyatt, E. (August 2008). *Tax Rates and Tax Burdens in the District of Columbia—A Nationwide Comparison 2007*. Washington, D.C.: Office of Revenue Analysis, Office of the Chief Financial Officer.

12

Communicating Liberation in Washington, D.C.

Jared A. Ball

This is DC you might think that you own it, a piece of South Africa on the Potomac. . . . See you can't vote, but you got to pay taxes, not a city or a state because their scared of the blacks. Fuck "Chocolate City," imagine a chocolate state with two chocolate senators in the debate.

DJ EuRok[1]

And so, today, we have this irony: engraved over the entryways to the headquarters for many of the largest corporate media firms (and of the entryways to many of the journalism schools that dutifully train employees to serve these same corporations) are lofty quotations from John Stuart Mill, Thomas Jefferson, Abraham Lincoln, and other greats from the liberal pantheon—all of them invoking the necessity of a free press to establish an informed citizenry and a viable democracy.

Robert McChesney[2]

INTRODUCTION

It is a widely held concept that in order for democracy to thrive there must first be an informed populace. The idea is simple of course. Public policy, that which largely determines the distribution of societal resources and benefits, is largely impacted by civic engagement and, specifically, the electoral vote. Voting, therefore, should be a highly involved process where an aware citizenry can regularly cast votes on the various issues of the day in order to have their interests represented. However, equally well-known is that should a media environment be meticulously constructed, one designed to limit the extent

225

to which a population is "informed," then that same "democracy" could easily be managed so as to never truly threaten the kinds of imbalances in power seen today. In no place is a microcosm of our national dilemma more on display than in Washington, D.C., where residents very much exist like the fish who it is said did not discover water because "an all-pervasive environment is always beyond perception."[3] Residents of the nation's capital, "The Diamond District," are forcibly held in a media environment largely devoid of the kind of media which might foster a greater degree of the kind of civic engagement which encourages higher levels of informed decision-making and results in community concerns being more substantively met. Public policy concerns, of which the city has many, can only be addressed when communities are themselves politically aware to the point of activity and this kind of awareness must be communicated via some form or another of mass media.

Public policy, again, that which determines who gets what in society, has powerful material ramifications. Nationally, racialized struggles over policy have been described in terms of the protection of "white nationalism" in which has evolved a sophisticated "public policy racism" designed to protect those interests.[4] This kind of national manipulation of public policy has prompted legal scholar and professor Derrick Bell to conclude:

> If the nation's policies towards blacks were revised to require weekly, random round-ups of several hundred blacks who were then taken to a secluded place and shot, that policy would be more dramatic, but hardly different in result, than the policies now in effect, which most of us feel powerless to change.[5]

This kind of public policy equivalence in result is nowhere better witnessed than in Washington, D.C. The very public policy of continued (and under-reported) police brutality, gentrification (read: forced relocation), and health care and wealth disparities remains omitted from popular discourse or held in such a fixed/limited form that necessary shifts in political consciousness expressed via civic engagement have yet to be successful. This is a city where "even amid an economic boom. . . . The District's poverty rate is the highest in nearly a decade, and the employment rate for African American adults is at a 20-year low." This employment-rate low, which in 2006—prior to this most recent crisis—dropped for black adults to 51 percent,[6] means that black unemployment in Washington, D.C. at 49 percent is *higher* than the 45 percent in all of Gaza—said by the United Nations at that time (2008) to be the "highest in the world."[7] And yet, despite these and many other worsening conditions—in this city and abroad—the question remains, "Where have all the protests gone?"[8]

However, protests or any measure designed to impact public policy means higher rates of politically conscious communities, which, it has long been noted, require that these concerns be more popularly considered and more often. This is precisely what this nation's architects of mass media, its practice and study, have fought against for decades. The origins of the field of mass communication research are found in government-sponsored propaganda studies where control of national communication was/is seen as a "fourth arm" of the military[9] and where manipulation of people's political acumen was seen as essential to the protection of an "invisible government" through managed elections.[10] It then becomes essential to consider the impact on policy by a societal media environment and, in this case, the media or communications environment of Washington, D.C.

If, as Noam Chomsky has said, "propaganda is to democracy what violence is to totalitarianism,"[11] then within an *un*democratic colony media must truly then be that wing of colonial rule described by Frantz Fanon as "psychic violence." Often Washington, D.C., has been referred to not as a democracy but as "the nation's largest plantation,"[12] or "America's last colony."[13] These, of course, are references to a majority black city which has no voting representation in Congress, lacks internal control of its economy, suffers high rates of gentrification, borrows policing techniques from the state of Israel, and has police officers who suggest that it is improper for African American residents to be in the more affluent and white areas of the city. However, were these analogies of enslavement and colonialism extended as the lens through which mass media in the city today are considered, then new analyses and responses might develop to grapple with naturally resulting questions, such as what would media in a colony look or sound like? Or how would a community perceiving a need for liberation and, therefore, a desire to communicate that need go about doing so and with what potential impact? If communicating liberation, however that is to be defined, is seen through the lens of anticolonial struggle or as the practice of "revolutionary media"—that which is "illegal and subversive mass communication utilizing the press and broadcasting to overthrow government or wrest control from alien rulers"[14]—or as simply a way of communicating ideas which legally threaten the undesired genuine democratic restructuring of city governance, then how would such communication take place?

To fully appreciate this dilemma, the way in which many see media must be challenged. Comedian Chris Rock has for many exemplified their views of media when in his hilarious, if not accurate, routine on "black people v. niggers" he explains that too much emphasis is placed on the importance of media as a major purveyor of negative imagery regarding black people, none of which override the power of individual or communal behavior. Parroting conservative positions of individual or collective responsibility, he concludes this segment describing his concerns when at "the ATM late at

night I'm not looking over my shoulder for the media, I'm looking for niggers!" This, of course, discounts the well-documented history of media being
seen as that which encourage forms of behavior and also how that behavior is
promoted and then interpreted. Media have long been seen as necessary for
the construction and maintenance of "public opinion," or, regarding African
America, as part of a "war of images" waged against African-descended
people here and abroad and used to justify the oppressive treatment suffered
by these communities.

So Rock's often poignant commentary misses the mark here. The concern is not the "organized technologies" by which media are often defined
(i.e. television, film, radio, newspapers, etc.). Media are more accurately
understood by their function and historical use as mechanisms of rule. They
establish cognitive norms, acceptable ranges of thought or discussion, and are
the primary disseminators of elite ideology. So it has never been about who
to fear at an ATM in the middle of the night as much as it has been about
shaping how people will interpret or how media play a role in developing
that fear.

The fundamental challenge presented in Rock's argument is the relationship media have with society. Attendant to that is the fundamental confusion
over the form this society has taken or its intent. If one accepts the popular
mythology of this nation being a democracy whose goal is freedom and
equality for all, then it does follow more easily that media would play a more
or less benign role. However, if another version or tradition of analysis were
to be applied, one that critically challenges this popular mythology, media
and their role is reinterpreted. The oft-repeated colonial analogies applied
to Washington, D.C., offer a point of entry into a discussion of a tradition
of scholarship whose view is that this nation as a whole has a relationship,
particularly with its black population, more akin to colonialism, which creates
"subjects," as opposed to a liberal democracy, which creates citizens. The
difference in treatment based on race or class is at its essence no accident,
but instead the natural outcome of a relationship between a colonial elite who
needs in varied ways to suppress any liberating aspirations of those whose
function as subject (as opposed to citizen) is to serve and produce the wealth
of that elite. This has long since required that popular mass media be used
toward that end. Media, far more than the technology which delivers them
(radio, television, film, etc.), are disseminated ideas. Media are the ideology
of those who control them, not necessarily those who appear in them. Simply
stated, the person we see, hear, or read in popular media is the *least* powerful
person in the process of producing that media. DJs do not choose the music
they play, news anchors do not select or necessarily even write the stories
they read, nor do actors have much (or any) input into their scripts. Their role

is to ensure that the intended meanings in the media they disseminate or are a part of have the greatest impact upon their audience (victims).

Within colonies media play a role second only to their militarized physical counterparts as the "psychic violence" which maintains order. They are used to encourage identification with the state, individual, and community identity and even as mechanisms of calming ease to the settler populations. Today they are seen as that which will ensure U.S. empire, as explained by Zbigniew Brzezinski:

> The American global system emphasizes the technique of co-optation . . . to a much greater extent than the earlier imperial systems did. It likewise relies heavily on the indirect exercise of influence on dependent foreign elites, while drawing much benefit from the appeal of its democratic principles and institutions. All of the foregoing are reinforced by the massive but *intangible impact* of the *American domination of global communications, popular entertainment, and mass culture* and by the potentially very tangible clout of America's technological edge and military reach. *Cultural domination has been an underappreciated facet of American global power.* . . . America's mass culture exercises a magnetic appeal, especially on the world's youth. . . . American television programs and films account for about three-fourths of the global market. American popular music is equally dominant, while American fads, eating habits, and even clothing are exceedingly imitated worldwide. The language of the internet is English, and an overwhelming proportion of the global computer chatter also originates from America, influencing the content of global conversation.[15]

Similarly, and more recently, the former president George W. Bush called upon Congress for a $75 million boost in funding for "propaganda" targeted at Iran[16] and the former secretary of defense Donald Rumsfeld made clear the role mass media are to play in the continuing "war on terror":

> "In many ways, many critical battles in the war on terror will be fought in the newsrooms and the editorial board rooms," continued Donald Rumsfeld. "Unlike the Cold War, this is an era of far more rapid communications, with the Internet, and bloggers, and chat rooms, and 24-hour news channels and satellite radio. Just as millions who were trapped in Eastern Europe during the Cold War were given hope by messages that filtered in from the West, similarly, I believe there are reformers in the Middle East who have been silenced and intimidated, and who want their countries to be free."[17]

In fact, the historical development of the entire field of communication studies is marred by a need to study and develop effective propaganda for the maintenance of control over ever-increasing populations nationally and globally. Their goal has long been the propagation of elite interests and the suppression of "dissident communication" or that which might encourage behavior found to be unacceptable to those in power.[18] Therefore, it is politically naive to assume a general ineffectiveness of media to affect consciousness and behavior or their particular function within a colony.

Further, this has been the point of media scholars for quite some time. It is the very focus of those, like Harold Innis, whose intellectual gaze was directed at how the advent of communication technology historically has meant suppression of "abstract thought" as knowledge becomes monopolized "to the point that {societal} equilibrium is disturbed."[19] For Innis, this disturbed equilibrium or imbalance is the coalescing of power among a tiny elite and is inextricably linked to the historical shift in mass communication from oral traditions to ones based in the technology of writing (and then later radio, television, film, etc.). It is this which has allowed for the establishment of civilizations which "could be disciplined to the point of effective political unity."[20] Again, "effective" refers to that which supports the rule of those in power. Once communication became organized by advanced technology, it also meant that those in control of that technology could determine which forms of communication would be spread en masse, to whom, and, to a great extent, to what effect.

Musically, for example, this is the equivalent of the industry deemphasizing improvisation in order to organize music, format it to the needs of commercial media, and destroy its potential to generate thought or behavior deemed unacceptable. As Ian Carr writes, "all qualities necessary for jazz [or the "freestyle" in hip-hop[21]]—individuality, spontaneity, autonomous control, trust in one's chosen associates—have always been anathema to totalitarian regimes" which quite necessarily require restraints on thought.[22] Today's form, described a bit more below, manifests in rigid song playlists which are determined by record label payments to radio stations which then reduce the DJ or host to blind sycophancy as opposed to independent fonts of musical wisdom and diversity (never mind quality). The journalistic, equivalent is the imposed self-censorship of editors, journalists, and media workers who "know" where their boundaries lie in terms of stories covered, perspectives taken, and so on. False balance and "objectivity" as a professional cult become restraints on journalists which prevent great accuracy in reporting. If an issue is to be covered, "both sides" must be given, attention which fraudulently assumes that there are only two sides to an issue or that one side is as legitimate and deserving of equal attention as another.

Within a professed "free democratic" society these same communicative limits must be applied—even more so—according to Noam Chomsky, who has said that "propaganda is to democracy what violence is to totalitarianism."[23] Despite such claims of freedom and democracy, D.C.'s microcosmic description as a colony helps to isolate how media function to maintain disparate communities both physically (in terms of socialization, gentrification, etc.) and psychologically (in terms of ensuring that different communities receive similar messages from the same entities but fashioned to their specific "tastes"). Here, again, comes the local application of Brzezinski's point of the use of media to maintain empire. In D.C., many—including Ben Bagdikian—have noted how the massive consolidation of ownership of mass media over the last twenty to thirty years has meant a reduction in the "diversity of cultural goods in circulation."[24] Only five CEOs currently head companies that own more mass media outlets than were held twenty years ago by fifty corporations, which has given them what "no imperial ruler in past history" has ever had, comprising "multiple media channels that included television and satellite channels that can permeate entire societies with controlled sights and sounds."[25] Such consolidation does suggest more than a tendency toward the monopoly of thought described by Innis as being necessary to maintaining order.

Nationwide mass media are highly desired properties which are consolidated in ownership for the purposes of ensuring both financial profit and social order. Fragmentation, or the dispersal of audiences into conceptual ghettoes all to be fed specifically tailored media developed by the same ownership, allows for fewer people to be involved in wider dissemination and penetration of audiences than ever before. All of this led the Pew Research Center's Project for Excellence in Journalism to reach the following conclusion in 2007:

> News consumers may have had more choices than ever for where to find news in 2007, but that does not mean they had more news to choose from. The news agenda for the year was, in fact, quite narrow, dominated by a few major general topic areas. Together, coverage of U.S. foreign policy and U.S. politics and elections accounted for almost one-third of the overall newshole for the year. It gets even narrower if we look at the specific news stories that drove coverage in each of those topic areas. Year-long coverage of the 2008 presidential campaign pre-empted most political attention. And coverage of U.S. foreign policy topics was dominated by the war in Iraq and the debate over war strategy.[26]

In Washington, D.C., a similar trend in media ownership emerges with predictable results. Popular media are consolidated in their ownership and revenue-generating (advertising) structure, and, therefore, as suggested above, establish serious challenges to anyone interested in disseminating counter-hegemonic communication. The largest media outlets in the city are, predictably, owned by the largest national media companies and conglomerates. *The Washington Post*, owned by The Washington Post Company, may attempt to appear as a "family-owned" entity but its board of directors (which includes billionaire investor Warren Buffett[27]) and its obedience to "the establishment"[28] belie any such claim. General Electric has WRC/NBC, Disney has WJLA/ABC, News Corp. has WTTG/Fox, Viacom has WUSA/CBS, and Infinity Broadcasting has D.C. radio stations WPGC 95.5 FM, WPGC 1580 AM, WARW 94.7 FM, WHFS 99.1 FM, and WJFK 106.7 FM. And, of course, as is rampant in media (as well as all business), "competitors" at times work with one another, so News Corp.'s WDCA airs Viacom's United Paramount Network (UPN). Radio One, the nation's largest radio provider to African Americans, owns WKYS 93.9 FM, WMMJ 102.3 FM, WOL 1450 AM, and WYCB 1340 AM. And not to be outdone or left behind, Clear Channel, the nation's largest radio station owner, has D.C.'s WASH 97.1 FM, WBIG 100.3 FM, and WWDC 101.1 FM, among others. Adding to this is Clear Channel's dominance over the media landscape of the city's (and nation's) billboards, bus kiosk signage, and so on. D.C. has become one of its "branded cities" where "brandscaping" turns communal spaces into "controlled environment[s]" where "brands [are] to be experienced" and unavoidably interwoven into people's daily lives.[29]

This consolidated ownership, and the larger political and economic context in which it exists, results in the apparent disparate relationship between the majority population of the city and the media available to them. The city's demographic being majority black and defined as "liberal" exists within a media structure which has recently been described as "an elaborate and heavily subsidized right-wing media machine in the city" which is buttressed by right-wing think tanks whose goal, through the publishing of reports, emails and press releases, is to influence the press or to drag the mainstream further to the right. This, according to Thomas Frank, allows this right-wing minority to greatly influence the popular mainstream while maintaining the appearance of professionalism and objectivity.[30]

Alternatives, however, do exist. There remain, for example, any number of smaller community and ethnic journals, magazines, and newspapers. There is *The Afro-American Tribune* (Afro) newspaper, which overall has maintained circulation numbers in the face of a national drop in newspaper readership. There is WPFW 89.3 FM, the liberal Pacifica Network's affiliate and a host of smaller "alternative" media outlets, low-power FM, and even the author's own attempts at an underground press using the hip-hop mixtape.[31] However, these sources are forced to struggle—to the extent they reach or penetrate only smaller audiences—against what is established as the norm or primary selection of stories, topics, and interpretations all set by dominant media. So, as in all cases, these smaller outlets must compete against a norm established to be that against which all else must be measured. That is, for example, even with recent drops in *Washington Post* circulation, their D.C.-area paid circulation is still 635,000[32] compared to the *Afro*'s 20,000.[33] Though broadcasting from a fifty-thousand-watt tower, WPFW's impact is lessened by its lack of commercial advertising, and the vast multitude of the marginalized whose disparate and eclectic—isolated—voices fail in amassing any powerful or collective movement.

To the contrary, the power of mainstream mass media's consolidated ownership and its subsequent fragmentation (one owner of multiple stations, channels, publications, etc.), or its ability to tailor its more or less monolithic message to a variety of specific audiences broken down along lines of race, gender, age, sexual orientation, and so on, is magnified by a similarly consolidated advertising industry whose ability to promote and disseminate its content in such a cost-prohibitive environment is more than any one form of the alternative media (be it WPFW or any other) can compete against. Similarly, low-power FM with its unsanctioned limited signal (roughly a three-mile radius) or the low production count of mixtapes (no more than three thousand per edition) all demonstrate the historical pattern of uneven distributive or promotional capacities. And while many claim the Internet is a great leveling medium, it too is limited in its capacity due to uneven promotional revenues for various websites (including those supported by their parallel in other media, i.e., CNN can promote CNN.com), which even in its general usage among individuals mimics their preexisting interests and political biases.[34] There is also the ongoing battle over "Net Neutrality,"[35] which threatens to result in premium web speed going only to those websites owned by corporations large enough to pay telecommunication companies the premium rates for access while the rest become marginalized by slow speed, which effectively kills their ability to compete in what many continue to mistakenly believe is a free or liberating medium. Consider also the recent battles over Internet radio, which threaten the same kind of limiting constrictions we face in regular or terrestrial radio.[36]

The emergence historically of a commercially driven mass media where content is determined and managed by those who pay the advertising revenue sublimates particular ownership and ensures that media will perform their colonizing function. It validates Marx's claim that "the ruling ideas of any epoch are the ideas of the ruling elite" and offers the deception described by Chomsky as "propaganda is to democracy what violence is to totalitarianism."[37] So it is that the prideful "brandscaping" of Clear Channel is not simply about advertising for sales or products but for what advertising is known to be, the sale of people's consciousness—"the higher value of eyeballs"[38]— from one to the next. In fact, this system of advertising driving or determining media content not only is a mechanism of negating the power of ownership, it forces "the formal right to establish a free press [to be] exercised by dissidents on the margins, but the commercial system is such that these voices have no hope to expand beyond their metaphorical house arrest."[39] Advertising, product placement, and branding are processes of imposing ideology so as to encourage and ensure acceptable forms of behavior. All of this is, of course, buttressed by the ever-impending use of "physical violence" should there be any breaks with that which is acceptable behavior, hence, the police brutality,[40] mass incarceration, overt statements about where those colonized should or should not go,[41] the covert transportation,[42] and architectural impediments[43] to free form movement including the recent police cordoning off of neighborhoods.[44] Washington, D.C., is a place, as described by Antonio Gramsci, where "[e]verything which influences or is able to influence public opinion, directly or indirectly, belongs to {the ideological structure}: libraries, schools, associations and clubs of various kinds, even architecture and the layout and names of streets."[45]

What this does mean is that those interested in communicating counter-hegemonic ideas, that which would encourage the development of Sandoval's "oppositional consciousness"—that which must precede oppositional political organization and activity—cannot expect to use mainstream media to that end. To provide at least one more fully developed concrete example, and given the city's demographic makeup, a focus on the city's radio system, particularly that targeting black audiences, will be explored.

THE DIAMOND DISTRICT AND CORPORATE MEDIA MINING

Radio One is Black Power!

Cathy Hughes (owner of Radio One)
Remark made during keynote speech delivered
to Morgan State University's 2007 graduating class

Washington, D.C., provides an appropriate approximation of the previously described struggle surrounding the dissemination of unsanctioned, unauthorized cultural expression or journalism. It remains a predominantly black city (57 percent) and is surrounded by Prince George's County, which at 66 percent black[46] is also the wealthiest black community in the country. Given this demographic, in our current discussion of media and the potential to communicate, liberation radio is best suited for an analysis given the community's material condition and relationship to radio. Black America's use of black-targeted radio, with its roughly 80–90 percent household penetration rates,[47] is greater than any other community's relationship to radio targeting them.

And while, again, there exist various forms of media, radio remains the primary and most pervasive medium targeting African America.[48] Though Howard University's WHUR (96.3 FM) ranks number one in citywide ratings, it cannot be said to be so rated among black youth nor can it be said to have any more oppositional content than the two stations that dominate among black youth—a key demographic long sought after by activists to maintain or evolve radical politics and by those seeking to blunt those same efforts.[49] For younger audiences there are really only two radio stations: Viacom's WPGC (95.5 FM), ranked third in the city, and Radio One's WKYS (93.9 FM), ranked fifth.[50] Part of the overall problem, a problem to be more fully developed below, is summarized by Glen Ford, former editor of Black Commentator.com and current editor of Black Agenda Report.com. He says:

> In 1973, 21 reporters from three Black-oriented radio stations provided African Americans in Washington, DC a daily diet of news—*hard, factual information vital to the material and political fortunes of the local community.* The three stations—WOL-AM, WOOK-AM and WHUR-FM—their news staffs as fiercely competitive as their disc jockeys, vied for domination of the Black Washington market. Community activists and institutions demanded, expected, and received intense and sustained coverage of the fullest range of their activities.[51] (emphasis added)

This, according to Ford, was a response to "the voices of an awakened people" whose involvement in variations of the civil/human rights and black liberation struggles mounted an undeniable challenge to mass media institutions to diversify staff and content. And specific to our immediate focus on Washington, D.C., and the impact of radio on African America, Ford notes the fact that "Black ownership has relatively little to do with the phenomenon. . . . According to the National Association of Black-owned Broadcasters (NABOB), there were only 30 African American–owned broadcast facilities in the United States in 1976." "Today," Ford continues, "NABOB boasts 220 member stations—and local Black radio news is near extinction." Not allowed to meddle with the role media play, black ownership does not significantly affect content or in this case news gathering/reporting. Again, Ford explains that "black-oriented radio journalism in the nation's capitol has plummeted from 21 reporters at three stations . . . to four reporters at two stations." Three of these reporters work for Howard University station WHUR 96.3 FM and one at Viacom's WPGC. Radio One, the largest national chain and owner of the enormously popular WKYS 93.9 FM in Washington, D.C., staffs no reporters. According to Ford, while the "great homogenizer of American radio" on a national level remains Clear Channel, with its more than 1,100 stations, "the queen of Black broadcasting is Radio One [with well over sixty stations], and her dictum is, 'Let Them Eat Talk'" (Ford, 2004, emphasis added).[52]

Ford touches upon a number of serious concerns facing proponents of progressive political struggle and certainly those seeking to expand the reach of liberating communication. First among them is that Radio One, the leading provider of black-targeted radio,[53] follows precisely the established model of dominant-society radio. Its FM stations follow the same payola-based playlist format assuring "homogenization" of the music and there exists no attempt at investigative journalism or news gathering. What Radio One offers, as is the case with Washington, D.C.'s WOL and Baltimore's WOLB AM stations, is talk radio. While the latter is not without benefit, it does not replace news gathering, particularly the kind Ford describes as being related and necessary to political movements. In response to these concerns are statements from Victor Starr, program director at Radio One's Baltimore FM station 92.3, who dismisses that station's need to deliver news to its audience "in an information era" where one can easily go to "CNN.com" to get the important news not covered in the two-minute segments each hour, that is unless it is something on the order of "Anna Nicole's death" in which case mention will be made.[54] Or from Lee Michaels, at that time the program director of Radio One's XM169 "The Power," the response was that "radio is business" and, therefore, Radio One need not nor *cannot* continue any tradition of black progressivism in radio (or that particular role for black America). Also, in statements strikingly similar to those engaged in "media reform" efforts, Michaels too suggests that change can only come from the people appealing to the Federal Communications Commission (FCC).[55]

However, it is precisely these disparate approaches, each calling for mass appeals to the FCC as the primary (only) mechanism for change, one from an ostensibly "outsider media reform movement," the other from one situated well within that institution (and in no insignificant position), that demand attention be paid to the *systemic* nature of colonialism. The final mass media product, that which hits the air, is predetermined to be limited in scope, safe, and functionally supportive of that which determines its shape. Neither race nor gender nor title of "owner" or "program director" in the end is of any significance. And strategies for change which focus exclusively on or tend to overemphasize the importance of appeals to the FCC are the political equivalent to the hen's appeal to the fox or better still Malcolm X's chicken laying, of course, a chicken egg. If it were to lay a "duck egg it would be one revolutionary chicken."

The FCC, whose nominal role is regulation of the public's airwaves, has, since its inception in 1934, never been able to assure that black images were anything other than that described in endless criticism as "Uncle Toms, Mammies and Aunt Jemimas."[56] Its five-member body consisting of appointees of the president with the tie-breaker going to that president's party along with its limited funding for in-depth study assures its impotency as an agent for change. Its oversight of the initial multibillion dollar giveaway of the public's airwaves has been followed by decades of policy or inaction which have sustained the control of those airwaves securely within the most elite segments of our society. "'The function of the FCC,' as one former chair informed William Kennard as he assumed the chair in 1997, 'is to referee fights between the wealthy and the super wealthy.'"[57] It is currently overseeing the further billion-dollar giveaway of our airwaves and digital spectrum which will likely relegate the new technologies of digital television and the Internet to a fate that is predictable—inevitable—in an ongoing process of colonization.

Since the 1996 Telecommunications Act further deregulated airwaves (paving the way also for Radio One to accumulate more stations), the situation has worsened as diversity of media content has lessened.[58] The impact of this, particularly—though not exclusively—on black youth, has been explored in a number of ways. One recent study from University of Chicago showed,[59] among other results, that most black youth did not like the hip-hop and R&B they heard on commercial radio and yet, as other studies, conducted in part by this author, show, the prevalence of that limited range of cultural expression (matched by almost zero news content) remains the norm. Colonizing media does not require liking; it only requires recognition as the norm or as the popular form of that which it claims to represent, be it music, news, or whatever else.[60]

Radio and television monitoring projects conducted (by this author's own classes) at the University of Maryland at College Park and continuing now at Morgan State University[61] resulted in dozens of FCC complaints being filed by students with no significant response or action. However, with no expected structural change coming from student monitoring projects and/or letters to the FCC, the real value of these studies is their coerced focus on content which results in higher levels of clarity among students as to what they are hearing and how, even why, what they hear makes it to air.

Students, listening to one of the two dominant commercial radio stations (with an option to select any other commercial radio station as their second choice for monitoring), created pie charts detailing what was heard, when, and for what duration. They only monitored programming at one-hour intervals, between 5 a.m. and 10 a.m. and again from 5 p.m. to 10 p.m. on weekdays. The results clearly demonstrate the aforementioned lack of news (most charts collected in the last run of this project contained no slots depicted as "news" and none which consisted of news departing from the variety described above by Victor Starr) and an adherence to the supremacy of advertising and major record label selected music. WPGC and WKYS, which dominate youth radio listening (ages twelve to seventeen), much like all dominant mainstream radio, have their content determined by a three-corporation "musical OPEC"[62] which is ultimately responsible for nearly everything we hear on radio (or see on music video channels). This leads to nationwide airing of songs, or spins, which reach the tens of thousands in a month, ten thousand in one week, or once an hour, every hour, every day.

Student reports again demonstrated a concern facing those interested in counter-hegemonic or critical thought related to or in advocacy of societal change (liberation). Described as "concision,"[63] the issue is time allowed for substantive discussion or dissemination of ideas which might counter those promoted by the powers that be and, therefore, made the norm. With so much of an hour consumed by sanctioned, paid-for,[64] major-label music, advertisements, and "news," any time allowed (even hypothetically) would be greatly limited so as to make the spokesperson defending or explaining ideas so little discussed or understood seem strange or delusional. With no time to make an unpopular argument, the system resets or protects itself in perpetuity from becoming what it has never intended to be. If, in popular media, a discussion is held which simply repeats popularly held "wisdoms," there is no time needed to clarify or explain and, therefore, those comments are easily made to fit within limited media space. However, to challenge popular notions requires time to detail, argue, and demonstrate those unpopular positions in a manner which would seem clear, sane or cogent. This is not easily done in the two-to-five-minute windows left for any discussion, news or reporting. It is a structural impediment to disseminating oppositional views which, again, maintains popular illusions of normalcy, objectivity and professionalism. Here, again, is the original intent behind mass media, that is, to produce that which already has been determined to be accepted fare for the audience/target and not as a source of anything new, controversial, or system-changing. As legendary establishment scholar Walter Lippmann said regarding the importance of "manufacturing consent," public opinions "must be organized *for* the press if they are to be sound, not *by* the press."[65]

This, of course, determines that not only will so much time each day be spent on airing these paid-for songs, but it also means that this time is taken away from the airing of other music. And certainly then the kinds of information so necessary to communities facing the worst of this nation's economic, social, cultural and racial policies would need more air (or print) time to help support or encourage more adequate responses. The radio applauded by Dr. King in 1967 for having assisted the civil rights movement exists, if at all, in a tremendously weakened or limited capacity.[66] This issue is the subject of a recent documentary from radio legend Bob Law called "Disappearing Voices—The Decline of Black Radio." In it Law traces the devolution of black radio from that which at one time would allow for "political and social activists [to] mobilize thousands of people by simply putting the word out over the radio about a protest or rally"[67] to today where, as radio host and hip-hop historian DaveyD has noted, no rally or political event is known to its target audience in most major cities usually because black-targeted radio is promoting "50 Cent" or some other apolitical commercial artist.[68]

So it is sadly ironic for a question like "Where are the Petey Greenes of today?"[69] to appear in *The Washington Post*. It is sadly ironic that an establishment paper would raise a question meant to elicit consideration of the poor state of black talk radio or the absence of people who, like Greene,[70] could use the radio to electrify audiences and encourage organized response to existing conditions. It is particularly dispiriting considering the question was raised in the context of praising the rise of Radio One and its adherence to the black talk radio tradition with its inclusion of WOL AM talk radio, five days prior to the sudden dismissal of politically progressive hosts Ambrose I. Lane Sr. and Mark Thompson (Matsimela Mapfumo) from the network. As the *Washington Post* raises the question of the quality and power of black talk radio, the genre's leading provider was simultaneously undercutting its own potential. However, even were this an attempt to move closer to the political middle where the most revenue is to be gained, it has apparently not been enough as recent financial troubles at Radio One have led to the selling off of further stations, a loss of its deal with XM satellite, and even the exodus of top executives, including Lee Michaels.[71] Here, again, are the limiting effects of advertising revenue which ultimately undercuts any individual owner's will. This is assuredly connected to the recent trend in media purchasing toward private equity groups, themselves involved in widely diverse international holdings.[72] So as more media becomes owned by fewer people who then invest in diverse businesses around the globe, the less room there is for dissident communication and less recourse for audiences interested in challenging existing media practices. Whereas it may have at one point been politically savvy to boycott local media or its sponsors, today this is less likely to be an effective option given that the immediate entity against which people would want to protest is likely but one piece of an international collection of holdings. Similarly, the major advertisers are likely to also have such a diverse portfolio as to severely limit any potential damage caused by a boycott by one community. This means such an effort would likely need to be organized on a national or international level to have the desired impact.

There is yet another consequence of media-encouraged apathy among the colonized audiences. This apathy, described by Fanon as so

> universally noted among colonial peoples is but the logical consequence of this operation. The reproach of inertia constantly directed at "the native" is utterly dishonest. As though it were possible for a man to evolve otherwise than

within the framework of a culture that recognized him and that he decides to assume.[73]

This inertia was made yet again popular, albeit unwittingly, when in January 2007 Oprah Winfrey popularly stated that

> [i]f you are a child in the United States, you can get an education. I became so frustrated with visiting inner-city schools that I just stopped going. The sense that you need to learn just isn't there. If you ask the kids what they want or need, they will say an iPod or some sneakers. In South Africa, they don't ask for money or toys. They ask for uniforms so they can go to school.[74]

Aside from the anti-historical nature of the comment or her positioning as a "black leader" despite being a "neoliberal icon" with a primary audience of affluent white women,[75] her comments defy the reality of the media environment impacting these "inner-city" youths. Perhaps, to the extent that there is truth in these comments, she might investigate the content and messaging in her show or, more appropriately, explore the content and delivery mechanism of the media directed at these unappreciative black children. This desire for material goods Winfrey laments is as likely to occur from the formulaic, massively repetitive, and newsless radio imposed upon that community, an imposition which as previously noted occurs regardless of a particular community's desire to hear it.[76]

Few would argue that hip-hop has become today the nation's (and world's) leading cultural product. It certainly remains so for young people and African Americans in general. In 2005 the final *American Brandstand* report was published, which tracked the prevalence of product placement and name-brand mentions within hip-hop lyrics.[77] The sheer amount of airplay coupled with the infusion of product placement, leaves little confusion as to why so many young people might, as Winfrey thoughtlessly lamented, be more focused on material goods than deeper intellectual pursuits. Perhaps were this matched with assessments of the modern "education" facing most African American students,[78] the concern would shift from blame to radical change. According to the 2005 *American Brandstand* report, Mercedes Benz topped the product placement "mentions" with one hundred separate references in hip-hop lyrics.

Magnify this by songs which routinely gain weekly spins nationwide in the six-to-ten-thousand range and its potential impact on audiences becomes clear. Winfrey's reference to "sneakers" being so desired by black youth—to the extent that any of her claims are true—would be of no surprise given that Nike, number two on the list, had sixty-three separate "mentions" that year. Rounding out that top ten list are AK 47 assault rifles which had thirty-seven "mentions" that year. It bears repeating that this result comes at the end of a process of music selection and promotion which has nothing to do with artist or audience choice. Artists who routinely produce more humane or community-supportive music are all but banned as they are not seen as marketable. Therefore, they are not signed or promoted as it is quite correctly understood to be antithetical to the needs of business and colonization to promote artists protesting corporate dominance, conspicuous consumption, or self-directed, anti-revolutionary violence.

Further, that anyone would blame societal flaws on its youngest and most powerless members speaks to the more deeply ingrained flaws in their own analysis. It might behoove those in agreement with Winfrey to question a media system which imposes this kind of repetition on its audience, particularly its children who have enough products officially licensed for them—not counting the Mercedes and AK 47s—which has now become a $132 billion "global market." The goal here, as has long been well understood, is to attach young people to products "before their brand decisions have been made, and before their defenses to advertising are well developed."[79] If this, again, is reinterpreted for a domestic colonialism and through centering the experience of young, mostly black, colonized residents of Washington, D.C. (or elsewhere), dangerous trends emerge where the brands to which these young people are attached, more than the products themselves but the very ideological underpinnings thereto, include the most deleterious self-concepts and negative anti-community behavior.

CONCLUSION

Complacency is a far more dangerous attitude than outrage.

Naomi Littlebear

To suggest that goals of "democracy," "freedom," and "equality," and, therefore, the existence of an informed population be challenged is to encourage a more critical reanalysis of the function of mass media and the challenges which result. The extent to which Washington, D.C., is seen as that "last colony" begs the continuation of that thought into an anti-colonial analysis and response to that system's mass media. Such a re-analysis demands that there be a grappling with the intended oppressiveness in the limited range of thought and cultural expression made available. Some, in the face of such criticism, naturally respond in the defensive, seeking to conjure media which does not fit the previously discussed forms.

In regular responses to questions of media conduct, the "liberalness" of National Public Radio (NPR), housed in Washington, D.C., is mentioned as part of the balance against the kinds of media practices described herein. While not mentioned above in the constellation of D.C. media, it certainly can be challenged in terms of its claims of serving the public. More specifically, given the current context, it can be seen as analogous to the function of national broadcasting described by Fanon in his consideration of the function of radio in a colonial setting. Fanon so presciently described NPR in his own critique of Radio-Alger, the French national broadcasting equivalent in the former French colony of Algeria. In his chapter on the subject, "This is the Voice of Algeria,"[80] Fanon focuses on the role of radio in maintaining both the identity of the colonized and, perhaps more importantly, the attendant identity of the colonizer. Playing its established role as a national voice, NPR does precisely what Fanon said of Radio-Alger: it "reminds the settler [colonizer] of the reality of colonial power and, by its very existence, dispenses safety, serenity."[81] Hence NPR's overall soft tone and careful balancing of any challenging content with that of a far more light, and white, middle-class content variety (cooking, movies, music, etc.). Its existence (particularly its often publicly criticized, or somewhat self-admitted, "liberalness") provides further cover for its primary function: reassuring the settler with what Fanon calls a "daily invitation not to 'go native,' not to forget the rightfulness of his culture."[82] For example, NPR does not produce or air one single show dedicated to labor, but has the weekday business program *Marketplace*—a listener-friendly, business newsmagazine designed to reassure American investors of the calm and order of the nation's economic hegemony—prominently placed on weekday evenings.[83]

The NPR-oriented struggles of African American liberal activist-broadcaster Tavis Smiley showcase this dilemma. He described the inherently contradictory position held by his now-discontinued nationally syndicated NPR show and its existence on a network whose "demographic [sic] is overwhelmingly white. So, every day, we have to do a show that is authentically black, but at the same time not too black."[84] Smiley's public concerns are similar to the claim made by cultural critic bell hooks—that once image and identity become part and parcel of the "machinery" of capitalist production, notions of authenticity are "meaningless."[85] So, too, is such a concept made irrelevant within a colonized/colonizer dialectic. The image of the colonized, in this case, becomes the product of the colonizer and, therefore, is authentic to that relationship. Smiley's acknowledged struggle, therefore, is that of combating the *function* of NPR. Fanon understood radio's role well. He called radio "a system of information, as a bearer of language, hence of message."[86] It is listened to, he argues, "solely by the representatives of power . . . solely by the members of the dominant authority and [who] seem magically to be avoided by the members of the 'native' society."[87] So the "authentic blackness" expected of the liberal Smiley (or any other host/producer from the non-dominant population) is that which appeases the larger need of the colonizing media: to put at ease its audience of authority.

Though NPR does receive federal funding of roughly $400 million annually, this seemingly robust amount accounts for only "15% of local station budgets . . . [m]ost shows are funded primarily by producers, viewer donations, private foundations and corporations."[88] The rest of what then must be about $2.7 billion a year comes from the largely affluent and, therefore, more than likely elite defenders of the status quo. There can be little doubt that NPR in 2008 caters to America's elite or dominant class. Twenty-six percent of its listeners fall within the top ten percent of national household income. Perhaps even more telling is the fact that NPR listeners are "139% more likely to live in a household that falls within the Upper Deck definition but does not derive most of its income from employment" which, of course, further indicates that they are part of society's ownership class.[89] However, even when measuring NPR listener income (as opposed to unearned income), 70 percent of NPR listeners earn more than $70,000 and 73 percent are "more likely than the average U.S. adult to have household incomes of more than $100,000."[90] Similarly, in a subsection titled "The Elite Majority," a report from Fairness and Accuracy In Reporting (FAIR) demonstrates the same.[91] "Elite sources dominated NPR's guest-list," the report states, which include "government officials, professional experts and corporate representatives—{which} accounted for 64 percent of all sources." Women were said to be represented at a one-to-five ratio to men and Republicans 61 percent versus Democrats 38 percent. Similarly, think-tank representatives to NPR's programming were said to be more "right of center" at a four-to-one ratio, and for its commentators overall 60 percent "are still white men."[92] Even by standards which (falsely) assume Republicans and Democrats to sufficiently cover the political spectrum, there can be said to be no "liberal bias" or clear attempt to upset the norm of mass media broadcasting of any kind at NPR.

The intentional nature can be found again in the way those actively struggling for progressive change in Washington, D.C., are dealt with via major media. This evidence, while not definitive, is suggestive of a lack of desire in or a lack of marketability of the promotion of anti-oppressive organizations. In interviews conducted with representatives of Empower DC and the Youth Education Alliance, respondents Parisa Norouzi[93] and Jonathon Stith[94] each noted their organization's inability to have local black-targeted radio in particular, and D.C. media in general, play a supportive role in bringing wider attention to or support for their work or the issues. Stith in particular noted the outright antagonistic relationship YEA has with the most popular commercial radio station in the city (WPGC) due both to their refusal to promote issues of concern to the organization but also to the antithetical fare offered day in and day out. With few exceptions,[95] black-targeted radio, "the people's station[s]," offer little support to organizations working to improve the material lives of D.C. residents, particularly youth.

The inability of black media to perform a supportive role in black community advancement is not particular to black America but is indicative of a larger pattern. When asked about the condition of the black press in the twenty-first century, former editor of *Emerge* magazine George Curry responded:

> I think that the problem of Black media is the same as Black business, period. Whether you look at Motown, Johnson hair care products, whether you look at BET or whether you look at *Essence*, you see the same thing; that our major institutions are being bought off by conglomerates and then homogenized.[96]

His concerns over a lack of "substance" can be extended to any form of popular media though the impact of that missing substance varies depending on the preexisting conditions and roles of the given community vis-à-vis the dominant society. Media professor, scholar, and veteran journalist with the black press Todd Steven Burroughs also cautions against seeing the black press today as providing a media solution to the struggles facing that community. "As a 'Black mainstream' institution, the Black press sees almost any mainstream advance as a progressive one—even, for example, Condi [Condoleezza Rice] and Colon [Powell]! The editorial and Op-Ed page will rail against them, but they'd NEVER be called 'Enemies of the People' the way, say, *The Black Panther* or *Muhammad Speaks* would."[97] The implicit suggestion as to a remedy is clear in the face of a tightly controlled corporate and ideologically elite media environment; the establishment of movement-based, organizationally supported alternative, or underground, press/media.

When asked precisely how corporations "control" the media, Noam Chomsky replied, "They don't have to control them, they own them." The point is simple. Media function in the service of those in power precisely to maintain existing power relationships. The trend of the black press is indicative of any press targeting an oppressed population. This description of black-targeted media and an analysis of NPR highlight the dialectic of the colonized who must be created and maintained as is also true of the colonizer.[98] Media targeting the elite does so to ensure that their rule appears natural, preordained, and necessary. Breaking convention means just that. Appeals to the FCC, letter-writing campaigns to newspaper editors, and even attempted boycotts can at best only be seen as contributing factors for change. In the tradition of all groups seeking to "Upset the Setup" of existing inequality, the colonized have developed their own media outlets designed to expand the intellectual reach of their organized efforts. Washington, D.C., is no different in that respect. Its media system has a political function and cannot be changed without first there being a fundamental reordering of society itself.

This means that public policy, itself the result of the popular political will of a society, can only be more positively impacted if those seeking redress in that arena have more ideas made more popular. This can only occur if means of communicating those ideas are created. Communicating liberation in this or any other city demands that space be acquired to do so, and such space cannot, by definition of the society and its media, be granted for fear that it would generate the "oppositional consciousness" required for radical or revolutionary movements. Those most negatively affected by public policy have little media being generated which targets them in a way that encourages more struggle around that policy. In fact, quite the opposite. These communities are most likely to be assaulted at the level of psyche and political awareness via limited discourse, repetitive and equally limited musical selections, and an absence of community-based/generated news.

Mark Lloyd, recently appointed as associate general counsel and chief diversity officer at the FCC, once said that "communications policy is a Civil Rights issue."[99] Perhaps. However, the fundamental right to communicate one's interests is a *human rights* issue and should be engaged on that basis. As a human right, one defined as such by the United Nations' Universal Declaration of Human Rights,[100] existing communications policy, currently operating in denial of those rights, must be vigorously challenged and circumvented by any means necessary so as to ensure that aggrieved communities can develop the kinds of organized public pressure that forces structures to change or fall.

NOTES

1. DJ EuRok (2004). *This Is DC!* upsetthesetup.wordpress.com.

2. Robert McChesney. (1997). Spry Memorial Lecture. "The Mythology of Commercial Broadcasting." Montreal, 2 December 1997/Vancouver, 4 December 1997. (www.ratical.org/co-globalize/RMmythCB.html).

3. Marshall McLuhan quoted in *McLuhan's Wake.* (2002). Kevin McMahon (Dir.). New York: The National Film Board of Canada. "It's like fish in the water. We don't know who discovered water but we know it wasn't a fish. A pervasive medium, a pervasive environment is always beyond perception."

4. Ronald Walters, *White Nationalism, Black Interests: Conservative Public Policy and the Black Community.* Detroit: Wayne State University Press. Walters describes a history of this nation which has been about the consolidation of power among a white elite whose expressed goals dating as far back as the mid-nineteenth century included the effectuation of a "racial purification" by carefully limiting (if not removing altogether) black populations geographically in a fashion which concludes today with the

aforementioned spatial separateness, gentrification or continued "racial cleansings," the history of which is described in *Buried in the Bitter Waters: The Hidden History of Racial Cleansing in America.* (2007). New York: Basic Books. Walters also details how "gains" accrued during the civil rights struggles have benefited *white Americans* more than African Americans or others.

5. "Great Expectations: Defining the Divide between Blacks and Jews" (1994). In *Strangers and Neighbors: Relations between Blacks and Jews in the United States*, edited by Maurianne Adams and John H. Bracey, 806. Amherst: University of Massachusetts Press, 1999.

6. Sylvia Moreno, (October 24, 2007). "Poverty Rate Grows Amid an Economic Boom D.C.'s Poorest Left Behind By Renewal, Report Finds." *The Washington Post.* www.washingtonpost.com/wp-dyn/content/article/2007/10/23/AR2007102302230.html.

7. July 28, 2008. "UN report: At 45%, Gaza unemployment is highest in the world." *Haaretz,* www.haaretz.com/hasen/spages/1006282.html.

8. Tom Engelhardt. (October 30, 2007). "Where Have All the Protests Gone?" *Alternet.org.* www.alternet.org/world/66433/.

9. Chris Simpson. (1993). "U.S. Mass Communication Research, Counterinsurgency, and Scientific 'Reality.'" In *Ruthless Criticism: New Perspectives in U.S. Communication History* (Eds. Solomon, W. and McChesney, R.). Minneapolis: University of Minnesota Press.

10. Edward Bernays. (1928/2005). *Propaganda.* Brooklyn: IG Publishing.

11. M. Achbar (Dir.). 1992. *Manufacturing Consent: Noam Chomsky and the Media* [film]. Canada: Necessary Illusions Productions.

12. July 3, 2003. "GOP Bullies DC on Vouchers, No Democracy for Black City." www.BlackCommentator.com.

13. Rupert Cornwell. September 16, 2007. "Rupert Cornwell: Out of America: It would be easier to promote political freedom around the world if DC's own citizens were finally able to vote." *The Independent.* www.independent.co.uk/opinion/commentators/rupert-cornwell-out-of-america-464338.html. Examples also include John Fortier, "The D.C. Colony," in *The Hill*, May 17, 2006, thehill.com/john-fortier/the-d.c.-colony-2006-05-17.html.

14. Juanita Darling, "Re-Imaging the Nation: Revolutionary Media and Historiography in Mesoamerica," *Journalism History* 32:4 (Winter 2007).

15. Zbigniew Brzezinski. (1997). *The Grand Chessboard: American Primacy and Its Geostrategic Imperatives.* New York: Basic Books, 24–25 (emphasis added).

16. Ewen MacAskill and Julian Borger. (February 16, 2006). "Bush Plans a Huge Propaganda Campaign in Iran." *The Guardian.* www.guardian.co.uk/media/2006/feb/16/usnews.iran.

17. www.globalsecurity.org/military/library/news/2006/03/mil-060302-voa08.htm.

18. "Dissident" is defined as that which threatens the power held by the nation's elite or government. Its complete definition, as the quote itself, can be found in Chris Simpson (1994). *Science of Coercion: Communication Research & Psychological Warfare 1945–1960.* New York: Oxford University Press.

19. Harold Innis. (1951). *The Bias of Communication*. Toronto: The University of Toronto Press, 4.

20. Innis, 10.

21. The same point is made regarding the removal of improvisational or "free-style" in hip-hop due to its co-optation by the music industry and all the politics and commercial demands therein. *Freestyle: The Art of Rhyme*. (2000). Kevin Fitzgerald (Dir.). Palm Pictures.

22. Ian Carr. (1998). *Miles: The Definitive Biography*. New York: Thunder's Mouth Press. 1998, 405.

23. M. Achbar (Director). (1992). *Manufacturing Consent: Noam Chomsky and the Media* [Film]. Canada: Necessary Illusions Productions.

24. P. Golding and G. Murdock. (1991). "Culture, Communications, and Political Economy." In J. Curran and M. Gurevitch (Eds.) *Mass Media and Society*. London: Edward Arnold, 23.

25. Ben Bagdikian. (2004). *The New Media Monopoly*. Boston: Beacon Press, 27.

26. *The State of the News Media 2007: An Annual Report on American Journalism*. Project For Excellence in Journalism. www.stateofthemedia.org/2007/index.asp.

27. He, in Jamie Johnson's *The One Percent*, can be seen disowning his grand-daughter for talking publicly about being born wealthy (www.theonepercentdocu-mentary.com).

28. Doug Henwood, "The Washington Post: The Establishment Paper," Fairness and Accuracy in Reporting, *FAIR.org* (January/February 1990), www.fair.org/index.php?page=1195.

29. www.brandedcities.com.

30. Thomas Frank, author of *The Wrecking Crew: How Conservatives Rule*, in an interview on Media Matters with Robert McChesney, August 10, 2008.

31. *FreeMix Radio: The Original Mixtape Radio Show* has been freely distributed in and around Washington, D.C., since 2004. The mixtape CD is itself used and formatted into a kind of radio program on CD, exposing listeners to music and ideas intentionally excluded from mainstream media. More information can be found on-line at voxunion.com.

32. www.bizjournals.com/washington/stories/2007/11/05/daily9.html.

33. "Afro-American Newpspers Testimonial." Software Consulting Services, LLC. Retrieved online July 11, 2009 (www.newspapersystems.com/pdf/testimonials.php).

34. For instance, Lee (2007), shows how political blogs follow topics and world-views established in mainstream presses, reducing the Internet's capacity to deliver new or counter-hegemonic politics to new audiences. The Internet simply reinforces, magnifies or extends the penetrating reach of the status quo.

35. www.savethinternet.com/-faq

The nation's largest telephone and cable companies—including AT&T, Verizon, Comcast and Time Warner—want to be Internet gatekeepers, deciding which Web sites go fast or slow and which won't load at all. They want to tax content providers to guarantee speedy delivery of their data. They want to discriminate in favor of their own search engines, Internet phone services, and streaming video—while slowing down or blocking their competitors. These companies have a new vision for the Internet. Instead of an even playing field, they want to reserve express lanes for their own content and services—or those from big corporations that can afford the steep tolls—and leave the rest of us on a winding dirt road. The big phone and cable companies are spending hundreds of millions of dollars lobbying Congress and the Federal Communications Commission to gut Net Neutrality, putting the future of the Internet at risk.

36. hiphopnews.yuku.com/topic/785.

37. M. Achbar (Dir.). 1992. *Manufacturing Consent: Noam Chomsky and the Media* [film]. Canada: Necessary Illusions Productions.

38. Louise Story, "Higher Value of Eyeballs," *New York Times*, November 5, 2007, C6.

39. McChesney, 2008, 257.

40. Deonte Rawlings and Ronnie White cases most recently.

41. Andy Solberg, Washington, D.C., Second District Police Commander.

I would think that at 2 a.m. on the streets of Georgetown, a group of three people, one of whom is 15-years-old, one of whom is a bald chunky fat guy, are going to stand out. They were black. This is not a racial thing to say that black people are unusual in Georgetown. This is a fact of life.

42. For example, there is no metro train service to Georgetown.

43. Consider the well-hidden upper northwest hideaway that is Dumbarton Oaks as an example of a beautiful "public" space that is not intended to be easily found or reached by those not intended to be there.

44. The Trinidad section of northeast D.C., where the neighborhood has several times been barricaded off to "unauthorized" vehicular traffic.

45. 381.

46. U.S. Census Bureau statistics, quickfacts.census.gov/qfd/states/24/24033.html.

47. Glen Ford, panel on Black Radio History, NPR, March 24, 2007. In-house panel, recorded but not aired.

48. As exemplified in the recent and first-ever report produced on ad revenue spent on black-targeted media, where it is stated that radio is used "more than any other medium" to reach black audiences. $805 million was spent between October 1, 2006, and September 30, 2007, on black-targeted radio or 35 percent of the total $2.3 billion spent on black-targeted media during that same time frame (www.insidebrandedentertainment.com/bep/article_display.jsp?JSESSIONID=2v0jHLkhpvwnxny2wTVtY1S382l9JSLNTbXsyTTLzRYTGHL32Wnl!1158789824&vnu_content_id=1003703403).

49. Point 5 of the 1966 FBI COINTELPRO (Counter Intelligence Program) document specifically targets black youth as potential threats and called for special efforts to protect against their radicalization (Churchill, Vanderwall).

50. The most recent (Winter, 2007) combined ratings (9.5) of WPGC (5.5) and WKYS (4.0) trump that of WHUR (6.9) (www.arbitron.com/home/content.stm).

51. Glen Ford. (2003, May 29). "Who Killed Black Radio News?" *BlackCommentator.com.* www.blackcommentator.com/44/44_cover.html, blackcommentator.com.

52. Glen Ford is now editor-in-chief of BlackAgendaReport.com: www.blackcommentator.com/44/44_cover.html

53. Radio One, after some recent sell-offs, owns "53 stations in 16 urban markets," according to its website (www.radio-one.com/properties/radio.asp).

54. Interviews conducted/videotaped by Leah Tayor, former student intern with the author, while at Morgan State University, fall 2007.

55. Comments made during the NPR panel on Black Radio History, March 24, 2007.

56. Barlow.

57. McChesney, 2008, 418.

58. Peter DiCola (December 2006). "False Premises, False Promises: A Quantitative History of Ownership Consolidation in the Radio Industry." Future of Music Coalition (www.futureofmusic.org/research/radiostudy06.cfm).

59. A University of Chicago study on the subject shows upwards of 60 percent of black youth dislike and want change to the popular hip-hop and R&B they are forced to hear due to the herein described process of popularization and apparent lack of awareness of alternatives (February 2007, blackyouthproject.com).

60. Hence Theodor Adorno's point that "like and dislike are inappropriate to the situation . . . familiarity is a surrogate for the quality ascribed to it."

61. Fall, winter, spring, and summer sessions from 2005 to 2006 and were conducted with the guidance and support of both Lisa Fager-Bediako of Industry Ears and Chanelle Hardy then with Consumers Union. The projects were designed to create awareness through detailed monitoring of content—precisely the kinds of images, stereotypes, and imbalances between substantive political content in music or "news." Students kept diaries and charts and sent written and phoned-in complaints to the FCC when thought necessary and then made end-of-the-semester presentations on their findings.

62. Greg Palast, 2002.

63. Noam Chomsky, 1992.

64. It is widely known but rarely reported that pay-for-play, or payola, is what determines song content in commercial radio. The costs are enormous, allowing only the largest of labels to be able to afford to have their songs added to radio station playlists for the kind of massive repetition necessary to convince listeners that they "like" what they hear. As industry insider and analyst Paul Porter has explained in a recent interview with the author: "Payola has replaced the ears and eyes of radio and video programmers. I have seen the process grow first hand, the industry has followed the nation, capitalism has replaced talent and creativity. Anyone who tells you anything else is stating a bold faced lie" (personal communication, June 28, 2008).

65. Walter Lippmann. (1921/1997). *Public Opinion*. New York: Free Press, 19 (emphasis added). In other words, for the news to make sense or to have the desired impact of limiting the thought of its audience/targets, general opinions of what is covered must already have been set. The news can never raise, discuss, or spend too much time illuminating various topics as it only exists to reify or amplify existing views.

66. Martin Luther King Jr. (1967). Speech given to black radio deejays in Atlanta, Georgia. *DaveyD.com*. odeo.com/audio/5430283/view.

67. Donna Lamb, "Disappearing Voices in Black Radio," July 7, 2008, *BlackStarNews.com*.

68. (2005). Speech given during a panel convened by Congresswoman Cynthia McKinney at the Congressional Black Caucus meeting. *COINTELPRO: A History.*

69. "'Talk,' in the Past Tense: Why There Are No More Petey Greenes on Local Radio." (July 22, 2007). *The Washington Post*, NO2. www.washingtonpost.com/wp-dyn/content/article/2007/07/20/AR2007072000478.html.

70. Ralph Waldo "Petey" Greene Jr. (23 January 1931–10 January 1984) was an African American television and radio talk show host. A two-time Emmy Award–winner, Greene overcame drug addiction and a prison sentence for armed robbery to become one of Washington, D.C.'s most prominent media personalities. On his shows he often talked about subjects such as racism, poverty, religion, sexuality, drug abuse, and government issues. His life was depicted in the film *Talk To Me* starring Don Cheadle.

71. blackpoliticalthought.blogspot.com/2008/05/two-top-executives-alejandro-claiborne.html.

72. "With a growing list of radio, newspaper and television assets on the auction block, some new players are on the verge of assembling the conglomerate of the twenty-first century: the private-equity media empire." Berman and McBride, 2006, "Private Equity May Face Snags in Media Hunt." *Wall Street Journal*, October 27.

73. Frantz Fanon. (1964). *Toward the African Revolution.* New York: Grove Press, 34.

74. "Oprah's Cosby Moment." (January 9, 2007). *Foreign Policy.* blog.foreign-policy.com/node/3007.

75. Janice Peck. (2008). *The Age of Oprah: Cultural Icon for the Neoliberal Era.* New York: Paradigm Publishers, and Daphne Brooks in Powell, K. (Ed.). (2000). *Step Into a World: A Global Anthology of the New Black Literature.* New York: John Wiley & Sons, Inc.

76. Cohen, et al, (2007). A University of Chicago study on the subject shows upward of 60 percent of black youth dislike and want change to the popular hip-hop and R&B they are forced to hear due to the herein described process of popularization and apparent lack of awareness of alternatives (February 2007, blackyouthproject.com).

77. L. Lucian James (2004). *American Brandstand Report.* San Francisco: Agenda, Inc.

78. Jonathan Kozol (2005). *Shame of the Nation.* New York: HarperCollins Publishers. See also Derrick Bell (2004). *Silent Covenants: Brown v. Board of Education and the Unfulfilled Hopes for Racial Reform.* Oxford: Oxford University Press.

79. Robert McChesney (2008). *The Political Economy of Media: Enduring Issues, Emerging Dilemmas.* New York: Monthly Review Press, 277–78.

80. Frantz Fanon. (1965). *A Dying Colonialism.* New York: Grove Press, 69–97.

81. Ibid., 71.

82. Ibid., 79.

83. "Marketplace" is produced by American Public Media. APM and Public Radio International are America's main syndicators of public radio programming outside of NPR. Both APM and PRI, not surprisingly, represent the same interests as NPR.

84. Bolling, Deborah (2002). "Tavis Smiley." PhiladlephiaCityPaper.net. November 21–27 (www.citypaper.net/articles/2002-11-21/om.shtml/). His comments could

also apply to his current nationally syndicated weekend radio program, "The Tavis Smiley Show," distributed by Public Radio International and aired on public radio stations across the nation.

85. S. Jhally (Director). (1996). *bell hooks: Cultural Criticism and Transformation* [Film]. Northampton: Media Education Foundation.

86. Frantz Fanon. (1965). *A Dying Colonialism*. New York: Grove Press.

87. Ibid.

88. Lyric Wallwork Winik and Mark Naymik. May 4, 2008. *Parade*. (www.parade.com/articles/editions/2008/edition_05-04-2008/Intelligence_Report).

89. www.kwmu.org/support/Underwriting/demographics.html.

90. www.kwmu.org/support/Underwriting/demographics.html.

91. S. Rendell and D. Butterworth (May/June 2004). "How Public is Public Radio?" *Extra!* fair.org.

92. Rendell and Butterworth, 2004.

93. Interview conducted during the author's radio program, *Jazz and Justice* on WPFW 89.3 FM, May 10, 2008.

94. Interview conducted August 10, 2007.

95. Interview with Zein Elamine of Save Our Neighborhood Schools Coalition who has spoken very highly of the support his organization has received from DJ and host EZ Street from WPGC (March 9, 2008).

96. Interview conducted with former editor of *Emerge* magazine, George Curry, June 7, 2008.

97. Personal communication, June 3, 2008.

98. Albert Memmi. (1964). *The Colonized and the Colonizer*. Boston: Beacon Press.

99. Mark Lloyd. (March 27, 2006). Communications Policy is a Civil Rights Issue. *Community Technology Review*. www.comtechreview.org/winter-spring-1998/r981lloy.htm

100. The Universal Declaration of Human Rights (adopted by the General Assembly of the United Nations December 10, 1948), Article 19, reads:

> Everyone has the right to freedom of opinion and expression; this right includes freedom to hold opinions without interference *and to seek, receive and impart information and ideas through any media and regardless of frontiers* (emphasis added). www.un.org/en/documents/udhr/.

BIBLIOGRAPHY

Allen, R. L. (1969/1990). *Black Awakening in Capitalist America*. Trenton, N.J.: Africa World Press.

Allen, R. L. (2008). Barack Obama and the Children of Globalization. *The Black Scholar*, Vol. 38, No. 4 (Winter).

Ani, Marimba. (1994). *Yurugu: An African-Centered Critique of European Cultural Thought and Behavior*. Trenton, N.J.: Africa World Press.

Ards, A. (2004). Organizing the Hip-Hop Generation. In M. Forman and M.A. Neal (Eds.). *That's the Joint! The Hip-Hop Studies Reader* (311–23). New York: Routledge.

Atkinson, P. (1993). *Brown vs. Topeka: Desegregation and Miseducation: An African American's View*. New York: African American Images.

Ball, J. A. (2008). Barack Obama, "Connected Distance": Race and Twenty-first Century Neo-colonialism. *The Black Scholar*, Vol. 38, Issue 4 (Winter).

Ball, J. A. (2009). FreeMix Radio: The Original Mixtape Radio Show: A Case Study in Mixtape Radio and Emancipatory Journalism. *The Journal of Black Studies*, vol. 39, no. 4, March.

Bell, D. (2004). *Silent Covenants: Brown v. Board of Education and the Unfulfilled Hopes for Racial Reform*. Oxford: Oxford University Press.

Bernays, E. (1928/2005). *Propaganda*. Brooklyn: IG Publishing.

Carr, G. (2008). *A Conversation About Race*. MSNBC (television). Retrieved July 19, 2009, from www.msnbc.msn.com/id/21134540/vp/24076911#24076911.

Cosby, B., and Poussaint, A. (2009) (Television). *Meet The Press*. Transcript retrieved July 19, 2009, from www.msnbc.msn.com/id/28605356.

Creamer, M. (October 17, 2008). Obama Wins! . . . Ad Age's Marketer of the Year. *Advertising Age*. Retrieved July 19, 2009, from adage.com/moy2008/article?article_id=131810.

Davis, A. (2003). *Are Prisons Obsolete?* Boston: Seven Stories Press.

Delaney, M. (1852/2004). *The Condition, Elevation, Emigration, and Destiny of the Colored People of the United States and Official Report of the Niger Valley Exploring Party*. New York: Humanity Books.

Downing, J., and Husband, C. (2005). *Representing "Race": Racisms, Ethnicities and Media*. London: Sage Publications.

Fanon, F. (1963). *The Wretched of the Earth*. New York: Grove Press.

Fanon, F. (1964). *Toward the African Revolution*. New York: Grove Press.

Ford, G. (2009). The Shrinking American Empire. *Black Agenda Report*. Retrieved July 17, 2009, from www.blackagendareport.com/?q=content/shrinking-american-empire.

Gaiter, C. (June 8, 2005). Visualizing a Revolution: Emory Douglas and The Black Panther Newspaper. *AIGA*. Retrieved from www.aiga.org/content.cfm/visualizing-a-revolution-emory-douglas-and-the-black-panther-new.

Galbraith, J. (2008). *The Predator State: How Conservatives Abandoned the Free Market and Why Liberals Should Too*. New York: Free Press.

Harris, W. J. (Ed.). (1991). *The Leroi Jones/Amiri Baraka Reader* (1991). New York: Thunder Mouth Press.

Hilliard, D., and Weise, D. (2002). *The Huey P. Newton Reader*. New York: Seven Stories Press.

INCITE! Women of Color Against Violence. (2007). *The Revolution Will Not Be Funded: Beyond the Non-Profit Industrial Complex*. Boston: South End Press.

Jackson, G. (1971/1990). *Blood in My Eye*. Baltimore: Black Classic Press.

Joseph, P. E. (February 2008). From Black Power to Barack Obama. *The Brooklyn Rail*.

Kamenka, E. (1983). *The Portable Karl Marx.* New York: Penguin Books.

Kofsky, Frank. (1970, 1988). *Black Nationalism and the Revolution in Music.* New York: Pathfinder Press.

Kouddous, S.A. (December 19, 2008). Katrina's Hidden Race War. *Democracy Now!* Podcast transcript retrieved from www.democracynow.org/2008/12/19/katrinas_hidden_race_war_in_aftermath.

Lewis, D.L. (1995). *W.E.B. DuBois: A Reader.* New York: Henry Holt and Company, Inc.

McChesney, R. (2004). *The Problem of the Media: U.S. Communication Politics in the 21st Century.* New York: Monthly Review Press.

Memmi, A. (1965). *The Colonizer and the Colonized.* Boston: Beacon Press.

Moreno, S. (October 24, 2007). Poverty Rate Grows Amid an Economic Boom: D.C.'s Poorest Left Behind by Renewal, Report Finds. *The Washington Post.*

Moyers, B. (November 23, 2007). James H. Cone. *Bill Moyers Journal.* Transcript retrieved from www.pbs.org/moyers/journal/11232007/profile.html.

Muhammad, D., Davis A., Leondor-Wright, B., and Lui, M. (2004). *The State of the Dream 2004: Enduring Disparities in Black and White.* Boston: United for a Fair Economy.

Nelson, J. (2001). *Police Brutality: An Anthology.* New York: W.W. Norton & Co.

Osayande, E. (2004). Art at War: Revolutionary Art Against Cultural Imperialism. *Black Commentator.* Retrieved from www.blackcommentator.com/108/108_guest_osayande_pf.html.

Palast, G. (2002). *The Best Democracy Money Can Buy.* London: Pluto Press.

Patel, R. (2008). *Democracy Now!* Interview (July 31), retrieved July 17, 2009, from www.democracynow.org/2008/7/31/raj_patel.

Peck, J. (2008). *The Age of Oprah: Cultural Icon for the Neoliberal Era.* New York: Paradigm Publishers.

Perkins, J. (2004). *Confessions of an Economic Hit Man.* San Francisco: Berrett-Koehler Publishers, Inc.

Pinderhughes, C. (April 10, 2009). *Robert Allen Celebrated: A 40th Anniversary Tribute to Black Awakening in Capitalist America.* Berkeley, California. Podcast retrieved from www.voxunion.com/?p=1089.

Rivera, A., Cotto-Escalera, B., Desai, A., Huezo, J., and Muhammad, D. (2008). *Foreclosed: State of the Dream 2008.* Boston: United for a Fair Economy.

Rose, Tricia. (1994). *Black Noise.* Middletown, Conn.: Wesleyan University Press.

Shah, H. (1996, May). Modernization, Marginalization, and Emancipation: Toward a Normative Model of Journalism and National Development. *Communication Theory,* 6(2), 143–66.

Shah, H. (2007). Journalism in an Age of Mass Media Globalization. June 2007. Retrieved from www.idsnet.org/Papers/Communications/HEMANT_SHAH.HTM.

Simpson, C. (1994). *Science of Coercion: Communication Research & Psychological Warfare 1945–1960.* New York: Oxford University Press.

UN report: "At 45%, Gaza unemployment is highest in the world." July 28, 2008. *Haaretz Service.* Retrieved July 19, 2009, from www.haaretz.com/hasen/spages/1006282.html.

13

Conclusion

Ronald Walters and Toni-Michelle C. Travis

The theme of the introduction is designed to illustrate the situations in which the District of Columbia has attempted to formulate public policy in the traditional processes followed by other cities, only to suffer from the frequent distortion of its aims by the intervention of the Congress. This has taken form in the historic prohibition of its movement toward some form of genuine political representation, as well as in the process that submits its budget to the Congress for review and enactment. It is this phenomenon that has been most acute and where this volume has posed questions about democracy and the satisfaction of the needs of citizens in the District who have been the most disadvantaged.

A companion chapter by Michael K. Fauntroy that also serves as an introduction to this subject shows clearly in its historical documentation that the status of the District in relation to the government of the country has always been fraught with ambiguity, but confirmed a point made in the introduction that the most serious modern challenge to empower citizens with self-determination came with the emergence of the civil rights movement. Its impact on the District of Columbia and the fact that so many local leaders were also involved in the national movement made this inevitable. Ironically, it also may have established the opposition to such empowerment by the fact that so many opponents of the movement were situated in strategic positions in the Congress. Fauntroy, for example, writes about the confrontation between the first congressional representative, Walter Fauntroy (uncle to Michael Fauntroy), and Rep. John McMillan, Democrat of South Carolina, who headed the House District Committee. But most important, he outlines the structure of the home rule legislation that was enacted and the extent to which the limitations of democracy were inherent in that structure. To that extent, he

expresses serious misgivings about the extent to which the home rule legislation mirrors the expectations of the citizens of the District and to what extent
it would allow the city to function in their interest. This is the primary reason
why the "Free D.C." movement was a mobilization for a more complete
model of home rule that ran throughout all of the mayors' administrations and
a force with which each one had to contend.

GOVERNING HOME RULE

The quest for political empowerment through self-rule was the environment
within which the administration of Walter Washington, the first elected
mayor, was born, the most urgent expression of which was the rebellion in the
city when Dr. Martin Luther King Jr. was killed in 1968. Toni-Michelle C.
Travis shows that the symbiosis between this demand in the form of violence
and its linkage to the birth of electoral power cannot be denied, as indicated
by the extent to which many considered the governing style of first elected
mayor, Walter Washington, to be too methodical and careful to suit the times.
Washington, however, a former government program manager, was aware of
the limitations he faced and, as a result, concentrated on the things he could
control that were under his direct supervision, such as setting a professional
tone for his administration, initiating projects for economic development such
as the convention center, and devaluing race in government administration
and civic affairs.

With the coming of Marion Barry, expectations grew because, as someone
previously involved in the civil rights movement—a former leader of the
Student Nonviolent Coordinating Committee—he was envisioned as a person
who matched the urgent expectations of the African American majority. So
Wilmer J. Leon III shows that despite the fact that the intractable problems
such as the lack of resources, the $100 million deficit Barry inherited, the
high levels of infant mortality, and poverty were as acute as they had been in
the Washington administration, his objective was to address them. He therefore proposed measures sensitive to self-determination for the city, such as
the ability to raise revenue through a commuter tax, a residency requirement
for those who worked in District government employment, and others. However, they would not be positively viewed by Congress; since they offended
the interests of Maryland and Virginia politicians, they were rejected as an
impudent attempt to acquire power beyond that allowed by Congress.

In fact, in his first administration some progress was made by Barry on his
agenda to redistribute government resources more robustly to social services,
a move that also was commensurate with the creation of a powerful politi-

cal organization. The political base he came to represent was served both by access to employment and the acquisition of services such as the nationally recognized summer youth jobs program. Leon shows, however, that as his second administration was tainted by his arrest and incarceration on drug charges, his effectiveness began to wane.

The one term of Sharon Pratt Kelly was undistinguished by its legislative achievements, despite her proposal to be a governmental reformer in the face of challenges such as a $300 million deficit, a restless Hispanic community, and a proposal to address the deficit by cutting two thousand workers from a bloated bureaucracy. Travis suggests that her role as a reformer was untenable by her outsider status in the District political and economic power structure and her lack of intimate attachments to a substantial political base among the people. Nevertheless, her reform agenda of streamlining District government also suffered as much from the complexity of governing and the lack of home rule, to the point that she led a mass demonstration down Independence Avenue in front of the House and Senate offices and the Capitol to raise public attention to this fact. Indeed, a theme of her term as outlined by Travis was the "intractable problem of congressional oversight" that was responsible for her administration's low productivity.

By Barry's third administration, the financial situation that faced many cities had clashed with the inadequate structure established by the original home rule legislation. And while Leon shows that many considered the financial debacle of the District as tied to the maladministration of the Barry administration, it is also undeniable that the restructuring of the financial responsibilities of the city by President Clinton's office of management and budget director, Frank Raines, produced subsequent budget surpluses. This, together with the tight fiscal control exercised by the Control Board, effectively extended the control of the Congress into the District, not only to administer its financial affairs, but also to exist as an alternative governmental structure with unprecedented and wide-ranging powers over most sectors of government.

Mayor Anthony Williams was considered an expert manager who could set right the fiscal situation of the District, and his "eyeshade" demeanor appeared to inspire confidence in citizens to elect him for two terms. In that role, Daryl B. Harris suggests that he privileged corporate interests, affected housing policies to the detriment of the city's underclass by spurring the growth of gentrification, and, in the process, devalued black interests in the city. Some criticisms by community leaders focused on his interest in balancing the budget to the point that it even took precedence over the needs of the most disadvantaged citizens. As an example of the latter, Harris points to the closing of D.C. General Hospital and the failure to replace it by breaking a contract with Howard University. In the end, Harris suggests that Williams remained an outsider of District culture and politics and reigned as essentially a caretaker of the District for congressional interests.

In summary, these authors illustrate the great difficulty of elected mayors and their administrations in exercising the kind of leadership that would effectively secure the interests of the African American majority in the city. In this sense, an acknowledged missing element of this picture in this work is the contribution of the City Council in the interplay of governance. However, as local representatives, City Council proposals, especially in the form of the city budget, were carried in legislation enacted at that level and approved by the mayor to Congress for passage and as such their work was reflected in the treatment by the Congress of their proposals.

The legacy of every administration is one in which the mayor had difficulty in both enacting proposals and fending off proposals by Congress in satisfying the financial and political interests of District citizens and their local representatives in the City Council.

THE OUTPUT OF GOVERNANCE: PUBLIC POLICY

The largest sector of the District budget, as in many cities, is education, and it is also the sector that has faced the most intervention and experimentation because of assessments of its lack of productivity with respect to excellent outcomes for students. Congressional proposals began the charter school movement in the District, now the largest in the country; former House Speaker Newt Gingrich proposed paying students to learn; and with the election of Adrian Fenty, an even more radical departure—mayoral control of schools—was adopted. The surprise was not only that mayoral control was adopted since it was linked to the strong accountability emphasis of the federal No Child Left Behind program that became the national standard, but that it dispensed with what had been the self-determination aspect of local democracy. For example, in a move approved by the Congress, the mayor was supported by the Council in eliminating the Board of Education and, as such, the direct role of the major stakeholders in education was excluded.

ReShone L. Moore indicates that School Chancellor Michelle Rhee's administration ran into some difficulty with respect to the way in which accountability was being fashioned; changes produced strains in the political culture of the educational institutions and the political structure of the city. In any case, she points out that the stakes of the experiment in mayoral control and the new structure are considerable, since bridging the achievement divide has been one of the more secure routes to participation in the democratic system for all citizens. Since this is surely true for children in the District much is also riding on the reforms brought about by the administration of Barack Obama through his secretary of education, Arne Duncan. The resources made available and the manner in which they are utilized will be even more important to empower minority children who comprise the majority of students in the system.

Darwin Fishman's chapter on the political socialization of District youth places the issue of school reform in the context of how it impacts on the attitudes and behaviors of the students. In general, students are not aware of the specific administrative changes in the structure of the way in which they receive their education because the social environment of poverty, police-community relations, school status, and so on are more dynamic in their direct effect. Nevertheless, the Summer Youth Program of Mayor Barry, which had a direct effect on students and their families, made an impact on their evaluation of him and his administration.

Because it shapes their outlook, Fishman suggests that black youth in D.C. link the absence or presence of opportunities to the fact that they have fewer political options than other Americans. This is the route to the cynicism that often affects low school performance, such as dropout rates, but also lowers levels of civic engagement in voting and other forms of political participation.

Throughout the history of home rule, the reduction of the District population has been felt most severely by working-class blacks who have been attempting to remain in the city by having access to affordable housing. William G. Jones indicates that the history of rent control and the establishment of the Housing Trust Fund were instruments created to affect this goal, but they have also become targets of those sympathetic to gentrification by the expansion of middle- and upper-income white residents and the developers who service them with higher-priced housing in hot markets.

Thus, a race and class problem has existed in which mostly working-class blacks have been slowly pushed out into Prince George's County by the laxity of the enforcement of District home building codes, rent control laws, and, as Jones argues, sharp increases in property taxes. Thus, the Rent Control Reform Act of 2006 was passed in an effort to stabilize low-income housing markets and increase family access to housing.

As Angelyn Flowers suggests, the economic status of the District of Columbia, the nation's capital, is distinguished by one of the highest poverty rates in the nation, second only to that of Mississippi. Thus the subject of governmental democracy leading to effective public policy delivery is fundamental to securing the needs of the group we have referred to in the introduction as those who "need government most." The face of poverty, she finds, is a "face of color." Flowers also found the inability of the city to successfully meet the service needs of this population to be based in the structure of prohibitions levied by Congress in establishing home rule.

The three most important federal constraints she delineates that deliberately undermine home rule are the prohibition on the District to tax income earned by nonresidents, the prohibition on a residency requirement, and the tax-exempt status of the federal government and nonprofit institutions. Indeed, while the annual federal payment to the District is meant to compensate for some of these factors, neither this payment nor personal and family incomes have grown to cover the increase in the cost of living in the District. The result is that a substantial part of the population is "living on the edge" due to their lack of skills and education, having a criminal record, poor service delivery, and other things, including the lack of sufficient investment in human needs that would create a real safety net.

Poverty is very closely associated with crime and thus, ninety percent of those held in the criminal justice system in the District are black. In the District, the federal government administers the prison system and the funding for many attendant services such as rehabilitation, whereas typically localities have control over such institutions. But while many prisoners are held in District jails, most are farmed out to other communities in congressional districts that derive a benefit from their prison population in the funds directed to support criminal justice institutions by the state and federal governments.

This problem, Kevin L. Glasper says, is a nightmare of administration. The District has thirteen combined local and federal levels of responsibility, since, as we have seen, for some funding purposes, the District is treated as a state. Nevertheless, he finds that the lack of efficiency of such a system puts a glaring focus on such issues as drug treatment, rehabilitation services, job placement, health care, and so forth in regard to the well-being of prisoners and ex-offenders who return to their communities. In short, it complicates the already dire situation of inadequate service delivery for a needy population—services that could keep a significant segment of the population from frequent encounters with the criminal justice system.

To a large extent, many of the problems of governance we have surveyed lend themselves to a more effective governmental regime of reform and for others it requires a more sophisticated and involved citizenry. That raises a question of the sources and nature of information that citizens receive and whether it is the kind that motivates them to become involved in projects of self-determination or not. Jared A. Ball has presented an analysis that places some of the citizens of color in the District in a "colonial environment" that suggests the need for their "liberation." Because Washington, D.C., is one of the major media capitals in the world, citizens have access to a variety of sources of information, but in terms of sources which are directed at their specific needs, there are few, and even fewer, as Ball says, that include the voice of the powerless.

Most of the major media devalue the disadvantaged by pretending to pursue "balance and objectivity," but insofar as this merely invites the powerful to the table once again, for Ball, it amounts to a "false balance." He says that the amount of community-oriented news from radio, newspapers, and television has shrunk by degrees in a withering response to the profit motive of the large corporations that control them, even nonprofit organizations, such as National Public Radio. The rise of hip-hop and the diversification of the media, he suggests, are positive trends, as a progressive entertainment voice is given space in some media and the alternative sources of news adds perspective to events that are often consistent with the lives of those consuming it. Yet he says that the danger of even progressive forces achieving significant space either in entertainment, such as hip-hop, or the Internet is that as they gain substantial audience, they become targets for commercial interests bearing their own messages of recolonization.

CONCLUSION

The election of Democrats in November of 2008 to the control of both the White House and the Congress could substantially improve the prospects for self-determination in the District of Columbia. As this volume is being drawn to a close in the first session of the 111th Congress, the House of Representatives passed an appropriations bill that would restore many of the bans on social programs enacted when Republicans controlled the Congress. For example, the District government could fund abortions for the poor using its own tax money, legalize medical uses of marijuana, restore the needle exchange program for intravenous drug users to fight the spread of HIV/AIDS, phase out the school voucher program favored by Republicans, and register same-sex partners to provide them with benefits. One observer said, "Republicans routinely used Congress' authority over the District to impose conservative social policies on the overwhelmingly Democratic city."[1] The measure passed 219–208, reflecting the fact that some anti-abortion Democrats voted against the measure, complicating whether it will survive the House-Senate conference later on in the session. Moreover, an amendment was added to the needle-exchange aspect of the bill that would prohibit such exchanges one hundred feet from the nearest school or park, severely limiting its effect. And although Rep. Jack Kingston of Georgia submitted the amendment ostensibly to protect children, the effect is to limit the scope of needle exchanges and continue the conservative war on those affected with HIV/AIDS. District Delegate Eleanor Holmes Norton said of this amendment, "The Republican minority wants to bring back the old days when they had a field day with D.C.

appropriations, imposing their personal views or those of their constituents on a self-governing jurisdiction of 600,000 residents in the nation's capital."[2]

Similarly, Norton was confident that the District would finally have a vote on the floor of the House, until an amendment was inserted by Republican Senator John Ensign of Nevada that would repeal most of the District's gun control laws. The bipartisan support for the amendment sponsored by the National Rifle Association caused Democratic leadership in both the House and Senate to shelve the bill, making its outcome uncertain.

During the presidential campaign, Barack Obama pledged that if a voting rights measure for the District representative in the House reached his desk, he would support it, leaving the impression that he was unable or unwilling to spend much political capital on the measure with such other weighty issues at hand. In any case, it is possible to assume that if changes in the political structure that characterizes the District's relationship with Congress, which has affected democratic outcomes for its citizens, come about, they will do so in the political environment of change in which the Obama administration was elected. They may not come as swiftly as desired or as fundamentally necessary, but they could come. Otherwise, the legacy of the administration with respect to the District could be as symbolic as others have been, rather than substantive.

NOTES

1. Andrew Taylor, "House Spending Bill Allows DC Abortion Funding," *The Associated Press*, July 17, 2009.

2. "AIDS Activists Prepare to Battle Against Needle Exchange Restraints," July 17, 2009, News Channel 9 Television, Washington, D.C., www.news8.news/stories/0709/641440.html.

Index

Abernathy, Ralph, 54
abortion, 8
Abramson, Paul, 143
activism: local black, 49–50; shift in strategies, 66–67
"The Adolescence of Political Socialization" (Merelman), 139–40
advertising, 233–34, 237
advisory neighborhood commissioners, 36
African American male: criminal justice system and, 183; incarcerated, likelihood of becoming, 191; incarcerated in District of Columbia jail system, number of, 186; rehabilitation resources for, 181–82
African Americans, 4–5; class division, 182; defined as "liberal," 232; democratic participation, 5, 47; in development of District of Columbia, role of, 67; Eagle Scouts, 62–63; as government employees, 46; health care services, 112–13; Home Rule Act and, 29; liberation of, 68; as majority population, 12–13, 47–49, 64–65, 184; media and, 226–28; middle class, 71, 75, 88, 167–68; national perspective of crime as relating to, 191–92; North

v. South, 67–68; on police force, 9; in position of power, 52–53; predatory and subprime lending to, 171; radio, relationship with, 234–35; rate of incarcerated females, 198; targets of neglect, 113; voters, role of, 25; Williams, A. and, 116. *See also* black; race
The Afro-American Tribune, 232–33
agenda: conflict, 3; denial, 4
Agronsky, Jonathan, 64
Alexandria, Virginia: housing in, 167; as independent city, 30–31
Allen, Anita, 74
Alley Dwelling Authority, 49
ambulance service, 79
American Public Media, 250n82
American Recovery and Reinvestment Act of 2009 (ARRA), 134
anti-discrimination laws, 32
anti-Vietnam War demonstrations, 50–51
Archer, Dennis, 110–11
Arlington, Virginia, 162
Armstrong Amendment, 10
Army Corps of Engineers, 45
ARRA. *See* American Recovery and Reinvestment Act of 2009

Asher, Robert, 49
assisted housing policy, 159–61
Atlanta, 150

Bagdikian, Ben, 231, 247n25
Bailey, Milton, 163–64
Baker, Ella, 63
Ballou Senior High School, 133
Banfield, Edward, 5
Barras, Jonetta Rose, 96, 104
Barry, Marion, Jr., 29, 37–38, 69–71,
    76–79, 110–11, 116; as activist,
    53, 62–64; administration, 88–89,
    94; agenda, 256–57; background,
    61–64; campaigns, 80, 90–91; critics
    of, 103–4; early years in District of
    Columbia, 64–66; gun wound, 76;
    health, 81; home rule and, 68–69,
    74–76; v. Kelly, 98; legal trouble,
    11–12, 78–79, 87–88; Nation Builder
    Award granted to, 82; personal life,
    82; from protest to electoral politics,
    55, 71, 73–74; as responsible for
    fiscal crisis of 1990s, 39; return from
    prison, 79–83, 96; on School Board,
    55, 74; Transit Strike and, 66–68; v.
    Williams, A., 103; youth backing,
    148–49, 154n23
Baumgartner, Frank R., 2
Bell, Derrick, 226
Benning Road bus line, 66–67
Bernstein, Carl, 58
Bevel, James, 62
Bilbray, Brian, 9–10
black: activists, local, 49–50; bourgeois
    citizens, 53, 89; colleges, 62
"Black codes," 31
black empowerment, 104; under
    Williams, A., 108–15
black-oriented radio, 235–36, 243–44,
    248n47; devolution of, 238–39
Black Panthers, 72
black politics, 5, 103; city, 6–7;
    independent v. coalition based, 74–
    76; shift in, 73

Black Power, 53, 66, 234
Black United Front, 72
black youth, 138; hip-hop and, 249n58,
    250n75; political socialization
    process, 143, 150–51, 153; potential
    for social change, 145; radio and,
    235, 240–41
Bloomberg, Michael, 126–27
Board of Aldermen, 31–32
Board of Commissioners, 33–34, 45
Board of Common Council, 31
Board of Education, 123, 258; Barry
    and, 74; right to elect members of,
    35, 109
Board of Trade, 46, 48, 70; campaign
    against home rule, 68–69
Bond, Jack, 92
Booker, Clarence T., 70
Branham, Thomas, 168
Braybrooke, David, 2
Brown v. Board of Education, 88
Brown, Ronald, 220n26
Brownback, Sam, 9
Broyhill, Joel T., 34–35
Brzezinski, Zbigniew, 229
budget, District of Columbia, 9, 12,
    221n32, 255, 257, 258; control over,
    28–29, 36; crisis, 104; deficit, 94,
    98; power over, 7, 58; proposals, 75;
    surplus, 132–33
Burroughs, Todd Steven, 244
Bush, George H. W., 12, 37
Bush, George W., 22, 126, 193–94
business: Barry relations with,
    community, 77; generation, 218–19;
    gentrification, 214–15; owners after
    riots, 56
Byrd, David, 91

Campbell, Bill, 111
"Can D.C. Schools Be Fixed?", 129–30,
    133
Carmichael, Stokely, 53, 72
Carr, Ian, 230
Carson, Clayborne, 67

CBC. *See* Congressional Black Caucus

Center for Information and Research on Civic Learning and Engagement (CIRCLE), 149–50

Chalk, O. Roy, 66

Chandler, Walter, 63

charitable models, 206

Children First, 126–27

Chomsky, Noam, 227, 230–31, 244

CIRCLE. *See* Center for Information and Research on Civic Learning and Engagement

citizen participation, 5, 7; African Americans, 5, 47; democracy and, 22; youth and, 149–50

citizens, District of Columbia, 226; limitation to, 83; limited political rights to, 138; needs and public policy, 14; significance of local representation to, 32

City Council, 38, 62, 256, 258; appointed, 70; 1871-1874, 33; housing policy and, 161, 172; Johnson, L. B. appointments to, 50; Kelly and, 93, 97; power of, 27, 36; right to elect, 28, 75, 109

city manager, 50

civic competence, 154n12

civil rights movement, 5–6, 70, 235, 238, 255; approaches in fighting for, 53; home rule and, 12; national momentum, 46, 49–50; Southern role in, 63, 68

Clarke, David A., 9

class: African American middle, 71, 75, 88, 167–68; division, 182; dynamics, 69; homeownership and, 162–63; issues, 53; white middle, 167

Cleveland, Ohio, 74

Clinton, Bill, 11

coalition politics, 74–76

Cobb, Roger W., 3–4

Cohen, Sol, 128

Committee on Finance and Revenue, 75

Committee on Higher Education, 220n25

communication, limits, 230–31

communications, dissident, 230, 239, 246n17

commuter tax, 36–37, 75, 99, 172, 215–16; exclusion, 207; federal prohibition against imposition of, 216–17

Comprehensive Housing Strategy Task Force, 165–66, 175; membership, 166

Comprehensive Merit Personnel Act (1978), 217

"concision," 238

Congress, 56–57, 217, 255; colonialist tendencies in, 116; Democratic control of, 261–62; Kelly and, 92–93; power of, 30, 36, 68, 80, 82, 104–5, 109, 221n32; relationship with District of Columbia, 1–3, 53, 58, 81, 262; Republican control of, 12; Southern members in, 5, 53; statehood bills introduced during 80th and 107th, 37, 43nn41–43; Washington, W. E. and, 58–59

Congress of Racial Equality (CORE), 47, 65

Congressional Black Caucus (CBC), 5, 7–8

congressional intervention, 7, 8–10, 115–16; impact of, 14

conservative assault, 113

Constitution. *See* United States Constitution

constitutional home rule, 24

Control Act (1995), 109, 115–16

Control Board, 38; administrative responsibilities of, 38–39; driving force in creating, 38; expiration of, 39

Cook, John, 32

CORE. *See* Congress of Racial Equality

Cornwell, Rupert, 246n12

Couch, Linda, 161, 170

Council of Governments, 174

Court of Appeals, District of Columbia, 28

courts: control over, 81; intervention by, 10–11; power of, 27–28

Court Services and Offender Supervision Agency (CSOSA), 181, 186–87, 198–99

Craig, Bill, 25

crime, 188; national perspective of, as relating to African Americans, 191–92; prevention, 187; as public policy issue, 181–82; rate, 51, 158

criminal code, 28

Criminalizing a Race (McIntyre), 191

criminal justice system, District of Columbia, 182–83, 194, 198–99, 260; discrepancies, 183, 189–90; local and federal agencies, 185–86

Cropp, Linda, 97–98, 164

CSO, 187

CSOSA. *See* Court Services and Offender Supervision Agency

cultural domination, 229

Cumberland, Maryland, 189

curriculum planning, 121

Curry, George, 244

Curry, Wayne, 162–63

Dada, Mukusa, 66

DaveyD, 239

Davis, Danny, 193–94

D.C. v. Heller (2008), 10

DCHA. *See* District of Columbia Housing Authority

DCPS. *See* District of Columbia Public School System

DC-TAG. *See* District of Columbia Tuition Assistance Program

decision-making, 7

DeLay, Tom, 12

Dellums, Ronald, 7–8

democracy, 14, 225–26, 241; citizen participation and, 22; limited, 255–56; at local level, 182–85; propaganda and, 227, 233–34; as structured by relationship with Congress and District of Columbia,

2–3, 21; under Williams, A., 115–16

Democracy in America (de Tocqueville), 128

Democratic Party: Congress, control of, 261–62; home rule and, 39–40

Democratic Platform Committee, 64

Department of Corrections (DOC), 185

Department of Housing and Urban Development (HUD), 160

desegregation efforts, 64

de Tocqueville, Alexis, 128

Detroit, 150

developmental policy, 111

Didden, James, 160

Diggs, Charles C., Jr., 5, 7–8, 27, 29

Dillon, John Forest, 106

Dillon's Rule, 105–6

"Disappearing Voices-The Decline of Black Radio," 238–39

dissident, 246n17

District of Columbia Emancipation Act, 67

District of Columbia Financial Responsibility and Management Assistance Act (1995), 37–38, 80

District of Columbia Financial Responsibility and Management Assistance Authority, 80, 109

District of Columbia Housing Authority (DCHA), 160–61, 174

District of Columbia Public Education Reform Amendment Act (2007), 122

District of Columbia Public School System (DCPS), 122, 127; academic performance of, 132; ARRA, benefits from, 134; major studies that examine, 124; political culture and issues impacting, 128–34; statistics, 129–30; students in, 138

District of Columbia Self-Government and Reorganization Act (1973), 221n32

District of Columbia Tuition Assistance Program (DC-TAG), 214

District of Columbia Voting Rights
  Amendment (1978), 37
Ditton, Paula, 193
Dixon, Arrington, 89, 91
Dixon, Julian, 8
Dixon, Sharon Pratt. *See* Kelly, Sharon
  Pratt
Dixon, Vanessa, 112–13
DOC. *See* Department of Corrections
Donaldson, Ivanhoe, 78
Donley, Kerry, 166–67
*Dream City: Race, Power, and the
  Decline of Washington, D.C.* (Jaffe
  & Sherwood), 146–47
Dugas, Julian, 56
duller students, 142
Dunbar High School, 51, 88
Duncan, Arne, 134, 259
Duncan, Charles, 56
Duncan, Douglas, 166–67

Eagleton, Thomas F., 27
economic stability, 167–68
economy, District of Columbia, 37–38;
  growth of, 39; September 11, 2001
  on, impact of, 39–40
education, 258; erosion of, 124; federal
  involvement in, 123, 126, 133–34;
  Fenty's, initiatives, 122–23, 127,
  132–33; higher, 220n25; high-need
  area, 127; income comparisons
  by, level attained, 212–13, *213*;
  investments in, 134; K-12, 126; as
  platform, 122, 133–34; in political
  socialization process, 137–53, 141;
  poverty and, 212–14; reforming,
  132; state-level decisions for, 123;
  strategies for improving, 121–22. *See
  also* public school system
Edwards, Don, 37
Elementary and Secondary Education
  Act (1965), 126
employment: efforts to provide, 217;
  prospects for ex-offenders, 197; rate,
  183, 226

Ensign, John, 262
establishment of District of Columbia,
  104–5
ethnography, 145
EuRok (DJ), 225
Evictions with Dignity Amendment Act,
  81
ex-offender reentry, 181–82, 186–87,
  192; health related concerns, 196;
  programs, funding for, 193
Ex-Offender Reentry Steering
  Committee, 188
ex-offenders, 194, 195, 200; housing
  and, 197; restrictions within society,
  187–88; skills received by, 192;
  transition into society, 197–98

Fager-Bediako, Lisa, 249n60
FAIR. *See* Fairness and Accuracy In
  Reporting
Fairness and Accuracy In Reporting
  (FAIR), 243
Fanon, Frantz, 227, 239–40, 242
Fauntroy, Walter E., 5, 24–25, 37,
  43nn41–42, 69, 72, 255; election of,
  55
FCC. *See* Federal Communications
  Commission
Federal Bureau of Prisons, 184–85
Federal Communications Commission
  (FCC), 236–37
federal government: cities place in,
  105; criminal justice system and,
  185–86; District of Columbia and,
  relationship between, 215–17;
  education and, 123, 126, 133–34;
  housing policy and, 159–61, 172–73;
  prison system and, 184–85, 188;
  rehabilitation services and, 188;
  responsibilities for District of
  Columbia, 38; v. state government, 2
federalism, 105–8; democratic or
  paternalistic, 4–7; structured issue
  conflict, 3–4
"Federalist No. 43," 32

Fenty, Adrian, 1–2, 39, 122, 131, 165, 175, 258; education initiative, 122–23, 127, 132–33

finances: control over, 11, 78; responsibility of, 38. *See also* revenue generation, District of Columbia

Financial Control Board, 11, 14, 80

financial crisis (2007-2009), 170–72, 176–77

financial emergency in District of Columbia, 38

financial service industry, deregulation of, 171–72

Firearms Control Regulations Act, 10, 40

Fisk University, 63

Fletcher, Thomas, 50

Ford, Glen, 235–36

Forman, James, 64, 65

Free D.C. Movement, 69

FreeMix Radio: The Original Mixtape Radio Show, 247n31

free press, 233–34

Garry, Indiana, 74

General Hospital, District of Columbia, 112–13, 116, 257–58

gentrification, 157–58, 172, 211, 214–15, 226–27, 257–58; business, 214–15; trends in, 170, 257

Georgetown, 30–31

Georgetown University Task Force on District of Columbia Governance, 14

Gillette, Howard, 111

Gingrich, Newt, 258

globalization, 212

governance, District of Columbia, 6–7, 14, 45, 58, 260; 1801-1871, 30–32; 1871-1874, 32–33; 1874-1967, 33–35; 1967-1973, 35; 1973-1995, 35–37; 1995-2001, 37–39; 2001-present, 39–40; authority over, 38; division of power and, 50; history of, 1–7; resources and, obtaining, 182–83; studies on, 42n36

governance, urban: market-oriented construct of, 106–7; nature of, 105–8

governor, 33

Graham, Jim, 170

Gramsci, Antonio, 234

Greater Southeast Community Hospital, 112–13

Great Reconstruction, 31–32

Greene, Ralph Waldo "Petey," Jr., 250n69

Hamer, Fannie Lou, 62

Harlow, Caroline, 193

Harrigan, John J., 128–29

Harris, Patricia Roberts, 90

Harvey, Carroll, 72–73

Hatcher, Richard, 73

health care services, 112–13, 226; to ex-offenders, 196

Hechinger, John, 72

Helms, Jesse, 9

Henderson, Lenneal J., Jr., 6

Henley, William Ernest, 83

hip-hop, 240–41, 261; black youth and, 249n58, 250n75; freestyle, 247n20

Hispanic men, incarceration rate, 191

H.J. Res 554, 37

Hobson, Julius, 47, 55

home equity loans, 171

homeownership: affected by financial crisis, 170–71; disparities between race and class, 162–63; low- and moderate-income, 172; project to promote, 160–61; rate, 211; tax burden on, 168

home rule, 11, 48–50, 152–53, 256–58; Barry and, 68–69, 74–76; campaign against, 68–69; civil rights movement and, 12; current form of, 24; definitions of, 41n2; Democratic Party and, 39–40; evolution of, 30–40; fight for, 24–26; future of, 40; "grace period," 8; legislative v. constitutional, 23–24; limited, 75, 182; opposition to, 5, 11

Home Rule Act (1973), 6, 26–30, 73, 108, 215; African Americans and, 29; Congressional intervention and, 7; criticisms against, 36–37; House District of Columbia Committee, 29; negotiations, 28; passage of, 22, 24, 35–37; poverty rate and, 13; section 602, 216; Senate and, 28; strengths and weaknesses, 29; Voting Rights Act (1965) and, 24–25
homestead deduction, 168
Homestead Housing Preservation Amendment Act, 81
homicide rate, 91
Hoover, J. Edgar, 54, 58
HOPE VI, 160–61
Horsky, Charles, 68–69
House District Committee, 7–8, 45–46; as governed by Southern Democrats, 5; Home Rule Act and, 29; H.R. 4644 and, 34; ideological makeup of, 26; role of, 24
House of Delegates, 33
House of Representatives, 55; right to elect delegate to, 35, 109
housing, 177; abandonment, 158; affordable, 157–58, 162–63, 206–7; affordable, federal funding for, 173; boom, 167–68; for ex-offenders, 197; increased cost of, 170; inspecting, 164–65, 176; market, 164–65; poverty and, 211–12; predatory and subprime lending in, 170; racial discrimination in, 64; strategies to address high price, 165–66; subsidized, 170; in Washington metropolitan area, 162–63. *See also* gentrification; homeownership; public housing
Housing Act (2002), 165–66
Housing Choice Voucher, 159
Housing and Community Development, 163–64
housing policy: assisted, 159–61; City Council and, 161, 172; federal v. local, 159–61, 172; issues in, 175; mayor and, 172–74; national and local objectives, 157–58, 173
Housing Preservation Rehabilitation, and Production Omnibus Amendment Act of 2001, 164, 175
Housing Trust Fund, 158–59, 259
Howard University, 51, 88; WHUR, 235
Howard University Hospital, 112–13
H.R. 4644, 34
H.R. 10115, 34–35
HUD. *See* Department of Housing and Urban Development
Hughes, Cathy, 234
Hyman, Herbert, 139–41, 144

incarceration rates, 190–91, 206–7; among African American females, 198; among African American males, 186; components related to high, 184
income: comparisons by educational level attained, 212–13, *213*; homeownership and, levels, 172; household, 210, *210*
infant mortality rate, 79, 211, 256
infrastructure, 45
Ingram, Helen, 2–4
inmates, District of Columbia: disparities in treatment of, 189; physical location of, 190
Interagency Collaboration and Services Integration Commission, 123
interest rate policy, 171
Internet, 233, 247nn34–35
Istook, Ernest, Jr., 10

Jackson, E. Franklin, 47
Jaffe, Harry S., 137, 146–47
James, Doris, 193
Jenkins, Timothy, 214
Jenrette, John, 26
job cuts, 94
Jobs for D.C. Residents Amendment Act, 81–82
Johnson, Karen, 78

Johnson, Lyndon B., 5, 35, 90; civil
    rights agenda, 70; home rule and,
    48–50; H.R. 4644 and, 34, 68
Jones, Bryan D., 2
judges, appointment of, 36

Karberg, Jennifer, 193
Kelly, Sharon Pratt, 79–80, 87, 96,
    97–98; administration, 92–96;
    agenda, 257; background, 89–90;
    campaigns, 88–89, 90–92; legacy
    of, 98–100
Kennard, William, 237
Kennedy, Edward, 43n41
Kennedy, John F., 48
King, Martin Luther, Jr., 5, 63, 115,
    238, 256; riots after assassination of,
    50, 52–56, 58, 71–72
Kingston, Jack, 261
Klein, Joel, 127
Kneier, Charles, 23–24

land and water area, 42n39, 215–16
Lane, Ambrose I., 239
Lanier, Cathy, 181
Lao Tzu, 212
Lappin, Harley G., 189
The Last of the Black Emperors
    (Barras), 104
Latino community, 94, 208, 257;
    violence in (1991), 95–96
Law, Bob, 238
legislative home rule, 23
LeMoyne College, 63
Lew, Allen Y., 131
Lewis, John, 64
liberal integrated organization, 74
Lindbloom, Charles, 2
Lindsay, John V., 49
Lippmann, Walter, 238, 249n64
Littlebear, Naomi, 241
Lloyd, Mark, 245
local government: democracy, 182–85;
    housing policy and, 159–61, 172;
    power, 106; rehabilitation services

and, 188; as unique in District of
    Columbia, 108–9
Lorton Prison, 184–85
low-income neighborhood, 163
lunch counter sit-ins, 63
Lyon, Schley, 150–51

Madison, James, 32
Mall, demonstrations on, 54
March on Washington (1963), 5, 65
Marketplace, 242
Marshall, Thurgood, 53, 77
Maryland, 34–35; bills to retrocede
    District of Columbia to, 37, 43n43;
    property assessments (2005), 168;
    revenues, 216–17. *See also specific
    places in Maryland*
Mason, Hilda, 79
mass culture, 229
mass media, 241; challenge to,
    235; original intent behind, 238;
    ownership and control over, 231–33;
    role of, 229–30
Mayfield, Rufus "Catfish," 70
mayor, 58, 105, 111, 256, 258;
    education as platform issue, 122;
    housing policy and, 172–74; power
    of, 27, 36; president-appointed, 30–
    31; public housing and, 161; public
    school system, autonomy over, 125–
    26, 258; right to elect, 18, 36, 109;
    transition from appointed to elected,
    87. *See also specific mayors*
mayor-commissioner, 48, 50, 54–55, 70;
    president-appointed, 35
McChesney, Robert, 225
McGary, Howard, 191–92
McGrath, James, 159
McIntyre, Charshee C. L., 191
McKenzie, Floretta Dukes, 121
McKinnie, Lester, 72
McLuhan, Marshall, 245n3
McMahon, Kevin, 245n3
McMillan, John L., 24–25, 45–46, 48,
    255; defeat of, 26–27; home rule

and, 49–50; racial hierarchy and, 51–52

media, 34, 103–4, 226, 227, 243–44, 260–61; African Americans and, 226–28; black-targeted, 248n47; colonizing, 237; corporate mining, 234–41; corporation control over, 244; delivery of, 240–41; demographics and, 234; functions of, 230–31; ownership, 247n25; political functions, 245; power of, 230; private-equity, 250n71; public opinion and, 238; reform, 236; repetition, 240–41; revolutionary, 227; small community and ethnic, 232–33; society, relationship with, 228. *See also* mass media; *specific kinds of media*

Meeks, Kenneth, 183–84

Memphis, TN, 62–63, 64

Mendelson, Phil, 170

mental health disorders, 196–97

Merelman, Richard, 139–40, 141–42, 144; quantitative/qualitative research methods, 154n17

Metropolitan Planning Organizations, 174

Michaels, Lee, 236, 239

Middle East policy, 21–22

Miller, Lisa, 3–4

Miner Teachers College, 51

minority, 153n5; students, 142

mixtapes, 232–33, 247n31

Model Cities Administration, 5

monitoring projects, 237, 249n60

Morrow, Sharon, 93

mortgage banking regulation, 171

Mortgage Disclosure Amendment Act, 81

Multer, Abraham J., 34

multiplier effect, 218

Mumola, Christopher, 193

municipal power, 106

murder rate, 79

Murphy, Patrick V., 52

musical OPEC, 237–38

NAACP. *See* National Association for the Advancement of Colored People

NABOB. *See* National Association of Black-owned Broadcasters

Natcher, William, 9, 46

National Association for the Advancement of Colored People (NAACP), 47, 62, 64–65

National Association of Black-owned Broadcasters (NABOB), 235

National Black Caucus of State Legislators (NBCSL), 82

National Capital Housing Authority, 49

National Capital Revitalization and Self-Government Improvement Act, 38

National Capital Service Area, 37

National Commission on Excellence in Education (1983), 124

National Low-Income Housing Coalition, 161

National Public Radio (NPR), 241–42, 261; function and funding for, 242–43

National Treatment Accountability for Safer Communities (TASC), 193

National Urban League, 65

NBCSL. *See* National Black Caucus of State Legislators

needle exchange programs, 261–62

Neighborhood Youth Corps, 65

"Net Neutrality," 233

"The New Black Politics," 6–7

news ownership, 231–32

The New Teacher Project (TNTP), 131–32

New York City Public School System, 126–28

Niemi, Richard, 142–43

Nixon, Richard, 2, 57, 74–75

No Child Left Behind Act (2002), 123, 126, 258

nonviolent offenders, one-year reduction for, 190

Norouzi, Parisa, 243–44

North Carolina, 189

Norton, Eleanor Holmes, 11, 39–40,
    43n41, 99, 153, 189, 199, 214,
    261–62
NPR. *See* National Public Radio

Obama, Barack, 259; education
    platform, 133–34; voting rights for
    District of Columbia and, 262
Omnibus Public Safety Ex-Offender
    Self-Sufficiency Reform Act,
    187–88
Operation Pipeline, 183–84
"oppositional consciousness," 234, 245
Organic Act: 1801, 30; 1878, 221n32

Pager, Devah, 197
Paige, Rod, 126
parole, 181–82; delivery of, 187
Parris, Stan, 9
Parthenon Group, 124
Patterson, Kathy, 187
Peterson, Michael B., 6
Peterson, Paul, 106–7, 111
Pew Research Center, 190–91; Project
    for Excellence, 231
Pharr, Shaun, 170
police brutality, 183–84, 192, 226
police-community relations, 52, 53, 184,
    198, 259
police force, 48; African Americans on,
    9; control of, 28; racial composition
    of, 51–52; Spanish speakers in,
    95–96
policing: racial disparities in, 184, 190–
    92; strategies, 197–98
policy: development, 114; effectiveness,
    7; evaluations, 14; racism, 226. *See
    also specific policies*
policy intervention: by courts, 10–11;
    motivation for, 11–12; pattern of,
    7–11; presidential intervention, 8.
    See also Congressional intervention
political compromise, 26
political culture, 128–34
Political Culture (Rosenbaum), 129

political socialization, 137–53;
    academic scholarship on, 146; Black
    youth and, process, 143, 150–51,
    153; definitions and examinations
    of, 140–41; difficulties in field
    of studies, 152–53; District of
    Columbia and, historical significance
    of, 146–49; education in, process,
    137–53, 141; ethnographic approach,
    145; families on, role of, 147–48;
    historical and theoretical origins
    of, 139–40; peer groups on, impact
    of, 148; qualitative v. quantitative
    research, 144–46; voting rights and,
    147; of youth, 149–51
Political Socialization (Hyman), 139–40
"The Political Socialization of Ghetto
    Children: Efficacy and Cynicism"
    (Lyon), 150–51
political sophistication, 154n12
*Politics and Policies in State and
    Communities* (Harrigan), 128–29
Poor Peoples' Campaign (1968), 5
population and demographics, 4–5, 47–
    49, 64–65, 138, 146–47, 184, 215,
    232, 259; media and, 234; between
    1950 and 1970, 12–13; 1950s, 47;
    of poverty, 208–9; within prisons,
    185–86, 190–93, 198; shift in, 148
Porter, Paul, 249n63
poverty in District of Columbia,
    205–21, 256, 259, 260; approaches
    to eliminate, 206; demographics,
    208–9; education and, 212–14; face
    of, 208–15, 259–60; housing and,
    211–12; juveniles living in, 209–10;
    map of, *209*; race and, 208; selected
    indicators, *211*, 211–12; symptoms
    of, 206–7
poverty rate, 12–13, 158, 226; Home
    Rule Act and, 13; two-year averages
    (1997-2007), *13*
Pratt, L. D., 69
predatory and subprime lending, 170,
    176–77; African Americans and, 171

pre-service experience, 121
presidential intervention, 8, 14
Price, Hollis, 63
"The Price of Neglect," 130–31
Pride, Inc., 69–71; creation of, 71; financial collapse of, 72–73
Prince George's County, 174, 234, 259; affordable housing opportunities, 162–63
prisons: control over, 81; disparities in resources and organization of, 189; inmate population and demographics, 185–86, 190–93, 198; return to, 188, 194–95. *See also specific prisons*
prison system, 199; federal involvement in, 184–85, 188
probation services, 181–82; delivery of, 187
propaganda: democracy and, 227, 233–34; funding for, 229
property: taxable, 99; tax-exempt, 36–37, 168–69, 172, 205, 217–18; tax relief, 175–76
public housing, 49, 174; demolitions, 162–63; revitalizing, 159–60, 161
Public Law 93-198 (1974), 2
public policy, 226, 245, 258–61; articulation, 4; citizen need and, 14; crime as, issue, 181–82; race and, in District of Columbia and, 2–3
Public Radio International, 250n82
public rights-of-way, 42n39
public safety, 186–87; director of, 53; ex-offender reentry and, 192; Kelly and, 94
public school system, 14, 121, 129; approach for managing, 123–24; heating in, 130–31; mayor-centric reform, 125–26, 258; in New York City, 126–28. *See also* District of Columbia Public School System
Puryear, Paul, 6

race, 150–51; dynamics, power of, 69; homeownership and, 162–63;
motivation for intervention and, 11–12; poverty and, 208; public policy in District of Columbia and, 2–3
racial issues, 51, 64; 1801-1871, 31; McMillan and, 24–25; policing and, 51–52, 184, 190–92; southern congressional control and, 53
racial profiling, 183–84, 190–92
"racial purification," 245n4
racial relations: long term status of, 56; post King, 54
racism, 65; institutional, 189–90, 199; policy, 226
radio, 234; African American relationship with, 234–35; black youth and, 235, 240–41; monitoring projects, 237, 249n60; music selection, 240–41; song content, 249n63; youth and, 237–38. *See also* black-oriented radio; *specific programs*
Radio-Alger, 242
Radio One, 234–37, 239
Raines, Frank, 257
Rarick, John R., 5
Rauh, Joseph, 47
Ray, John, 91, 97–98
Reagan, Ronald, 8
real estate boom, 167–69, 171
Regula, Ralph, 43n43
rehabilitation resources: for African American male ex-offenders, 181–82; re-offenders and, 195; restricted access to, 199; unequal distribution of, 194–95
rehabilitation services, 188, 260; CSOSA and, 187; local and federal, 188
Reid, Robert, 168
rent control, 158–59, 169–70, 175–76, 259
Rent Control Reform Amendment Act (2006), 169–70, 176, 259
re-offenders: efforts to reduce, 198; risk factors of, 195–97

reorganization of District of Columbia, 50–52

Reorganization Plan No. 3 (1967), 35

representation, District of Columbia, 1–2, 255; constitutional silence on, 22–23; exclusion of, in national legislature, 22–23; significance of, 32; tax and, 215–16

Republican Party: Congress, control of, 12; conservative government through, 9

residency requirements, 75

Retinas, Nicolas, 162

revenue generation, District of Columbia, 215–19

Revolutionary War, 22–23

Rhee, Michelle, 131–32, 258

Right of First Refusal, 170

right-wing minority, 232

riots, 147; business owners after, 56; efforts to prevent, 71; after King's assassination, 50, 52–56, 58, 71–72; Latino community, 95–97; national inner city, 70; Washington, W. response to, 52–55

Risher, John, 56

Rivers Correctional Institution, 189–90

Rock, Chris, 227–28

Rockville, Maryland, 167

Rolark, Wilhelmina, 80

Rosenbaum, Walter A., 129

Ross, Marc Howard, 3–4

Sandalow, Terrance, 41n2

Schattschneider, E. E., 3–4

school(s), 51; conditions of, 130–31; reform, 259; segregation in, 88

School Board, 55, 62

Schwartz, Carol, 110

SCLC. *See* Southern Christian Leadership Conference

Second Amendment, 40

Second Chance Act (2007), 193–94, 198

segregation, 45; intra-racial, 69; in schools, 88

The Semisovereign People (Schattschneider), 3–4

Senate: electing members of, 41n1; Home Rule Act and, 28

September 11, 2001, 39–40

service(s): bilingual, 96; delivery, 14, 58; funding, 98–99; privatizing local, 94, 112–13. *See also specific services*

Seventeenth Amendment, 41n1

Shackelton, Polly, 47

Shepherd, Alexander "Boss," 33

Sherwood, Tom, 137, 146–47

Sisk, B. F., 34–35

Smiley, Travis, 242–43

Smith, Steven Rathgeb, 4

SNCC. *See* Student Non-violent Coordination Committee

Sobieszek, Barbara, 142–43

social problems, 159; interrelated, 183

social services, 79, 206

socio-political problems, 151

South Carolina, 25–26

Southern Christian Leadership Conference (SCLC), 47, 68

Southern sit-in movement, 64

Spaulding, William, 213, 220n25

State Board of Education, 123

state charters, 105

state government: education and, 123; v. federal government, 2; powers of, 106

statehood, 3, 99; bills introduced during the 98th and 107th Congresses, 37, 43nn41–43; movement, 37; objections to, 12; protesters seeking, 54–55

Steen, Leslie, 175

Stephens, Claude, 25

Stewart, Carter, 32

Stith, Jonathon, 243–44

Stokes, Carl, 73

Stone, Clarence, 106–7

street vendors, 215

Student Access to Treatment Act, 81

Student Non-violent Coordination Committee (SNCC), 47, 61, 256–57; formation of, 63; visibility in District of Columbia, 65–66
substance abuse, 188, 197
subway system funding, 57
Superior Court, District of Columbia, 28
Swaim, Marty, 74

TASC. *See* National Treatment Accountability for Safer Communities
Tate, Katherine, 73, 74
tax, 205, 215–16, 260; cuts proposals, 75; homeownership, burden on, 168; recordation, 165–66. *See also* commuter tax
tax-exempt: entities, 36–37, 207; properties, 36–37, 105, 168–69, 172, 217–18
Taylor, Charles, 9
teacher(s), 123–24; preparation, 121; shortage, 131–32
techno-manager, 110–11, 116
Telecommunications Act (1996), 237
TENAC. *See* Tenants' Advocacy Coalition
Tenants' Advocacy Coalition (TENAC), 159
Thompson, J. Phillip, 113
TNTP. *See* The New Teacher Project
"Townhomes on Capital Hill," 160
Transit Strike, 66–68
Tredwell, Mary, 71, 73
Tucker, Sterling, 47, 55, 75–77
Turner, Maurice T., 91

unemployment, 183
United Federation of Teachers, 127
United Planning Organization (UPO), 65
United States Bureau of Prisons, 189
United States Constitution, 22–23
United States Department of Education, 123, 126

United States Government Accountability Office, 205
UPO. *See* United Planning Organization
urban administration, 105
urban governance: market-oriented construct of, 106–7; nature of, 105–8
Urban League, 47
urban policy, 106–7
urban revitalization, affordable housing and, 157–58
U.S. v. Barry, 79

Virginia: Commonwealth of, 31; revenues, 216–17. *See also specific places in Virginia*
vocational training, 214–15
voter: action, 25; registration, 80, 138, 141; youth, participation, 149–50
voting, 225–26; age, 154n23
voting rights, 1–2, 6, 35–37; history of, 148; limited, 138; Obama and, 262; political socialization and, 147
Voting Rights Act (1965), 24–25

Walters, Ronald, 245n4
War on Poverty, 70, 206
Ward Eight, 80
Washington Area Housing Partnership, 174–75
Washington Area Housing Trust Fund, 166–67, 174
Washington Bee, 67
The Washington Post, 66–67, 110, 239; on Barry, 61–62, 103–4; circulation, 233; endorsement of Barry, 77–78; endorsement of Kelly, 90–91; on District of Columbia housing market, 164–65; investigation of public school system, 129; ownership, 231–32
Washington, Walter E., 14, 45–60, 70, 72–73, 76; administration, 87–89; agenda, 256–57; appointment of, 49–50; congressional response to, 58–59; early career, 49; legacy, 55–59; race

for mayor (1974), 55; reorganization of District of Columbia, 50–52; riots, response to, 52–55
Weaver, Robert C., 53
welfare recipients, 51
white middle-class, 167
White, Mike, 110–11
"white nationalism," 226
WHUR 96.3 FM, 235
Wilkins, Robert, 192
Wilkins, Roy, 63
Williams, Anthony, 39, 104, 163, 175, 188; agenda, 257–58; v. Barry, 103; corporate interests of, 107–8; critics of, 114–15; early life, 110; Housing Trust Fund and, 166–67; policy interests, 108–15; state of democracy under, 115–16
Williams, Maurice, 76
Wilson, James Q., 5
Wilson, Jerry V., 52
Wilson, John A., 93, 94, 97
Wilson, Willie, 114
Winfrey, Oprah, 240–41

Wirtz, Willard, 70–71
WKYS 93.9 FM, 235
WOL-AM, 235, 239
Wolf, Frank, 11–12
Woodrow Wilson International Center for Scholars, 212
WOOK-AM, 235
work force, over-employed, 78–79
"workhouse" movement, 206
Worthy, Patricia, 92–93
WPFW 89.3 FM, 232–33
WPGC 95.5 FM, 235
Wright, Jim, 8
Wright, Richard, 67

youth, 152; Barry, backing, 148–49, 154n23; contemporary struggles, 149–51; cumulative disadvantages, 210; development, 141, 146; in political socialization process, 149–51; radio listening, 237–38; voter participation, 149–50. *See also* black youth
"youth of color," 141, 152, 153n5
Youth Pride Economic Enterprises, 71

About the Authors

Jared A. Ball, Ph.D., is assistant professor of communication studies at Morgan State University. He is editor-at-large of *The Journal of Hip-Hop and Global Culture* from Words, Beats and Life, Inc. He is also the founder and producer of *FreeMix Radio: The Original Mixtape Radio Show*, and can be found online at voxunion.com.

Michael K. Fauntroy, Ph.D., is assistant professor of public policy at George Mason University. He is the author of *Republicans and the Black Vote* (2008) and *Home Rule or House Rule? Congress and the Erosion of Local Governance in the District of Columbia* (2003).

Darwin Fishman, Ph.D., is assistant professor in the Department of African American Studies at the University of Western Illinois.

Angelyn Flowers, J.D., Ph.D., is professor of criminal justice in the Department of Urban Affairs and Social Science and Social Work at the University of the District of Columbia. Her most recent publication is *Crime in the District of Columbia: 2008 Report*.

Kevin L. Glasper, Ph.D., is assistant professor in the Department of Management, Marketing, and Public Administration at Bowie State University in Bowie, Maryland.

Daryl B. Harris, Ph.D., is associate professor and chair of the political science department at Howard University in Washington, D.C.

William G. Jones, Ph.D., is adjunct professor at Howard University. He has been a research consultant in housing and community development policy issues for more than fifteen years.

Wilmer J. Leon III, Ph.D., is a full-time lecturer in the political science department at Howard University in Washington, D.C.

ReShone L. Moore, Ph.D., is adjunct professor in the Department of Management, Marketing, and Public Administration at Bowie State University in Bowie, Maryland.

Toni-Michelle C. Travis, Ph.D., is associate professor of government and politics at George Mason University. She is the editor of the *Almanac of Virginia Politics* (2008) and coauthor of *The Meaning of Difference* (2008).

Ronald Walters, Ph.D., is professor of government and politics emeritus at University of Maryland, College Park. The most recent of his ten books is *The Price of Racial Reconciliation* (2008).

Breinigsville, PA USA
02 September 2010
244729BV00001B/1/P